Peripatetic:
A Memoir

*A French-American Citizen's Perspective on
His Jewish Heritage and War, Love and Politics*

by Daniel Dorian

ISBN: 978-0-692-48167-7

Cover designed by Sean Montgomery
Interior Layout & Design by Scribe Freelance

Published in the United States of America

If you do not tell the truth about yourself,
you cannot tell it about other people.
—VIRGINIA WOOLF

The author wishes to express his profound gratitude to his wife Maria Pon, Joe Dorman, Jean-Claude and Michele Héberlé, Larry Holofcener, Robert Kimmel, Eliane and Jean-Pierre Laffont, Barbara Markenson, Mark Rosenthal and the members of the Bucks County Writers Workshop, particularly Don Swaim, Chris Bauer, Jim Brennan, Natalie Dyen, Jackie Nash, Alan Shills and Sharyl Volpe.

per·i·pa·tet·ic

/perēpəˈtedik/

adjective

1. Traveling from place to place, especially working or based in various places for relatively short periods.

—OXFORD ENGLISH DICTIONARY

Prologue

Born in 1937, at the American Hospital in Neuilly, I was one of World War II's 'war children' who lived through starvation, bombings and the brutality of a merciless enemy. Those of us who survived the ordeal and did not suffer physical wounds were psychologically scarred for life.

In my early teens, I yearned for role models whose accomplishments made me forget the miseries I had witnessed when I was a little boy. The hero I most identified with was Blaise Cendrars, the Swiss poet and writer who blossomed at the turn of the twentieth century. This fearless adventurer, who had been blessed with unappeasable curiosity, had started out as a mediocre student. His peregrinations enflamed my imagination. He had been a film producer in Italy, France and the US, while circling the globe and writing great novels.

I too had been at the bottom of my class. I was incurably inquisitive, couldn't stand still, hated the status quo, occasionally flirted with danger, loved passionately and tried my hand at several trades, some more successfully than others. Like Cendrars, I never hesitated to reinvent myself when urged by an irresistible desire or faced with no other alternative.

Like him, I fell in love with a country other than my country of origin. For Cendrars, it was France. For me, it was America.

Never would I have ever thought that my new life in the USA would give me first-hand access to celebrities and movie stars and to heads of state as an actor, journalist, publicist and filmmaker. Nor could I have imagined what lay ahead: the opportunity to chronicle so many of the major events that shaped the second part of the twentieth century in the most unpredictable ways.

Contents

The Old Continent

1

True Origins
(The Cat's Out of the Bag)

*I am by heritage a Jew, by citizenship a Swiss, and by makeup
a human being, and only a human being, without any special
attachment to any state or national entity whatsoever.*
—ALBERT EINSTEIN

After our separation in 1978, my ex-wife Annick left the United
States for Paris, taking with her our daughter, Cécile and our son,
Stéphane. We decided that both children would spend their
vacations with me in the United States.

One summer, Cécile came to live with us for the month of July at the
Manhattan apartment I shared with my second wife, Maria. She loved to
lose herself in other people's drawers, in search of crusty secrets that if
found, would give her immense pleasures. One day, she discovered hidden
in one of my closets, a very old, beaten black suitcase I had brought back
from Paris after my mother's death. It contained love letters my parents
exchanged at the beginning of their relationship and copies of my father's
naturalization papers.

That same evening she questioned me, "Dad, is Dorian your real
name?"

I had dreaded the day I'd be asked that question. Cécile had unearthed
a secret I had always kept to myself, a secret so well hidden, I thought, that
it would die with me.

I resented her for having infringed on my private life like a common
thief. I felt betrayed. My anger wouldn't subside for many years, but, as I

write these words, I now see my daughter's indiscretion as a blessing that gave me the motivation to extract myself from the state of denial I was in.

During my entire youth, my parents shielded me from my Jewish identity.

Years after my father passed away, I got hold of his death certificate and discovered that his real name was Goldschlager. It was a shock, not so much because it confirmed my true origins, but because of the name itself. Goldschlager sounded so odious, so foreign and Jewish. It made my dad even more Jewish than he was.

No one ever told me I was Jewish, including him, but deep down, I always suspected he was. Many of my parents' friends were Jewish, the food we ate at home was Jewish, the dishes my mother prepared so skillfully were often Jewish, the jokes my father told were Jewish. These exterior signs of Jewishness notwithstanding, never was I brought up as a Jew, according to Jewish traditions. My parents were staunch atheists.

I was also led to believe that my mother was Catholic of German descent. Consequently, some people saw me as half Jewish and those who considered you had to be born to a Jewish mother to be a Jew saw me as a gentile. "My father is Jewish," I'd admit, "but my mother is Catholic." The "but" said it all.

When I recently revisited the documents stored in the old black suitcase, I examined my mother's naturalization papers more closely. Their content left no doubt as to her extraction. She too was Jewish. I could not pretend anymore that I had gentile blood flowing in my veins. I was Jewish after all... *juif à part entière*, one of the chosen ones, a M.O.T., a Member of the Tribe. Who wants to become the member of the most persecuted tribe in man's history? I had so far gone through life unharmed, unbruised, untouched, never had to bear the stigma of being a Yid and all of a sudden, here I was, defenseless against the pangs of anti-Semitism. There was no advantage to be gained in being one of the children of Israel aside from the fact that I did not have to live in a state of denial anymore. I also cringed at the thought of having inherited some of the Jewish stereotypes people make fun of—the whining, the arrogance, the rudeness or the cliquishness. I had enough quirks of my own.

The inner crisis caused by the discovery proved to be ephemeral.

Maybe I was too old when I made it—I was already in my fifties—too old for it to have a deep and lasting impact on me. It was a shock at first, no doubt, but once I realized there was nothing I could do about it, my uneasiness subsided. Yes, I was a Jew, whether I felt like one or not, but that did not mean I had become a different person. Only the label had changed, not the man.

I had always rejected sectarianism and the ghettoization Jews often inflict upon themselves. I had always shunned any restrictions imposed by religion, ethnicity, nationality, tradition or even fear. I will remain open until my last breath, surrounded, as I have always been, by friends of all creeds and cultures.

I never wanted to belong to a tribe, to a sect, ethnic, religious or otherwise. I have no patience for extremists, be they Hassidim or members of the Evangelical Right. I do not relate to Jewish traditions or to Jewish beliefs, but I love my Jewish friends and my Israeli family. I understand and respect Jews who feel it is crucial for them to affirm their Judaic roots. I recognize the intelligence, creativity, talent and the genius Jews display in so many fields and while I concede without arrogance that I might have inherited some of these qualities, I still feel that I do not belong to the tribe.

Do I condemn my parents for having lied to me about my origins? I am sure their initial intention was to raise me as a Jew. The fact that they had me circumcised at birth attests to that. They tried to make me less Jewish than I was when they felt they had no other choice. My father bore a name that, in the forties, would have brought a death sentence upon the three of us. If the Nazis had been convinced that my mother was Catholic, they might have shown leniency.

My father's parents, David and Fanny, were Jews of modest means. They resided in Iasi, a university town bordering Ukraine in the Moldavia region, southeast of Bucharest, the capital of Romania. David was a salesman. His father had been smuggled from Russia in a sack when he was a teenager, so that he wouldn't be recruited in the czar's army.

David's wife Fanny, whose maiden name was Feingold, was twenty-two when she gave birth to a son she named Sanil, in 1897. Thirteen years later, she had another child, a baby girl she named Zica.

I have no knowledge of my father's life in Iasi. He only confided to me that his parents were poor. Occasionally, he evoked a few childhood memories, making a point to remind me that he had been an A-student and recalling with some pride the time when he had worn out the seat of his pants on the same bench Edward G. Robinson sat at his primary school. He remembered him well. Robinson, born Emmanuel Goldenberg, immigrated to America from Romania at the age of ten to become one of Hollywood's most popular movie stars.

My grandfather nourished high hopes for his son. In those days, most Romanians saw France as a cultural Mecca. A great many of them spoke French, a natural, given the fact that Romanian is a romance language even closer to Latin than French.

After Sanil graduated from high school, David sent him to Paris to study medicine. He gave him just enough money for food and modest accommodations.

My father arrived in the French capital a couple of years after the Armistice, in a country still weakened and traumatized by four long years of war. He wound up in a *chambre de bonne,* one of those tiny little rooms still used today to put up servants under the roofs of most five or six story buildings in Paris. His first address was 3 Rue des Carmes, in the heart of the Latin Quarter. The place had no running water, was barely heated. The johns were down the corridor.

Dad studied medicine in that closet eighteen hours a day, falling asleep in the wee hours of the morning, exhausted and numbed by the small amount of opium that could be found in the Camels he chain-smoked.

For him, to start from scratch and to study in a language that wasn't his mother tongue was challenging. His fight for survival in an environment that was foreign to him seemed so romantic, but the reality of it was not always idyllic. As Hemingway wrote in *A Moveable Feast,* "Paris was a very old city and we were young and nothing was simple there, not even poverty, nor sudden money, nor the moonlight, nor right and wrong, nor the breathing of someone who lay beside you in the moonlight."

Father always had "the breathing of someone who lay beside him," a sweetheart who lifted his spirits and made him forget the hardships of poverty and loneliness. Finding lovers was easier than making friends in this city that spurned foreigners.

He must have been popular with the so-called *sexe faible*, judging from a few passionate letters I still possess. The language of love was so remote from the way lovers communicate today. The naiveté, the freshness, the inventiveness of these monologues—aren't love letters monologues, after all?—the poetry, sensuousness and charm that emanates from them belong to the twenties and thirties just as much as art deco, surrealism or poetic realism do.

"I waited for you and you didn't come. You will never come," wrote one of his many conquests. "I had grown accustomed to your presence. I loved your way of thinking. I loved to see you. I loved to hear your voice. I loved... I loved everything that was yours... Know that I regret nothing. I abandoned myself to you with all the fervor of my delirious senses and shared with you divine moments. Adieu my passing fancy, adieu my delicious fantasy. Your friend in bad days, your lover in happy days. Marcelle."

If he was foolhardy and unreliable in love, my father was most dependable in friendship. Modest, often too modest in society, he felt ill at ease when his achievements were recognized. He was tight with money, but incapable of asking those of his patients who were not as wealthy as most of his others to pay his fees. Many took advantage of a kindness that his wife construed as weakness. His aloofness when it came to money annoyed her. She had no qualms about going after the defaulters.

"I see that van Dongen hasn't paid his bills. How much does he owe you?" she asked my father on a Sunday morning. No answer. Kees van Dongen was an illustrious Fauves painter then. My mother picked up the phone and dialed. Van Dongen answered. "My husband tells me you haven't paid your bill. How about giving us a couple of paintings in exchange?" Pause. "Are you home?" Pause. "I'm jumping in a cab."

She returned with a large oil painting depicting the artist's townhouse garden and a magnificent watercolor of a flower bouquet.

Both pieces had adorned the walls of our living room in our Paris apartment for as long as I could remember. When Father died in 1960, my mother gave me the oil painting. I brought it to the United States. Two years later, financial hardship led me to put up the masterpiece for sale.

Sotheby auctioned it. It sold for eighteen thousand dollars. The money was spent in less than six months.

Twenty years later, as I was strolling down Fifty-seventh Street, I saw a van Dongen in Wally Findlay's art gallery showcase similar to the one I had sold. So, I entered the gallery and asked, "How much is the painting in the window?"

"A million eight."

My father would have had a seizure had he been with me that day. He was so uncomfortable with money. Like most Catholics, this Jew considered the lure of money a sin. What a paradox!

Given his professional success, Sanil should have died a rich man. He was broke when he passed away. For a long time I felt he had exercised his generosity at the expense of our well-being.

In medical school, he had befriended a man by the name of William Davenport. Billy was an American expatriate, tall, handsome, elegant, a sort of Douglas Fairbanks who happened to be very, very rich. Billy was ambling through his medical studies like a dilettante, more interested in some beautiful woman's anatomy than by Anatomy. He was a womanizer, but contrary to my father, a lazy one and one who married all the women he fell for. Billy had four wives.

Billy and Sanil rarely saw each other socially after medical school, but their professional collaboration endured for almost four decades.

Sanil made sure that Billy studied hard enough to get his diploma. The two of them graduated the same year. They both chose stomatology, a form of advanced dentistry considered in France a medical specialty like cardiology or urology. So, when they entered the job market, Billy was so grateful that he proposed a partnership to my father. He offered to cover the expenses of the rental of a dental office. They settled for the entire third floor of a building located half a block off the Champs-Elysées, at 63 Avenue Franklin D. Roosevelt (formerly Avenue Victor Emmanuel III), in Paris' most affluent and glamorous arrondissement.

From the start, Billy and Sanil expanded. They took another partner, hired medical assistants, secretaries and technicians for their prosthesis lab, and, last but not least, a Korean majordomo who would greet their patients in style, always wearing a black tuxedo and immaculate white gloves.

Such pomp was more a reflection of Billy's style than of my father's. Sanil bore modesty in his genes. Billy was ambitious, driven, as a good old American entrepreneur ought to be. The Yank was determined to take Paris by storm. And he did.

Their practice fast became *the* place to have your teeth fixed. Their reputation spread throughout Europe. The royal families of Great Britain, Netherlands and Belgium flocked there; so did poets, writers, politicians, musicians and Hollywood stars. I was impressed by some of the 63 Avenue Franklin D. Roosevelt regulars, like the Duke and Duchess of Windsor or Eric von Stroheim, the famous Austrian-born actor/director of the thirties, a true Hollywood legend. He had taken a liking to my father, had even offered to send me a signed picture of him when I was attending summer camp in England. A few words were written on the back of the photograph that showed a stern, Teutonic von Stroheim, his face bearing scars from his saber fencing at the university.

I flaunted the precious document to my British friends at the camp. Only seven years had passed since Germans had showered them with V-1s and V-2s. In the early fifties Brits didn't feel particular empathy for anyone with a name preceded by Von.

My father's famous patients are too numerous to list here at the risk of my being labeled a name-dropper, but I'd be remiss not to mention the stunning Barbara Stanwyck. She had been more than just Dad's patient, she had been his mistress, according to my mother, a revelation that filled me with pride, I hate to confess.

Thirty-five years later, I told the story to my now deceased friend Axel Madsen, who had just written an extensive biography of the movie star. He first rebutted the assertion, reminding me that Stanwyck had been a member of Hollywood's *sewing circle*. Then he added that she had probably been bisexual, lending a bit of credibility to my mother's allegation. That being said, my mother never lied.

Her name was Milly. She was born on November 13, 1901 in Bucharest, one of three daughters of Eliza Teitlebaum and Heinrich Maurer, a Jew of German descent.

Her family was far better off than my father's, but both had something in common: their shared admiration for France. So, Heinrich and Eliza also sent Milly to Paris.

The moment she arrived in the French capital in 1919, a year after the end of World War I, Mother took private singing lessons. She was nineteen when she was accepted to the Paris Music Conservatory, a true achievement in and of itself.

In July 1925, at age twenty-four, this newly arrived Romanian immigrant signed a contract with the Opéra-Comique where she made her debut under the stage name of Milly Morère, in the part of Javotte, in Jules Massenet's *Manon*.

She was an attractive woman, judging from old photographs and from the two portraits Boris Pastoukoff painted of her. Pastoukoff had been Clark Gable and Marlene Dietrich's official portraitist.

Milly's long neck, her posture, her self-assurance, her haughtiness, her elegance, bestowed upon her a queenly bearing. She displayed sharp, evenly carved features, a thin face lightened by gazelle eyes. Like a rock star, she had her share of groupies. She counted hundreds of suitors, but few lovers. It would have been out of character.

In 1929, she joined the Palais Garnier. She was twenty-nine when she made her debut on January 7, 1930, in Wagner's *Die Walkürie*, in the part of Helmigue. She became a diva, but was first and foremost a great artist hard at work. Franco Zeffirelli, the Italian director, once said, "Diva is a title you must earn." Milly had. I remember listening to her as she vocalized for hours, hammering the same notes over and over on the keys of her grand Steinway, her powerful voice filling the entire apartment.

As Georges Clemenceau, a former French Prime Minister, once put it, "when one has character, it is always bad." My mother was loaded with character. She also possessed a sharp sense of humor. She told raunchy jokes with the verve of a general. She had the common sense of a peasant and the will and perseverance of an Olympic champ.

Like the ultimate pro she was, Milly would not compromise on quality. A few days after she suffered a stroke, my daughter and I visited her in the nursing home where she spent the last days of her life. Cécile aspired to becoming a pop and jazz singer. She had brought a demo cassette with her, hoping to get her grandmother's professional opinion.

We entered her room and sat next to her bed. My mother was laying flat on her back, her eyes closed, a plastic tube coming out of her nose. "Cécile recorded a song for you. She'd love to have your opinion," I ventured. Milly kept silent. I nodded to Cécile. My daughter hit the playback button of her small cassette player. She had the enthusiasm and the self-confidence of youth, but she also felt stage fright, just as if she had auditioned at Carnegie Hall. The song ended. Mother kept her eyes closed and remained as expressionless as a sphinx. Impatient to hear her comments and secretly hoping that she would receive praise for her performance, Cécile stared at me, on edge. Not a word. The heavy silence lasted for an endless minute. Then Milly, her eyes still shut, whispered, *"Beaucoup de travail."* (Needs lots of work)

Cécile failed to realize that she had received a valuable piece of advice.

My mother was strong and could be mean and intransigent. She hated complacency and stuck to her guns when she felt that she was right. She stood her ground in moments of adversity. She never minced her words. "I always say what's on my mind," was her motto. Well, saying what was on her mind got her into more trouble than she bargained for. She ruffled her share of feathers in her lifetime. Yet, she never regretted having given a piece of her mind to those who had offended her, even if it meant some sort of setback. She never compromised on her beliefs, no matter the consequences.

I was at her bedside a week before she passed away. She was immobile, hooked to an oxygen tank. She knew as I did that she was dying. At one point, I gathered the little courage I had in me and asked, "Mom, I know you've always been an atheist. But, I have to ask you, have you changed your mind?" Milly opened her eyes, looked at me defiantly and uttered, *"Je ne crois qu'en ce que je vois."* "I only believe in what I see." She then closed her eyes, exhausted by the overwhelming effort she had to exert to let out these few words. Her inner strength was unshakable.

On August 2, 1928, Milly wrote a letter bearing the Opéra-Comique letterhead. She addressed it to *Docteur* Dorian. My father had graduated from medical school three months earlier, on April 23, 1928, at the age of thirty-one. He had taken the month of August off to visit his parents in Iasi. "Life is so sad. I miss you tremendously," she wrote. "I send you all my affection, my tenderness and my biggest kisses, your Milly."

My father got sentimental too. He was in love when he wrote, "My Darling Milly, A thousand thanks for your letter and for the photos. Seeing you in the company of dogs, I couldn't help thinking, here is *the Beauty and the Beast*. My friends ask about you and we all wait for your return impatiently.

"I will at last be able to tell you, and to make you realize, how much I have missed you."

Two years later, on March 1, 1930, Sanil and Milly were married. He was thirty-three years old. She was twenty-nine. On March fourteen of the same year, Sanil was officially appointed Assistant Surgeon at the Hartford British Hospital in Paris.

By 1931, Sanil and Milly knew that they would never return to their homeland. Paris is where they lived. Paris is where they were going to stay. Sanil could not keep his Romanian nationality if he wanted to practice medicine in France. They both were naturalized on February 3, 1933. It is then that my father changed his name to Dorian.

What an awkward choice. Dorian didn't even sound French. Why didn't he pick a name like Durand or Dubois if he wanted to assimilate? Why Dorian? There was some logic behind that choice, though. Dorian contained the French word *or,* which translated in German, means gold as in Goldschlager. So, Sanil had retained part of his original name, sort of. He also adored Oscar Wilde's *The Picture of Dorian Gray*.

I never quite knew how to answer people when they asked about the origins of the name. I'd come up with some cockamamie explanation that would never satisfy the inquisitor. I hoped I would not have to deal with that issue in the United States, where the name Dorian, you would think, wouldn't raise an eyebrow. I was wrong. When they realized that I was French, some wondered why a French boy like me would bear such an Anglo-Saxon name. Others took me for an Armenian. I am still inundated with junk mail from Armenian organizations.

My father's purpose bore no ambiguity. He just wanted a gentile's name like most Jews who emigrated from central Europe. For some there might have been a more pressing reason, maybe a premonition in the wake of rampant anti-Semitism both in France and in Germany. After all, Volume Two of Hitler's *Mein Kampf* had already been published five years earlier. Some people, and possibly my parents as well, had sufficient foresight to sense the inevitability of what was bound to happen.

In the thirties, Milly and Sanil had reached the height of their professional success. My father's practice was flourishing. My mother's popularity was growing. They could afford more luxurious accommodations. They found the apartment of their dreams on the ground floor of one of the upscale freestone buildings that dated from the late 1800s. It was located a block from the Luxembourg Gardens, a few minutes walking distance from Montparnasse, the Latin Quarter and Saint-Germain-des-Prés. An ideal location.

When they settled in their new place, Sanil and Milly left their Bohemian life behind and turned into good old bourgeois, acquiring the best and the worst of the new social status bestowed upon them.

The apartment located at 4 Rue Joseph Bara, in the sixth arrondissement, was dark but spacious. Its living room was so large that my parents called it *le petit château*. Its layout and its proportions were indeed those of the *salon* of an eighteenth century castle. It had direct access to a long and narrow garden that would become my retreat, my fief, my magic kingdom during my early years, right after the war.

Few people could boast of a private garden in the heart of the capital. It was landscaped with tall gold dust Japanese aucuba plants that grew next to a metallic fence mounted atop a thick stonewall. On the other side of the fence laid a wider garden that had been let go. It had grown into a thick jungle of tall grass and weed trees. So close, yet so remote, the untidy universe exerted an immense attraction on my young mind, teasing my imagination. There lay an uncharted territory filled with hidden treasures that begged to be explored. I found the courage to climb the metallic fence, managed to avoid its sharp spikes and jumped into this wilderness, my heart pounding. Hidden by the wild vegetation that was twice my height, I felt as if I had been transported thousands of miles away, to some African savannah. My curiosity satisfied, I returned to my own Shangri-La and buried, in-between aucubas, a few time capsules that contained toys, coins and letters addressed to whomever would perform archeological digs, centuries hence.

My birth on April Fools' Day, in 1937, sealed my parents' happiness. He was forty. She was thirty-six. My late arrival was unexpected. Forty was considered old to be a father at that time, so was thirty-six to be a mother. I was going to be the only child of old parents.

The carefree and happy times came to an abrupt end. Sensing that war with Germany was imminent, the French government started mobilizing. Sanil was drafted on September 2, 1939. Six months later, on May 10, 1940, the German armies invaded Belgium, Luxembourg and northern France and within six weeks defeated the Western forces. In June 1940, France capitulated. It was what the French called *la debâcle.*

2
The War Years

Man is condemned to be free.
—JEAN-PAUL SARTRE

My father was demobilized July 14, 1940, on Bastille Day, a month after the German army invaded Paris. He had spent almost a year in the military at an undisclosed location and had missed the first days of an occupation that would last four interminable years. He wasn't in Paris when two trucks loaded with German soldiers and a few motorcycles entered the city through Porte de la Villette, in the wee hours of the morning of that first day of the occupation. At five thirty-five in the morning, German soldiers were seen on Avenue de Flandre, heading toward two railroad stations, Gare du Nord and Gare de l'Est. An hour later, German troops reached the Invalides. At seven-thirty, the German general in charge of Paris stepped out of his car on Place de la Concorde and entered the Crillon Hotel, which he would use as his headquarters. Paris had lost its freedom.

When Dad returned, the French capital appeared unchanged. The shops and the department stores, which had been closed for a brief period, had reopened for business. The brothels were booming, the terraces of cafes were packed, Les Grands Boulevards, the Champs-Elysees, the Tuileries Gardens were bursting with activity. You couldn't get a restaurant reservation. Cabarets and music halls like the famous Folies Bergère and the Moulin Rouge were booked solid. Paris had remained Paris, with significant exceptions. Fewer cars were roaming the streets. German soldiers in their green-gray uniforms were everywhere. People tried to go about their businesses as if impervious to the invaders' omnipresence, but an underlying malaise hovered over the city.

A giant swastika floated under the Arc de Triomphe, as other Nazi flags of smaller size had replaced France's blue, white and red emblems on all official buildings. The first German military parade on the Champs-Elysées was met with total apathy. A few rejoiced, but not all. Violette Wassem, a typical Parisian, felt the sting of defeat like most of her fellow Parisians.

"On June 14, there they were," she recalled in a letter dated July 1997. "It was eight in the morning and I was alone, walking to work on Boulevard Haussmann. They appeared so tidy as they were marching down the avenue, looking straight in front of them. They marched at noontime; they marched in the evening; they marched the following day and the day after that. We were looking at them horrified."

Many hid their tears, as the invader captured their beloved city. Deafened by the umpapas of the brass bands that could be heard throughout Paris, the vanquished had also to endure the ominous thump of boots hitting the pavement in unison, as the *Schleus*, that's what the French called the Germans at that time, performed their awkward goose steps with the primitive force and arrogance of victorious Huns.

At first, this arrogance manifested itself in military marches. But German soldiers and officers alike had received strict orders to avoid confrontation with the Parisians, to act "civilized." So they did. They behaved like gentlemen and often, as an American journalist put it then, like "naive tourists."

The old public buses with their open decks were the first victims of a severe gas rationing that would worsen until Liberation Day. Taxis came next and later on, private cars. Bicycles in Paris became as rampant as they were in China in the fifties. The entire city took to pedaling. Horse and buggies reappeared. Rickshaws replaced taxis.

Sanil had returned to civilian life, but could no longer ride his beloved # 83 bus, which so conveniently took him to the front door of his office building. He had to bicycle to work. To do so, he needed a permit issued by the French authorities. His partner, Billy Davenport, wrote an official letter addressed to police headquarters. In it he stated, "Doctor Dorian has to use his bicycle for house calls." The permit was granted.

Every weekday, Doctor Dorian had to pedal his way across the capital. The experience might have been enjoyable, particularly for someone who loved Paris as much as my father did, but the sight of German soldiers and armored vehicles must have filled his heart with fear and sorrow.

A curfew had been imposed. No one could ride a bike or walk in the streets after eleven o'clock without running the risk of being arrested.

On September 24, 1940, the German and French authorities issued a pass to Sanil written in German and in French, the left page titled *Ausweis*, the right page titled *Laissez-Passer*.

By November of the same year, Sanil could no longer practice medicine without an authorization from the Department of Hygiene. To secure it, he had to submit a complete file to the General Secretariat of Public Health, a branch of Police Headquarters. In a letter dated November 12, 1940, the head of this service acknowledged receipt of my father's request to practice medicine in accordance with the August 16, 1940 legislation. "The present document authorizes Dr. Dorian to practice medicine until a final decision is made concerning his situation."

General Pétain's Vichy Government, for which medicine was of primary importance, had ordered the French Medical Association to come up with a xenophobic and anti-Semitic legislation that would regulate the medical profession. The law of August 16, 1940, stipulated that only French physicians born of French fathers or naturalized before 1927 could practice medicine. No one ever protested or opposed the new measures.

The letter from Police Headquarters raised more questions than it provided answers. The authorities must have known that my father had been naturalized, but were they aware that he had become a French citizen six years after the deadline imposed by Vichy? Did my father lie, arguing that the new law did not apply to him? Why was he given a break? They authorized him to practice until further notice, but why didn't they grant him that license permanently? Did they suspect something? Did someone intervene in his favor?

Life was so precarious then. No one could tell what tomorrow would bring. A Damocles sword was hanging over the heads of people who were in my father's situation.

Rationing hit coal and food reserves. Basic products like milk, eggs and butter became scarce; endless lines formed in front of food stores; the *boulangeries* suddenly stopped producing baguettes, a serious setback for Parisians. Life had turned complicated and challenging.

I'll never know how my mother laid her hands on chickens, but one day we found six of them roaming our garden. Our luxurious apartment had morphed into a farm. Say what you want, but the birds provided us with the most basic sought-after staple: eggs, a rarity in occupied Paris.

We baptized one of the chickens Joséphine. Amazingly, Joséphine responded to her name. When called, she hopped over my parents' bedroom parapet, scurried on their Persian carpet to gobble the few grains of corn we'd throw at her. Satiated, she would hesitantly proceed to explore the rest of the apartment. I got attached to the fowl. She was my first pet.

One Sunday, my mother served chicken for lunch. As we were gorging ourselves, I caught her staring at my father, a strange look in her eyes. It didn't take long for me to find out what had happened to my dear Josephine, even though my mother never admitted that she was responsible for her demise. I was crestfallen. That loss was the first big sorrow of my life.

The winter of 1940 was difficult. Coal was scarce. Heating became a luxury few could afford.

At the start of the invasion, the Germans did not want to be accused of anti-Semitism. They did not want the French population to think they were responsible for the anti-Jewish measures that were about to be taken. They made sure that the local population would shoulder this responsibility. The future atrocities the Nazis would commit against Jews would be seen as a natural consequence of a legitimate wish of the people.

The Gestapo first helped foment spontaneous, grass root anti-Jewish demonstrations that would allow them to say, "French citizens, we heard you. You do not want Jews on your territory. We will help you get rid of them."

Au Pilori, a French language newspaper created by PresseGruppe, an arm of the Ministry of Propaganda of the Third Reich, was instructed to recruit young French men to lead anti-Jewish demonstrations. Two groups were born, one called *Le Jeune Front*, The Young Front, for men age sixteen to twenty; the other called *Guarde Française* for men twenty-one years and older. Their mission was to disseminate anti-Semitic leaflets.

On August 3, 1940, they shattered the window case of a Jewish-owned store. Four days later, they broke into several stores and vandalized them. On the twentieth, a group of youngsters threw bricks in the windows of all the alleged Jewish-owned stores on the Champs Elysées, in broad daylight.

Thomas Kernan, the French editor of *Vogue Magazine* and the representative for Condé Nast in Europe at that time, witnessed the incident. This is what he wrote:

> I happened to be chatting with my colleagues on my office balcony when we heard shouts coming from L'Etoile. A young man wearing some sort of uniform was driving a yellow roadster down the empty avenue. He was shouting "Down with the Jews," as he was leaving behind him a trace of shattered glass. Men in uniform posted in front of every targeted store had been throwing bricks wrapped in newspaper in the windows of these stores as the roadster was driving by them. There was, in front of my startled eyes, a million dollars worth of windows shattered. Most of these establishments had been closed for a while. Their faithful employees, who were watching the scene shaking and crying, had just reopened them.
>
> After having accomplished their ugly deed, the young men in uniform strolled down the avenue, reached the *Jeune Front* headquarters at 66 Avenue des Champs-Elysées, entered the building and reappeared at its windows, shouting and laughing at the crowd that had gathered, attracted by the noise.
>
> I saw a German officer walking out of the Claridge Hotel, as a brick was being thrown into a window nearby. The officer grabbed the perpetrator who pulled a piece of paper out of his jacket and showed it to him. The German officer checked it out and let the Frenchman go.

Was my father aware of what had happened, a few blocks from where he worked? How could he not have been?

Two months of anti-Semitic propaganda and unrest were followed by a period of discriminatory ordinances. Jews had to register with police and had to carry IDs stamped *Jew* at all times. Jewish-owned businesses had to post the inscription, "Jewish Enterprise" on their walls.

In May 1941, thirty seven hundred men, mostly Germans, Czechs and Polish, responded voluntarily to a notification requesting they go to several locations to have their immigration status checked. It was a trap. French police arrested them and took them to the internment camps of Pithivier and Beaune-la-Rolades from where they were sent to concentration camps in Germany several months later.

The French authorities first targeted Jews that weren't French nationals. Later, they targeted Jews born in France of foreign or naturalized parents.

I belonged to that category.

For my father, the threat of being arrested was real and ever present. Every Jew in Paris had waited in fear for that fatal moment when he would hear loud orders barked in German, boots rushing in the hallway, the rattling of weapons and those insistent and unnerving knocks at his door.

My father had to do something. He decided to renounce the Judaic faith, which he'd never embraced, and to embrace the Catholic religion, in which he had no faith. He was an atheist's atheist. That didn't stop him from being baptized on August 8, 1941, at the *St. Pierre du Gros Caillou* Parish, 92 Rue Saint-Dominique, in the seventh arrondissement. His was an act of survival.

It is not clear why Milly did not follow suit.

On August 20 and 21, 1941, French police backed by German soldiers rounded up two hundred and thirty-two foreigners and sent them to the new internment camp of Drancy, which was to become a stopover on the way to Auschwitz.

These operations failed to arouse the wrath of the French population. After all, the victims were foreigners. Most of them were new arrivals. Who cared?

In September, an infamous anti-Semite exhibit named *The Jew and France* was inaugurated at the Palais Berlitz, on Boulevard des Italiens. It was organized by the French.

Milly, who had been under the protection of Jacques Rouché, the Director of the Paris Opera, decided to convert to Catholicism too. She was also baptized at the *St. Pierre du Gros Caillou* parish on November 22, 1941.

Three months earlier, she had been asked by her employer, the Ministry of National Education, to sign a peculiar document, declaring upon oath that she had never been "... a member of the *Grand Orient de France*, the *Grande Loge de France*, the *Grande Loge Nationale Indépendante*, the *Ordre Mixte International du Droit Humain*, the *Société Théosophique*, the *Grand Prieuré des Gaules* or of any subsidiaries of the above-mentioned organizations," all freemason secret societies, "or of any organization under the August 13, 1940 legislation..."

Milly and Sanil's baptisms, though not a total panacea, improved our chances of survival, at least temporarily. If they could establish that I was born of Catholic parents, then they had made my life safer. But the risk that our secret might be uncovered at any time increased exponentially as the situation in France worsened. Friends, neighbors or acquaintances could inform on my parents. Their naturalization papers could be exposed.

Whenever my nanny fell ill or was off, my mother had to take me with her to the opera when she was performing. She would sit me on a stool in the wings, and would return to her dressing room to be prepped for the performance, leaving me by myself. According to her, I never budged, so mesmerized was I by the costumes, by the sets and by the dancers in tutus. Particularly by the dancers in tutus.

I endured many operas in that uncomfortable position, even long and tedious ones.

A masterpiece of baroque sensuousness designed in the Beaux Arts style by Charles Garnier, the Palais Garnier was built in 1862 during the Second Empire, under the reign of Napoleon III. Its architect decorated the mammoth building lavishly, with multicolored marble friezes, columns and lavish statuary, as well as deities from Greek mythology. The building featured a lavish *Grand Foyer*, corridors, stairwells, alcoves and landings that allowed the movement of large numbers of people. It had the biggest stage in Europe.

One evening, my mother made an exception. She used the main entrance of the Palais Garnier instead of the stage door in the back of the building, took me to a seat in the center of the orchestra and left. I remember being mesmerized by the opulence of the room rich with velvet, gold leaf, cherubim and nymphs. I couldn't keep my eyes off the scintillating six-ton chandelier hanging from the ceiling. The place was my Disneyland.

The entire theater filled up fast. It could accommodate twenty-two hundred spectators. I looked around. Not one woman in sight. Not one civilian. German officers in uniform had occupied all the seats. The orchestra, the boxes, and even *le poulailler*, the French name for peanut gallery, were packed. The top ranking officers of the invading forces had gathered in the landmark theater that evening.

The ones who were seated around me could not have been more solicitous, even affectionate. They smiled at me, made funny remarks that were punctuated by loud laughter. The sight of this little boy with blond curly hair and blue eyes must have been so out of place, so surreal to all these SS officers who were flaunting the collar patches, shoulder boards, sleeve cuff bands and diamond patches that adorned their impeccably pressed military garbs.

Under different circumstances, my well-groomed admirers would not have hesitated an instant to send me to a concentration camp if they had suspected I was Jewish, curly hair or no curly hair. I didn't fall for their cutesy manners. I knew who they were and I didn't like them.

The persecution of Jews and foreigners intensified. An ordinance dated May 19, 1942, made it mandatory for them to wear the yellow Star of David. It was implemented on Sunday, June 7, 1942.

No document indicated that my parents needed to abide by the new law. Conversely, no document indicated that they did not. I cannot imagine them wearing the yellow Star of David, he at his upscale practice, she as a diva. But these were no ordinary times.

Another ordinance dated July 8, 1942, barred Jews from restaurants, cafés, bars, theaters, concerts, telephone booths, markets, swimming pools, museums, libraries, sports events, historical monuments, racetracks... Well, from everywhere. "Jews wanted war," wrote *Le Petit Matin*, a daily newspaper, "The malfeasance of their race has thrown the entire world into this horrible conflict. Compared to this crime, the recent measures concerning them are benign."

They were indeed benign if you weighed them against what followed. In less than forty-eight hours, from the morning of July 16 at four in the morning, to one in the afternoon the following day, police arrested 12,884 German, Austrian, Czech, Polish and Russian Jews in Paris. Women and children, the old and the sick were all rounded up at the *Vél d'Hiv*, a huge sports arena in the fifteenth arrondissement, in the heart of the capital. An operation of that scope had required long and careful preparation. 9,000 French civil servants, including 4,000 policemen, had been mobilized for this roundup they ironically named "Operation Spring Wind."

The detainees were kept in the stadium without water and in appalling hygienic conditions from July 16 to July 22. All of them were deported to Auschwitz.

Following that incident, the implementation of Hitler's final solution became more pressing for the Nazis. Paris' Jewry had to be eradicated.

Serge Klarsfeld, the renowned French-Romanian Nazi hunter, claims in his *Shoah Memorial,* that 51,000 Jews of foreign descent and 24,700 French Jews (thirteen percent of all French Jews) were deported to concentration camps. An estimated 5,500 survived.

Not all Parisians were collaborators or anti-Semites. A handful of them revolted as early as July 1940. Graffiti reading, "Long live de Gaulle" or "Death to the invader" appeared on the walls of the city and reappeared after having been washed off. A pun on Maréchal Pétain's name read Maréchal *Putain*, which, literally translated, meant Marshal Whore. On November 11, 1940, a student protest on Place de l'Etoile was brutally put down. Nine months later, a German officer was assassinated. Those responsible for terrorist acts caught by French police or by the Germans paid with their lives. On April 14, 1942, twenty-seven communist partisans were executed at Mont Valérien.

The number of arrests, expedited trials, reprisals and executions grew as the resistance movement amplified and as underground warfare spread.

* * *

The pressure on my parents must have been tremendous, unbearable. By mid-1942, their friends advised them to vanish, to disappear, to leave Paris. Each day they delayed the decision increased the eventuality of a tragic outcome. They were lucky to have escaped the roundups so far, lucky to be alive. Many had fallen into German hands. Aware that they had pushed their luck, Milly and Sanil took the necessary steps to avoid the worst.

3

The Hideaway

Acquaintances of my parents knew farmers willing to provide a hideaway. Their farm was located on the outskirts of a tiny village bearing the bucolic name of Saint-Priest-des-Champs. It was tucked away in the heart of the Massif Central Mountains, an area described by Parisians as being *la France profonde,* deep France.

The decision to flee Paris was not simple. Mom had to interrupt her career; Dad had to close his practice. They abandoned their apartment and all the valuables in it.

Milly and I left Paris for Saint-Priest-des-Champ in the spring of 1943. My father was to join us at a later date. We took the train but could not travel beyond Orleans, sixty miles south of Paris. The railroad network was used for the transportation of German troops and material. Service to certain destinations was scarce, often canceled.

In Orleans, we experienced our first bombardment, the rush to shelters, the interminable moments during which we had to stand up pressed against one another in these dark and damp rat holes, the stale odors, the babies tucked in their mothers' arms crying their lungs out, the anxious faces, the fear in women's eyes as the muffled detonations of bombs falling nearby tested everyone's nerves. Then total silence would ensue, a loud, eerie, threatening silence. We would come up for air, crazed and numb. Orleans was not a good place to be. My mother had to press on.

We still had to travel a little more than two hundred miles, a short distance by today's standards, but in 1943, even fifty miles meant a long and at times dangerous journey. Milly and I covered the remaining stretch by foot, by car or by truck whenever she found good souls willing to give us a ride.

The images of long lines of women, of old people and children exhausted, dragging their feet on roads littered with vehicles that either were destroyed or that had run out of gas are carved in my brain forever. An entire humanity, displaced, humiliated, famished and scared was moving south, indifferent to the horrific sight of the decomposing corpses of donkeys and horses that lay in ditches. Some had packed horse-driven carts, old automobiles or pick-up trucks with all the personal stuff they could gather. My mother carried only a couple of suitcases.

Messerschmitt fighter planes were diving on us and spraying us with bursts of machine-gun fire. Milly knocked at doors, begging for milk. She was turned down like an undesirable bum more often than not. Thank God, there were exceptions. My mother's resourcefulness and her determination to survive saved us from starvation.

The journey had taken weeks, so what a relief for her to reach the farm where we would spend two years in precarious conditions.

One day, in the summer of 1991, I felt the urge to escape the pressure of New York City, saturated as I was by an overdose of noise, pollution, and cab drivers' insolence. I don't know why, but I could not get Saint-Priest off my mind. I had retained good memories of the small village where my mother, my father and I had hidden for two years, but time and my imagination had distorted them. I vividly remembered a pristine and primitive Shangri-La made of green pastures, unexplored valleys, old unshaven farmers, barns, cows, pigs, horses, chickens, ducks. Could life in that heavenly environment have been so blessed and carefree at a time when our civilization was on the brink of destruction?

I decided to call Jean-Claude Héberlé, a close friend who had been my colleague when I was a journalist in the sixties. He had been the CEO of Antenne II, a French TV network, and had just retired. He was living in Normandy with his wife. I explained to him that I was stricken by a hard case of nostalgia and that I wanted to go back to Saint-Priest. Would he be interested in accompanying me? His curiosity piqued, he accepted without hesitation. As soon as I hung up, I rushed to a ticket office and purchased a New York/Paris round trip ticket.

On a beautiful Friday morning, Jean-Claude and I drove south. France that year had been hit by an unusual heat wave. The sky had remained blue for days. It took us five hours to reach the village of Saint-Priest-des-Champs. We arrived early afternoon.

I looked around, searching for references, landmarks and felt disappointment at first. The village square bore no resemblance to what I had imagined it to be.

Then it all came back. "Would you like to see my school?" I asked.

The school stood a few yards from the main square. It took us seconds to reach it and there it was, in its simplicity, an unsophisticated, nondescript, one-story stone building and in front of it, the small yard where we used to play tag, fight or roll marbles during breaks.

It was a public primary school that looked like the one featured in *Au Revoir Les Enfants*, Louis Malle's masterpiece. My story was similar to that of the film's protagonist, a Jewish boy named Jean Bonnet. His real name was Jean Kipplestein. He too was hiding from the Nazis in a remote village. Like him, I was surrounded by Catholic kids who had no idea what a Jew was. Did their parents know? Of course they did. Did that put me in jeopardy? Anyone could have snitched on me. But no one did. If they had, I wouldn't be here to tell the story. Not all French were rotten. France had its heroes, many silent heroes who saved thousands of people from deportation. I owe my life to the entire population of Saint-Priest-des-Champs, that tiny village of less than seven hundred inhabitants, all heroes in my eyes.

Jean-Claude and I returned to the small square and strolled around. It was very hot. At one point we passed in front of a wide-open window located at street level. An old woman was beating a carpet. She must have been in her mid-eighties. "I beg your pardon, Madame," I asked, trying to draw her attention. She looked at me, still beating her carpet. "Can you tell us how to get to the Petit farm?"

Her arm froze. She stared at me with great intensity. She couldn't keep her eyes off me. After a long pause, she said, her voice filled with astonishment and delight, "But... but... you are my little Dorian." She paused, waiting for a reaction. Any reaction. "Do you know who I am?" she asked, a smile on her gentle face.

"No."

"I am your teacher. My name is Madame Bouchon."

"How did you recognize me?"

"You look so much like your father."

She trotted away, reappeared at her front door, and took me in her arms. Then, she went knocking at her neighbors' doors, yelling, "You'll never guess who is here. *Le petit Dorian. Oui, le petit Dorian* is here."

To her I was still the little Dorian.

The few old timers who had survived were surprised and happy to see me. They all insisted on offering us drinks. We had to do the rounds, pay a visit to each and every one, one house after another, one *pastis* after another. By the time we were done, Jean-Claude and I could barely stand. We parted and drove to the farm the best we could, a couple of miles outside the village.

I recognized the long dirt path bordered by oak trees to the left of the main road. At the end of it stood the farm, the barn to its right and the stables a few yards farther.

A cart filled with bales of hay blocked our way. We got out of the car and spotted, on top of it, a peasant in his mid to late forties picking up bales with a long fork and throwing them inside the barn. Sensing our presence, the man looked down and cried out, "*Vingt Dieu! Mais c'est Dorian... Dorian*! I'll be darned... Dorian!"

He was our savior's son, my partner in pranks and petty crimes, my good old buddy, André Petit.

Monsieur Petit, his father, had two sons, André, the youngest, René and a daughter, Marinette. They all lived at the farm, a stone building with a cement patio overlooking the fields. Its ground floor had a kitchen and a living room and behind the kitchen, a dark corridor that led to a small bedroom facing the barn. That room, basic, primitive, damp, had been our living quarters. Adjacent to it was a tiny space where my mother used to prepare meals.

The place had remained as untidy, muddy and smelly as it had been almost half a century ago.

Life at the farm was simple but rough. Winters were brutally cold. The stove that had been installed in our room just for us was barely sufficient to handle the extreme. Saint-Priest lay 4,000 feet above sea level and temperatures could plummet to lows of minus twenty to thirty degrees Fahrenheit. Three feet of snow was not unusual in these parts. The locals were used to it, but for us city folks, the white stuff was challenging, particularly when we had to move around. I remember walking to school during these major storms, with snow up to my torso.

Every weekday morning, rain or shine, I had to hike the two kilometers that separated me from the school by foot, even in the dark of winter. When I was passing by the old alcohol distillery, at the outskirts of the village, the workers would offer me a taste of their ninety proof schnapps, setting my mouth on fire. Sometimes, my mother accompanied me to school. Whenever we spotted headlights approaching, she pulled me by the hand, forced me to take shelter, usually in the ditch and to keep my head low, assuring we could not be spotted by some German patrol.

Under the terms of the armistice signed on June 22, 1940, the German army had occupied the north and west of France. The country was divided into an Occupied Zone and a Free Zone, overseen by a French government located at Vichy. Following the Allied landings in French North Africa on November 8, 1942, the Germans decided to occupy the free zone to avoid the risk of an exposed flank on the French Mediterranean. Thus when my mother arrived in Saint-Priest-des-Champs in early 1943, the Germans were everywhere. Although they were not stationed directly in the village, they had military headquarters in nearby Riom and Clermont-Ferrand and patrolled the area regularly.

My father was able to join us in the fall. He kept a low profile at first, limiting his outings to the countryside, always on the alert. It took awhile before he dared to show up in the village. When its people found out he was a physician, many sought his professional advice and before long, Sanil was treating the sick and attending to wounds for free. He became quite popular.

On occasions, he took me to the village at night to see a patient or to visit friends. I remember a few mysterious meetings that took place in different houses at night. The host always changed, but not the ritual. Only men attended. Such gatherings were risky during the curfew. A villager was posted outside, on the lookout for German patrols. Ten to twelve people formed a circle around an old wooden radio. I was relegated to a corner of the dark room and could only see the back of these farmers. They were all bent forward, their grotesque shadows projected on the walls. They appeared frozen, as if they were awaiting the words of a divinity. The volume of the radio had been set as low as possible. The drums of Beethoven's Fifth segued into the now famous, "*Les français parlent aux français*," "the French speak to the French," solemnly spoken by a male announcer. The crackled sound of his voice seemed to come from another planet. The Germans tried to scramble these broadcasts, but never succeeded.

Then came the litany of cryptic sentences that were often funny, always enigmatic, enunciated one after the other in neutral tones, each separated from the next by short pauses.

Tante Amélie fait du vélo en short (Aunt Amelia bikes wearing shorts)

Yvette aime les grosses carottes (Yvette likes fat carrots)

Ecoute mon coeur qui pleure (Listen to my weeping heart)

Veronese était un peintre (Veronese was a painter)

Berce mon coeur d'une langueur monotone (Cradle my heart with a monotonous languor)

La vache saute par dessus la lune (The cow jumps over the moon)

These atonic litanies were nothing short of an enigma to my young mind. I was not aware then that the radio program, broadcasted mostly at night by the BBC from London, was geared to the French Underground, to the Resistance. The arcane sentences were code for important military actions or decisions. They informed their targeted audience that weapons were about to be parachuted, that a plane was about to land, that a train had to be blown up, that a railway section had to be sabotaged. To be caught listening to them was punishable by death.

Most of the villagers who attended these gatherings had taken to the *maquis*. They had decided to rise up against the intruder and to fight the enemy every which way they could. The *maquisards* lived a clandestine life in forests and mountains, training, planning and fighting. They were the ones who sabotaged, attacked and killed the occupier, who interrupted their communication networks, who informed London of their activities. Not all were armed soldiers. Many fought the invader in more subdued ways. The telephone operator intercepted sensitive conversations. Farmers hid partisans from the Germans. Dedicated men and women informed on troop movements.

I was too young to realize or understand the sacrifices these people were making. When I reached the age of reason, I wondered how I would have reacted to the German Occupation had I been old enough to fight. What would have I chosen to do? Collaborate with the enemy for the sake of survival, or join the Underground and become one of the "soldiers of the night," as David Schoenbrun, the American journalist and historian, called the French Resistance fighters? I hope I would have had the fortitude to opt for the latter, but such a decision was far from being simple. I honestly do not know what I would have done.

In an interview I conducted for a documentary I had produced entitled, *A Reliable Ally*, Schoenbrun said, "The courage it took to form an underground movement in a country occupied by the Nazi army and the Nazi police is a courage that, even though I saw it, I knew it, is beyond my own comprehension."

The resistance fighters operating in and around Clermont-Ferrand, the largest city near Saint-Priest-des-Champs, were in desperate need of physicians to attend to the wounded and the sick. Surviving the long and cold winters was challenging, particularly for the *maquisards* who had no roofs over their heads. My father understood the urgency. He joined the *Forces Françaises de l'Intérieur*, the *FFI*, in the winter of 1943, two months after his arrival in Saint-Priest-des-Champs. They gave him the rank of captain.

From that moment on, he disappeared from our lives. I was often awakened by whispers and by the creaking noise of doors being opened in the middle of the night. I'd get out of bed, take a peek outside the window and discern the shadows of men in the courtyard armed with light automatic weapons. I could see my father taking my mother in his arms, telling her things I could not hear and then he would leave. The following day, my mother would mention his visit. We never knew when he would come back.

Sanil rarely talked about his life with the *FFI*. He despised the absurdity of war. He told me once that his men had captured a German officer who had been shot in the foot. The partisans could not afford to keep prisoners. They had scheduled the officer's execution the day after his capture. They still ordered my father to surgically remove the bullet that was lodged in his foot. My father was outraged, "Why go through the trouble? The prisoner will be dead tomorrow." "We want him to be in good physical shape and aware of what is happening to him when we execute him."

Left alone, my mother and I got by. Life was not always grim. We had many happy moments. The place was magic. On Saturdays and Sundays, I'd lose myself in the deep valley that extended below the farm to the *Viaduc des Fades*, a spectacular truss bridge that had been built at the beginning of the century. My long excursions were like safaris. I can still smell the musty scent of ferns and moss, their aroma enhanced by the morning dew, see those majestic oak trees under which we could harvest gigantic *cèpes* (porcinis), hear the sound of the rushing waters down below and the cacophony of ravens, sparrows, hawks and magpies calls.

I'd roam the fields with André, walk along hedges and look for sparrows that we tried to kill with our self-made slings. I never brought one down.

A farmer owned a beautiful, sturdy, muscular plough horse named *Bijou* (Jewel). He was the kindest, gentlest and friendliest of all horses. He loved children. He often came to school by himself, stopped in front of some elevation so that we could jump on him. He took us back to the farm at a very slow pace through fields and woods, stopping from time to time to graze or to drink at a waterhole or a brook. Once he reached his destination, he let us slide down his back and returned to his stall. Bijou was the talk of the town. Many were convinced that he was some sort of good spirit.

I had my first experience with the female anatomy in the semi-darkness of the barn, when I played doctor and patient with the farmer's daughter. Marinette was not very pretty, but boy, was she prematurely jiggy and willing to please.

On Sundays, we would all go to church, my mother, the entire Petit family and myself. In fact, my father decided to have me baptized by the local priest. The three Dorians were now reformed Catholics. The move had given my parents some provisional reprieve. I wasn't different from my peers anymore. I was going to church, to confession; I was attending catechism like the other kids. Had the Nazis observed us—and they didn't—nothing unusual or suspect would have drawn their attention. I was integrated on the surface, but no one saw me as a Catholic. Everybody at the village knew I was the Jewish boy from the city who had been baptized. Except me.

I am convinced that my parents had long-term motives. Having lived through the horror of war, having escaped the genocide of the European Jews, they wanted to protect me from being set aside, ostracized, victimized. And they hoped that such protection would last my lifetime. They were convinced that I had to blend if I was to thrive in a France that was not only Catholic, but so profoundly anti-Semitic too.

They grossly miscalculated. You can leave France and become an American citizen. But according to French law, you are still French. And you will remain French until you die. The same applies to Jews. Once a Jew, always a Jew. To paraphrase Sartre, there is no exit. "No Jew can escape by conversion, and not of trauma," once said Jean-Marie Lustiger, the recently deceased Cardinal of Paris, in trying to explain that the thirteen year-old Jewish child he was didn't convert to Catholicism to escape the Nazis. "I was born Jewish and so I remain, even if that is unacceptable to many," he bravely stated.

Paris was liberated on August 1944. The three of us traveled back to the capital in the fall of that same year.

4

The Bumpy Road

Why learn what's in books since you can find it there?
—SACHA GUITRY

he city was still celebrating its liberation when my parents returned to their beloved apartment. The people of Paris were partying day and night. Promiscuity was rampant. Women were offering themselves to their liberators. GIs were roaming the streets, surrounded by hordes of kids who were begging for chewing gum, Coca-Cola or cigarettes, yours truly included. Only a few days after our American friends had freed us, walls were covered with graffiti reading, "Yankee Go Home," a weird way of showing gratitude to our liberators. Old scores were settled. The hunt for collaborators was in full swing. Women who had slept with the enemy had their hair shaven in public and were paraded in the streets. The man who had fled to England to create and head the Resistance Movement had returned a national hero. General Charles de Gaulle became Prime Minister of the French Provisional Government.

I was eight years old in April 1945. Circumstances and luck had protected me from the worst. I had lived in a green cocoon made of forests and pastures while millions were being slaughtered. What did I know?

Six months had elapsed since our return from Saint-Priest when one day, my mother and I happened to walk down Rue d'Assas toward Sèvres Babylone, less than a mile from our apartment. When we reached Boulevard Raspail, a surreal sight took us aback. Skeletal men and women dressed in striped pajamas were assembled in front of the four-star Hotel Lutetia, hundreds of them, frail, ghosts in bright daylight, their eyes that too much horror had assaulted and dulled, lit by an imperceptible glow of hope. "Who are these people?" I asked my mother. I lifted my head and saw tears trickle down her cheeks. "Who are they?" I asked again. "I'll explain later, Daniel," she said almost choking.

The Lutetia, with its sculpted *Belle Epoque* façade, its welcoming statue of Gustave Eiffel, its opulent chandeliers, its thick carpets, its deep leather armchairs, its maîtres d'hôtel in tux, had been requisitioned by General de Gaulle as a welcoming center for the fortunate Jews and non-Jews who had survived and returned from hell. They were now corralled behind white fences, right in front of our eyes. The posh Lutetia had become a place of hope for so many who, sequestered on the other side of these fences, were holding photos, signs, shouting names, trying to locate disappeared husbands, brothers, daughters, nephews or cousins. Most had come in vain. Their loved ones would never return.

I failed to grasp the full meaning of what I had witnessed. How could I have understood the incomprehensible? How could anyone have? The extent, the scope of the horror hit me when, a few months later, someone took me to an exhibit on the Holocaust. It featured items that had been collected from several concentration camps, including lampshades made of human skins. The French knew of the existence of concentration camps at the end of hostilities. They were aware that atrocities had been committed, but they might not have fathomed the scope of these atrocities.

An event that happened on the day World War II ended might also have escaped their sphere of consciousness. On May 8, 1945, ten months after the liberation of Paris, French troops stationed in Sétif, in North-Eastern Algeria, fired on demonstrators killing somewhere between fifteen and twenty thousand unarmed protesters, setting the stage for two bloody colonial wars, the first in Indochina in 1946, the second in Algeria in 1954. The latter would affect my life significantly. Ironically, France had moved from oppressed status under the Nazis jackboot to oppressor status. Its colonial empire was about to crumble.

In the fall of 1944, the French had to face the daunting challenge of reconstruction. Hard choices and sacrifices had to be made. Women were given the right to vote and the French received significant social protections with the introduction of *la Sécurité Sociale*, also known as *la Sécu*, a government-sponsored program that would guarantee universal healthcare and more to all. France had turned socialist and remains so to this day.

Billy Davenport did not close his dental practice during the war. Therefore, my father had no difficulty resuming his professional activities. I can imagine how he felt when he rode the # 83 bus again on his way to work, the first time in what must have felt like ages.

My mother had lost her full-staff status at the Paris Opera but she managed to sing under yearly contracts until 1949.

My parents had to find a good school for me. They chose *Ecole Alsacienne,* a private establishment located half a block from Rue Joseph Bara.

Scientists and academics had founded it in 1870. They had fled Strasbourg following France's defeat in the Franco-Prussian War, when the German Empire annexed two French departments, Alsace and Lorraine.

That same year, they opened a one-room elementary school on Rue des Ecoles, in the fifth arrondissement to affirm their countrymen's will to remain French. The school then moved to Rue d'Assas, its permanent location, and expanded. It offered classes up to the fifth grade. Reputed for its avant-garde educational methods, it still caters to the well to do. André Gide, the French author and winner of the 1947 Nobel Prize in literature, was one of its illustrious alumni.

The three years I spent at *Ecole Alsacienne,* from 1944 to 1947, were the best school years of my entire life. My report cards read, "Excellent. Good grades." My parents were ecstatic.

I had everything a kid of my age could dream of, elegant clothes, fancy shoes, expensive toys, vacations in Normandy in the summer and in the French Alps in winter. My parents couldn't have been more proud of me. I was the greatest, the fairest and the smartest. They treated me like royalty. I was farting in silk sheets, as my drama teacher used to say.

After I graduated to the sixth grade, my parents had to find a new school for me. I was ten when I transferred to *Lycée Montaigne,* one of the capital's stepping-stones to *les grandes écoles,* prestigious higher education establishments whose purpose was to train France's elite.

Lycée Montaigne encapsulated the best and the worst of French education. Its academic level was one of the highest in the nation. To secure and preserve that reputation, it had zero tolerance for children who were not up to the task. You were of the required level or you drowned.

My transition from a private to a public school was brutal. *Ecole Alsacienne* had a system of education similar to the American model. It allowed self-expression and creative thinking. The public system was disciplinarian.

I failed from the start in the face of such rigidity. I was drowning and no one was lending me a hand. In less than three months I had regressed from model student to dunce. How could these teachers have displayed such poor skills? Their intransigence toward children who needed help, worse, toward children who had just survived the trauma of war, was unconscionable.

The Germans had trampled their soil, spoiled their women and wounded their honor. They had wiped out six hundred thousand of them. Cities had been flattened; infrastructures had been destroyed. The French had lost everything except their beloved culture. Culture kept the dream of greatness alive. You cannot kill the dead. Descartes, Pascal, La Fontaine, Molière, Voltaire, Zola were a reminder of France's *grandeur*. Instead of investing in the future, the French educational system turned to the nation's illustrious past, to more glorious times, to the Renaissance, to *Le Grand Siècle* (The Great Century) or to *Le Siècle des Lumières* (The Century of Enlightenment). It aimed at producing well-educated individuals with abilities that could serve not necessarily the interests of the individual, as is the case in a capitalist system, but of the state. The best students from the best universities such as *Polytechnique,* the French MIT, did not vie for jobs in the private sector. It wasn't in their culture. They aspired to becoming top-ranking bureaucrats, a tradition established by Napoleon Bonaparte. The few who achieved that goal were placed on a pedestal.

It has often been said that France was ruled by elementary school teachers. The *instituteurs* represented <u>the</u> first authority all French citizens had to answer to. Revered but also feared, they were inflexible disciplinarians who rarely gave children the opportunity to voice their opinion. They taught with an attitude and were the symbol of a pyramidal system in which decisions came from the top and trickled their way down, just like the French political system, one that is diametrically opposite to our grass roots. Their arrogance became contagious. Arrogance breeds arrogance. They passed on their complex of superiority to an entire nation. They created individuals in their own image, a people convinced that their way of life was superior to all other ways of life, that their culture was the richest in the world, that they undoubtedly were the smartest and that no one could possess their sharp and subtle sense of humor. Hubris in France had reached an unbearable level. When he came back to power in 1958, General de Gaulle made matters worse.

I turned as bad as Antoine Doinel, the troubled character of François Truffaut's *Les 400 Coups*.

My academic downfall created havoc on my family life. My father obsessed over my failures, threatened, begged, played the sentimental chord in the hope that I'd improve but wound up losing his trust in me. He told me that I was the cause of his failing health.

His love for my mother dwindled. My parents started arguing about anything and everything. The rift between them deepened. Their feuds increased in intensity. They were bickering with each other in the evening, shouting at each other in the morning. He often accused her of being dumb. "We are powerless when confronted with stupidity," he would always say to me. He had me almost convinced, but I knew that my mother was smart in many respects, even smarter than he was in some, particularly when it came to money. Their confrontations had sucked the air from where we lived.

I was rarely given permission to leave the apartment. Saturdays were better than Sundays because Dad would often take me along to events organized by the *Société des Amateurs d'Art*, a non-profit organization aimed at discovering new talents. They included visits to painter's studios or to well-known collectors, such as Maurice Chevalier who owned a splendid collection of impressionists. The *Société* also organized dinners once or twice a year during which an unknown painter was honored and awarded a prize. Some of these gatherings took place at a restaurant called *Chez Camille Renaud*, located in Puteaux, outside of Paris, a couple of miles from the Arc de Triomphe. Camille Renaud was a gentle character. When I met him, he had the body of an obese person, the blue eyes and the blond hair of an angel. He started his professional career as an apprentice pastry chef. During his free time, he would pay a visit to art galleries and draw inspiration from Gauguin and other Fauves to decorate his pastries. He opened his restaurant in 1925. Early on, he formed a friendship with Jacques Villon, the French cubist, and with Franz Kupka, an up-and-coming Czech painter. Together they created the *Puteaux Group,* an association made of artists interested in cubism and in gastronomy. Picabia and Léger were among them. Villon was the brother of Marcel Duchamp, the French/American Dadaist and surrealist. *Chez Camille Renaud* became the favorite eatery of *le tout Paris.* Everyone wanted to try Camille's *Poulet Gauguin,* his *Canard Van Gogh*, his *Croustades Kupka* or his *Turbot Villon.*

This talented chef fed many starving painters in exchange for their art. The walls of his huge restaurant were covered with portraits of himself signed by the greatest artists of the twentieth century. Renaud became one of the most generous patrons of the arts and allowed painters to exhibit and sell their work at the restaurant.

In 1967, bulldozers tore down his painter friends' studios for the development of a huge industrial and corporate complex named La Defense. Camille closed his restaurant and left Puteaux to open a successful gallery on Boulevard Haussmann.

The maid was off on Sundays. My mother always cooked a chicken. The three of us had lunch on a bridge table in my parents' bedroom. The afternoons were so dreadful that I could not wait for Mondays, even though I hated going back to school. My father's sole activity was to listen to concerts or operas on the radio and to read in bed all day.

My room was located across from theirs. It had to be neat and sparkling clean at all times, since it was also used as our dining room. I had to surrender it when we had guests and could not go back to it before they were gone. It wasn't furnished with the stuff that befits the room of a boy my age. My desk was a rare eighteenth century piece. Posters would have been more appropriate for a fifteen-year-old than the artsy paintings that hung on its walls. My parents had denied me the privacy that is so essential to a teenager.

I had to turn creative to find ways in escaping this golden prison. I volunteered to go buy the bread, to go buy the newspaper, to go buy just about anything; I even volunteered for coal duty, a task that was terrifying to me. At that time, we used coal for heating. A big pile of the black and dirty stuff was delivered every month and kept in our cellar. Somebody had to fetch it and carry it back to the boiler located next to the kitchen.

I exited through the back door and walked down to the basement, a lit candle in my hand. The cellar had no electricity. It was pitch dark and rat infested. I had to amble through an endless, windy, damp and smelly tunnel to reach our unit. There, I shoveled the coal hastily into a large bucket and returned to the apartment carrying the heavy load in one hand and the candle in the other. Drafts often blew out the candle. When it happened, I'd run as fast as I could, panic-stricken, guessing my way out, bumping into a rat or crashing into the wet and filthy wall. When I reached the bottom of the stairs and could see a ray of light, my heart was ready to explode. I then exhaled a huge sigh of relief, happy to have survived the ordeal.

On Sundays, I felt immense relief each time I escaped the apartment. I often bumped into the concierge's son with whom I occasionally hung out and wrestled on the doormat, in front of my front door.

His older brother, Michel, was a good-for-nothing punk who had carved for himself the reputation of being the poor people's Don Juan. His sole mission in life was to conquer the young and naïve female servants who lived on the sixth floor in tiny quarters, most without a sink, some without electricity. Michel would enter their rooms through their transom windows he accessed from the roof, waited for the poor girls to show up after work and tried to seduce them. His efforts were not always successful. They were, with Yvette.

Yvette was our servant, a farm girl in her late twenties who looked older than her age. She was neither pretty nor particularly smart, but she worked hard.

One afternoon, she confided in me that she had fallen in love with Michel. Our local Casanova had ignored her once he had gotten what he had been after. He had stopped visiting her after a few nights of hot romance. What could she do? The only way she could get him back, she thought, was to tell him that she carried his child. So, she asked if I'd agree to knock her up. She would make her loved one believe that it was he who had committed the act.

Without showing a trace of emotion, Yvette described to me, matter-of-factly, how she wanted to proceed. She gave me the rules of the game, no kissing, no undressing, just the act. I was fifteen at the time. This horny teenager was not going to let the prospect of losing his virginity pass him by, regardless of the crazy rules. I struck a deal with the girl. We chose a moment when we would be alone in the apartment.

It came. My father was at work; my mother had gone for errands. Yvette was busy in the kitchen. I was in my room unable to concentrate on my homework, so excited at the thought of getting laid for the first time. Yvette was procrastinating. I turned impatient. "Yvette," I shouted, "If we don't do it now, it'll be too late. " No answer. "Have you changed your mind? It's okay by me, if you have. I'm doing it for you, you know." Still no answer. I was dying with impatience.

A few minutes later she stepped in my room, pulled her skirt up, took off her panties, lay down on my bed and opened her legs, exposing her vagina. "Come on top of me," she directed. She then lowered my zipper, pulled my underwear aside, grabbed my penis and guided it into her. She was wet. I entered her with ease. She must have found the situation erotic in spite of her detached attitude. It took me a few seconds to come. She looked concerned. "Were you deep enough? We should do it again... Just to make sure."

It didn't take long to ready me for another try. I entered her a second time. As I was doing my back and forth, her eyes remained fixed at the ceiling. When she sensed that I was about to climax, she grabbed my ass and pushed me forward with all her strength, making sure I was as deep inside her as possible. She then stood up, put her panties back on, lowered her dress, said, "*Merci, Monsieur Daniel*" and left.

The following day, she behaved as if nothing had happened. To her, I was still *Monsieur Daniel* and remained so until the day my mother fired her for stealing some silverware. My mother always accused her servants of robbing her blind. It now occurs to me that dear Yvette would have been sent to jail for seducing a minor if we had been in the United States. But, hey, we were in France.

She did not get pregnant. I hate to think of what would have happened if she had.

I often paid a visit to Jean-Michel, a boy of my age who lived with his mother in a small two-bedroom apartment on the ground floor of a building adjacent to ours. The woman was a civil servant and a member of the French Communist Party.

Communism was rampant in France at that time. The PCF was the largest left-wing party in number of popular votes in national elections, from 1945 to the seventies. Its membership grew from three hundred and seventy thousand in 1944 to eight hundred thousand by the end of 1946. French communists looked up to Stalin and the party remained under the total influence of the Soviet Union until Khrushchev took power in 1953.

Not only did the party brainwash its members, its members also brainwashed the rest of their families. Too many swore allegiance to the Soviet dictator. Jean-Michel was one of them. And like most brainwashed people, he would rehash the same slogans over and over again. Our lively exchanges were most heated when they turned to the United States. Jean-Michel would then throw around the slogans he had heard from his mother, who had heard them from fellow party members who had read them in *L'Humanité*, the Communist daily paper. Americans were imperialists, capitalists, warmongers, racists, oppressors and expansionists. The sacrifices of the courageous GIs who had died for France's liberation had been forgotten.

Many French people disgraced themselves when they collaborated with the Nazis. Many shamed themselves when they looked up to Stalin and made the Russian mass murderer a hero and a role model. Thank God, they were not the majority.

France's appetite for social perks never quenched. The more its citizens were granted, the more they sought and the more they got, unemployment benefits, child benefits, family credits, housing benefits, thirty-five-hour work weeks, five-week paid vacations, free healthcare, early retirement. The French became a nation of scroungers. Its ever-growing social safety net stymied the people's motivation to work and to produce. The system created a generation of whiners who felt that the state owed them everything. And when the state or private employers failed to live up to their expectations, they went on strike. Even journalists went on strike. Strikes became a way of life in the land of Molière.

Michel was my closest friend. He lived alone in a maid's room in the heart of Montparnasse. His parents, who owned a small house in northern France, had abandoned him. They just sent him enough money to survive. Oddly enough, he had the self-discipline to study.

The games we played might have seemed anodyne, but deep down they were an expression of our anxieties and of our loneliness. Every afternoon after school, when the two of us reached the corner of Rue Vavin and Rue Notre-Dame-des-Champs, we tossed a coin. The loser had to accompany the other home. Michel lived alone. He craved the company of kids his age. So, he didn't mind losing. From that intersection, my building was much farther than his. Losing meant I'd keep him company longer. I too secretly hoped he'd lose. The more time I spent with him, the better I also felt.

I met two of my other best friends sometime in 1951. Claude lived with his divorced mother on Rue Vavin, a harsh and overpowering woman. Bernard resided with his rich parents on Boulevard Saint-Germain. His mother was cold and egocentric.

Michel was lonely. Claude resented his mom. Bernard needed warmth and affection. My parents' feuds tore me to pieces. We were not happy at home. So we created a warmer and friendlier environment for ourselves, a second family, if you will, less inclined to bear judgment, unwilling to criticize or to punish. We became inseparable.

5

The French, the Brits and the English Language

*The French and the British are such good
enemies that they can't resist being friends.*

—PETER USTINOV

My father insisted I learn German. I never understood why. English yes, Spanish certainly—enough people spoke it around the world—but German, after what they did to us... to him? Didn't we have an earful of it? Who wanted to speak German after the war? If you were heard speaking it in the Netherlands in the late forties, early fifties, you were "lynched." In his defense I must say that Dad acted like a true Frenchman. France and Germany had been at each other's throats for so long. Who knew when the language would come in handy one more time? So, I chose German as my first foreign language, English as my second as I was about to start the sixth grade.

My father who was on the board of directors of the Hartford Hospital in Paris and of the American Hospital in Neuilly felt it was important for me to be fluent in the tongue of Shakespeare. He decided to send me to camp in England.

I arrived in London in early July 1951 and traveled south to a seaside holiday camp in Selsey owned and managed by Helga Greene and Joan Gellner.

Joan Gellner was the daughter of Julius Gellner, one of the most famous German-speaking theater directors of the twenties and thirties. In 1924 and 1933, Julius was the Superintendent and Vice-Director of the

Munich Theater, the *Münchner Kammerspiele in Schauspielhaus.* A Jew born in Austria-Hungary, he left Germany when Hitler rose to power. He settled in Prague, and then escaped to England when Germany invaded Czechoslovakia. In London he was hired by Hugh Greene to work for the German Service of the BBC. Hugh Greene was Helga Greene's husband. He also was Graham Greene's older brother. So, when she married him, Helga became the famous writer's sister-in-law.

Sir Hugh Carlton Greene was a journalist and a television executive who produced news programs that made him a household name in Europe. In 1960, Hugh was promoted to Director General of the BBC. He and Helga had two sons, the youngest, James, a skinny, red-haired freckled boy and his brother they named Graham after the writer, also skinny, red-haired, freckled, but taller. Both wore the same pair of thin-rimmed, round spectacles that made them look like Charles Dickens' characters.

Few women exude the sort of powerful sex appeal and raw sensuality that transcend physical appearance. Helga was far from being pretty, but she had a certain je ne sais quoi that attracted men like a magnet. She was energetic, loved children and had a great sense of fairness.

Joan and Helga had rented a school in Selsey, a seaside resort and a civil parish in the Chichester District of West Sussex. They transformed it into a paradise for kids. The boys and girls' dormitories were located in four separate buildings, two dormitories for young boys and girls, two for older children. The property had a couple of tennis courts and stood a few minutes walking distance from the beach. For Helga the camp was not a business. She did not need the money. Her main purpose was to help Joan who wasn't as fortunate. She also wanted her two boys to be surrounded by children of diverse cultural backgrounds.

At the Greene-Gellner camp, I experienced three firsts:

I was taught how to play tennis by a pro, I learned how to ride a horse and I had my very first romance.

On the second night, the boys decided to pay a visit to the girls' dormitory, an excursion, I was told, in keeping with the camp's tradition. Though someone had slammed a door on my middle finger, crushing it to a pulp, I went along.

So, we waited an hour until the lights were turned off, wrapped ourselves in sheets or covers, exited the building on the sly and ran across the lawn that separated us from the girls' dormitory. It was close to midnight when we stepped into a big room that housed a dozen bunks. All the girls were awake, their hearts filled with great anticipation at the thought of experiencing the first romance of their young lives. In total darkness, we each felt our way toward the beds that belonged to our dulcineas. Whispers and giggles would break the silence of the night every time a boy found his beloved. I reached the wrong girl, apologized, and tiptoed to the next bed.

She was tucked in. I lay down next to her, on top of the sheets. Her name was Ghislaine. She was a cute, impeccably raised fourteen-year-old, the daughter of a French mother and a Dutch father. Boys did not interest her. She was old-fashioned and did not approve of these silly games. "We are too young," she used to say to me. "You will have plenty of time for all that." She had agreed to let me share her bunk because of peer pressure and on one condition, no hanky-panky. We would only talk. So, that's how we started the evening, by talking, or more accurately, by whispering. Soon whispers turned into kisses. I managed to slide under the sheets. My hand wandered surreptitiously. When it reached too far south, Ghislaine grabbed it and firmly brought it back north. I tried again and again. The struggle was exhausting. I fell asleep.

When we woke up at the crack of dawn, Ghislaine pushed the cover aside and screamed, "Daniel!" She looked horrified and accusatory, her eyes shifting back and forth from the bottom sheet to me, from me to the bottom sheet. It was covered in blood. "What have you done?" she exclaimed, almost in tears. Did she think I had deflowered her? For a second I also wondered. No way. How could I have not been aware of it? Pain brought me back to reality. My finger was killing me. I realized I had lost my bandage while wrestling with dear Ghislaine. All that blood had come from my injured middle finger. My girlfriend had not been spoiled after all. My bursts of laughter woke up the other girls in the dormitory. The episode ended in a massive giggle.

I was the only kid who dared to light a cigarette in the open. Joan and Helga were not keen on discipline, but Helga felt she had to tell my parents. She broke the news to them in a letter in which she revealed a great sense of humor.

> Now as I am writing to you, I have decided to tell you something. The important thing for <u>me</u> is that you and Madame Dorian are very careful not to let out that I have 'told tales,' which is not done in the best English circles. But sometimes one has divided duty towards parents and principles.
>
> It is not at all anything serious, but Daniel now smokes fairly regularly. He knows we do not approve. On the other hand, it is all done quite openly. Please, I must repeat, do not betray me, or you will destroy Daniel's faith in the English.

And how about their faith in us, the French? In Brighton, where Helga occasionally drove us so that we could fish on the pier, I saw signs hung on the fronts of ice cream parlors and coffee shops that read, "Dogs and French not admitted." Yes, the Brits had had it with our Gallic ways. I have to say, in all fairness, that the hordes of rich and spoiled French boys who were sent to England were often loud and unruly, exacerbating the historical aversion the English felt toward my fellow countrymen. We, on the other hand, didn't have much love lost for them either. Didn't the Duke of Wellington, Arthur Welsley, once say, "We are, always have been, and I hope always will be despised by the French"?

James and Graham Greene were my close friends. That did not stop them from applying the good old stereotypes that most Brits use to judge their nemesis, the French. In their eyes, I was a garlic-loving, snail-eating, skirt-chasing, shoulder-shrugging Frog. And for me they were tight-ass, rigid, puritan, hypocritical Brits. We still cared for one another and saw our respective pitfalls as being congenital flaws.

In 1953, Helga Greene accompanied her father, Sam Guinness, on a trip to France. My mother prepared an elaborate lunch for the occasion. She had told Helga to come *en toute simplicité*, which either meant "we have invited a few people" or "don't bother to dress up" or "we will serve a simple meal." When they had guests, the French never served a simple meal. A simple meal would bring eternal shame to the hostess. In America, you flaunt your brand new Porsche or the latest Mac. In France, you prepare an unforgettable dinner. And, when my mother cooked meals, they were unforgettable.

The moment they arrived, she offered Sam Guiness and Helga aperitifs and a few *amuse-gueules* in the living room. They were then taken to the dining room where foie gras was served as an *amuse-gueule*. A cold salmon and its *sauce verte*, paired with the right vintage white wine, followed. The servant then brought a shoulder of venison with three purées, accompanied by an old Bourgogne. A selection of cheeses handpicked by my mother came next. Her *Camembert* was always *à point,* soft and unctuous. The ten-year-old Bordeaux she had carefully chosen to accompany it contained just enough acid to dissolve the fat of this rich Normand treat. Millésimé champagne was served with dessert. Milly was a master pastry chef and could turn out a *Paris-Brest* that melted in your mouth. Helga and Sam were then taken back to the living room for a digestif. My parents were partial to a magnificent fifty-year-old Armagnac. That is what they meant by *en toute simplicité*, a full five-hour, five-course gastronomic feast that would send you to your cardiologist.

Sam Guinness belonged to the beer empire family that bore their name. He was an elegant octogenarian, still alert, with a sharp sense of humor; the way he dressed, his stiffness, his mannerisms were oh so British. He smoked one Players after another using the butt of the one he had just finished to light the next. He always had a cigarette between his lips.

My mother was horrified by her Anglo-Saxon guests' table manners. When she saw Helga and Sam spread butter on their bread and eat it before the meal, she almost fainted. Then these two had the impudence to ask for iced water. That did it. My mother tried to contain herself, but that last sacrilege was too much for her to bear. She had to speak up. She explained as calmly as she possibly could that bread would fill them up and the cold water would numb their taste buds, therefore preventing them from appreciating the subtleties of her cooking. As soon as she was done explaining, Sam Guinness grabbed a piece of bread, splashed an inordinate amount of butter on it and gulped it down.

My mother went out of her way to show Paris to the old man. They did it in style. Sam Guinness had brought his Rolls Royce and chauffeur.

The day after Helga left, Milly found out that my father was having an affair with her. She had uncovered a love letter. Her dignity had taken a terrible blow. When my father returned from work, she confronted him head on. "That bitch had the gall to come to my house, to sit at my table and to eat my food." She insisted that he end the relationship. Divorce was out of the question. My mother told me a few years later that my father had confided in her that Helga was a sex maniac who was perpetually unsatisfied. Milly blamed her for my father's declining health. "The British whore killed him," she kept repeating.

Many years later, I happened to be in London on a shoot and had one evening free. So I called Graham, who had become the curator of the British Museum. He had some professional obligations that evening and suggested I call his brother James. James said he'd love to see me. I jumped into a cab. He lived a half-hour north of Trafalgar Square, in a street lined with gray and uniform brownstones, similar to the ones you see in Mike Leigh's movies. I had not expected to find him in such an environment. I sensed that something had gone awry with his life.

His welcome was warm. He insisted on preparing dinner. I should have declined. The food was barely edible, not a surprise in this part of the world.

"Did you know that my father was your mom's lover?" I asked point-blank.

"Of course I did. As a matter of fact, my mother was always laughing when she was with your father. I never saw her so happy. Your father came to see her every weekend."

"Every weekend?" I asked, taken aback.

"Almost every weekend."

It hurt to learn the truth, even after so many years. It is not the fact that my father had a mistress that bothered me, but the lies. He had spent his summer vacations with Helga and not with me. Perhaps he had loved me too much and at times, not enough.

James went on explaining that his mother had many lovers. In 1955, she met Raymond Chandler, the Anglo-American novelist and screenwriter whose trademark character was Philip Marlowe, a name that became synonymous with private detective.

That year, Helga Greene became his literary agent and lover. He was then sixty-five years old, thirty years older than she. In February 1959, he proposed marriage to her but died on March 26 before they could tie the knot. Helga inherited his entire estate. When she passed away in the early sixties, her fortune went to Graham and James.

6

Hectic Times

Hanging around until you've caught on.
—ROBERT FROST

In the fall of 1953, I started my ninth grade at *Lycée Louis-le-Grand*. It prepared students for entrance to the *Grandes Ecoles*. Named in King Louis XIV's honor after he visited it and offered his patronage, the *lycée* was founded in 1563. Molière, Voltaire and Victor Hugo were among its most famous alumni.

Finding myself in such esteemed company did not boost my appetite for learning. I just about made it to the tenth grade after a mediocre second ninth grade I had been forced to repeat. I dreaded school more than ever. Had I become lazier? No child is lazy. Laziness has always been a code name for something else. A child can be preoccupied, disturbed, stifled or unmotivated, but not lazy. I lacked maturity, but not the ability to succeed academically. A devastating incident that occurred in the winter of 1952, three months before my fifteenth birthday contributed to my downfall.

It was around eight in the evening. I was in my room doing my homework. My father surprised me when he stepped in. I had not heard him enter the apartment. He looked drawn. He took hold of a chair, dragged it near me and sat down, his eyes filled with tears. "I want to discuss a matter of grave concern with you, Daniel," he said, "and I want you to listen."

Anxiety squeezed my heart. "I just had a check-up," he added, portentously. "My blood pressure is excessively high. My life is in danger,

Daniel."

I felt a knot in my throat. I gathered enough strength to ask, "What do you mean, Dad?"

"I don't know how much time I have left. But I want you to promise me that you will make an effort at school." He sighed. "What will you do when I am not around anymore? What will become of you if you do not get your *baccalauréat*? Promise me, Daniel, promise me you will change."

Overwhelmed by emotion and frightened at the prospect of losing him, I stuttered, "I... I... pro... pro... promise, Dad." He was telling the truth. He was gravely ill. Blood pressure medication had not yet been invented.

He took me in his arms, pressing me tight against his chest, then left the room leaving me numb and lost.

He honestly believed that the prospect of his demise was the necessary wake up call that would incite me to do better at school. It never occurred to him that he had injected me with a poison that would wreak havoc on my young life. The fear that he could drop dead at any time would haunt me for many years to come.

That night, I remained wide awake, curled in my bed like a fetus, my pajamas soaked with sweat, too frightened to move, my heart pounding at the sound of his heavy breathing that I feared would turn silent at any moment. Dad's room was just across from mine. The possibility that he could pass away filled me with terror. I lived in a perpetual state of fear from that night on. My bouts of anxiety dissipated when I left for the army, six years later.

The subject of his failing health came up whenever he had to sign my reports. Even my mother always said, "Think of your father's health." On my seventeenth birthday he wrote to me, "If my long struggle and my many sacrifices do not bear fruit, I do not want to survive your failures. I am even resolute to force destiny."

He was now threatening to kill himself if I did not earn good grades.

Life was not entirely bleak. I hated school, but I loved my neighborhood.

Almost every morning before school, I bumped into the sculptor Ossip Zadkine and his wife Valentine Prax. They lived in an artist studio on Rue d'Assas, just around the corner. I remember his white bushy hair waving in the wind. Zadkine always smiled at me. I did not realize how powerful a sculptor he was until I visited Rotterdam with my parents a few years later and saw his famous sculpture entitled *The Destroyed City*, a monument in which the arms of a large figure, a hole torn in the center of its body, are outstretched in horror. The piece conveyed so graphically and emotionally the intensity of the destruction of Rotterdam and the suffering of the Dutch people during World War II. Valentine Prax was also a talented painter. When they both died, their studio was made into a museum, *Le Musée Zadkine*.

The grounds I had to cross on my way to *Louis-le-Grand* were glorious. I'd exit my building, cross Rue d'Assas, take Rue Michelet to the *Petits Jardins du Luxembourg*, then enter the Luxembourg Gardens, walk along a promontory that overlooked a magnificent basin and the Senate. That's where I regularly bumped into Jean-Paul Belmondo. Bebel, as we called him, was heading to his drama school. He wasn't yet the movie idol he would later become. He was nineteen, four years my elder. During our brief encounters, he would say to me, "Why don't you drop the *lycée*? Come to drama school with me. It's more fun." The idea was tempting. I had thought about it often. He didn't need to convince me. It was my father who needed convincing. When I first told him I wanted to be an actor, Dad dismissed the idea with a shrug of the shoulders. When I told him a second time, a third time and a fourth time, he said, "Get your *baccalauréat* first, then we'll see." Nothing would ever happen in my life without that damn *baccalauréat*. Why was the *baccalauréat* so important? Was it a sort of Holy Grail that would miraculously open the doors to a free and exhilarating life... to stardom?

With the first downy hairs on my face came the first pimples and the first pubic hair and the first erection and the first masturbation and total self-absorption and that uncomfortable sensation of not being together. Once that nightmarish thing called puberty passed, I started shaving and paying more attention to others. I stopped masturbating, my pimples vanished, but my libido went through the roof. I had to get laid.

I remember my first kiss. Not my first kiss but my FIRST KISS. You know, the one that has nourished your every dream, the kiss you were too shy to steal or lucky enough to get when you least expected it. The kiss you didn't know whether you were going to love or hate since it was your first. The Bogey and Bacall kiss. The kiss you never wanted to end. The wet kiss, the interlocking kiss, the kiss full of promises, the one you give and the one you take with your eyes closed. No one should forget his or her first kiss. I remember mine so vividly; the sweet and sour taste of it, her probing tongue, and her soft lips that were open a little too wide for my taste. I remember its indescribable smell. Yes, the smell of it. I even remember her. She was red-haired, petite, frail and naïve. I also remember where it all happened, at the corner of Rue de Vaugirard and Rue Guynmer, just outside the Luxembourg Gardens. But I do not remember her name.

I do remember the name of the girl with whom I made love for the first time. Evelyne was a virgin. It is with her that I lost my virginity, not with Yvette. My brief and awkward sexual encounter with Yvette, the maid, had just been a mishap, a freak accident that did not count.

Evelyne had the body and the voice of a woman. She often behaved like one and yet she was fifteen. I had picked her up in an area of the Luxembourg Gardens where we liked to hang out, near the puppet theater and the merry-go-round. Her kisses, her embraces betrayed her impatience to discover *les plaisirs de la chair*.

On a warm spring evening, I called her mother and asked if I could take her daughter to the movies. Instead Evelyne and I headed for a little hotel near the Seine. It was the kind of establishment that rented rooms by the hour. We both felt a little nervous when we entered the lobby and faced the male receptionist. He gave us the once-over. I avoided his stare. When he handed me the room key while still gauging Evelyne from head to toe, I dared looking at him. He then smiled, a guy smile that said, "good for you."

We stepped in the room, closed the door behind us and faced each other for a while, hesitant, self-conscious, our hearts bursting with anticipation. I took the first step, put my arms around her and kissed her. She freed herself and dashed to the bathroom. She reemerged two minutes later wearing her panties. She rushed to the bed while trying to hide what looked like two nicely shaped, generous breasts. She lay down, modestly keeping her arms over her chest. My head was spinning. It was the first time I had been exposed to a woman's naked body. Mesmerized, I could not take my eyes off her half-hidden breasts, her thighs and her sheer panties that revealed the dark upside down triangle of her pubic hair. I don't know how I managed to undress, but I did it hastily and clumsily. I lay next to her. The moment she turned the light off, we fell in each other's arms. When I pierced her hymen, I felt whole.

My tenth grade French and Latin teacher had a significant impact on my life. He didn't make me an A student but he achieved what no other teacher had. He motivated me.

He was cool, never came to class wearing the old, worn out, dull suits, barely ironed shirts, saggy bow ties or dusty and bulky peasant shoes that were the accouterments of old-fashioned teachers. Monsieur Vincent dressed in designer suits, double-breasted pinstriped jackets, with matching pocket-handkerchiefs. And his shoes, yes his shoes were so hip.

He showed that he cared. He was a modern man who used modern teaching methods that were way ahead of his time. He had the ability to bring to life the most boring author and demonstrated to us how modern the classics were, how we all could relate to the miser in Molière's *L'Avare* or to Jean Valjean, Victor Hugo's character in *Les Misérables*. Our opinions never failed to peak his interest. Everyone got respect, whether you were a good student or not.

Monsieur Vincent had a weakness however. He was a gambler. Thoroughbreds were "his thing." He loved betting on horses at the Vincennes Racetrack or at the PMU, the French version of our OTB. That made him even more human and closer to our hearts. He was our hero. Every kid needs a "Monsieur Vincent" in his or her life, a man with enough humanity and generosity to awaken the curiosity that is often dormant in the hearts and minds of some children.

Monsieur Vincent was teaching at the Sorbonne when he passed away in 1965 at an early age. His death provoked great emotion. Mine wasn't the only life he had saved. Alas, I remained mediocre in math, physics, history, geography and Latin, particularly in Latin.

Latin was my nightmare. I was Latin-proof. I did not understand the language, never grasped the advantages of learning it and hated it with a vengeance, but was aware that I could not get my high school diploma without acquiring some basic knowledge of it. So, in desperation my father called upon his friend Solovine and begged him to help me.

Before the war, Maurice Solovine and my father were members of an epicurean society that held its regular meetings at the *Closerie des Lilas*, on Boulevard Montparnasse. The *Closerie*, a social and culinary magnet for the avant-garde, had opened in 1847. Gertrude Stein, Alice B. Toklas, Ingres, Henry James, Chateaubriand, Picasso, Hemingway, Apollinaire, Lenin and Trotsky were some of its illustrious patrons.

My father loved and admired Solovine, not only because he was Romanian like him, but also because he was a unique individual blessed with unique qualities. After the war, Dad renewed his friendship with him. He invited him to lunch a few times and before you knew it, the man had become a regular. He'd show up at the apartment every Wednesday at half past noon sharp always wearing the same open-collar shirt and the same old worn out jacket, in the heat of summer or in the cold of winter. Solovine had the health of an eighteen-year old.

He was skinny, bold and had protuberant front teeth that made him look like a rabbit. He wore pure kindness on his smile. He was soft-spoken and had a good sense of humor. His looks, his demeanor, his inquisitive eyes could have inspired the most sensitive poet or the wittiest cartoonist. He breathed bohemia but was also reminiscent of Professor Nimbus, for those familiar with Tintin.

When the servant brought him to our dining room, he never sat down before being invited to. He was extremely shy. He'd carry some small talk for a while and come dessert time, his face would lighten up. He'd put his glasses on, search inside his jacket and retrieve an envelope he handled like a rare crystal. This ritual was repeated week in week out.

"I just received a letter from Albert," he'd say with pride.

He then looked at us, making sure he had peaked our curiosity— Solovine had a great sense of timing—and showed us the letter ever so briefly. We could not touch it, God forbid. We were only allowed to look at it. It was hand-written in fonts that could not be found in any computer today. The calligraphy was even, round, a little stark but pleasant to the eye. Few people could have known that the letter was written in German and in Gothic characters. Gothic characters were still taught in high school during my time. The signature at the bottom read Albert Einstein.

Every week, Solovine brought us a new letter he had received from his friend, Albert Einstein.

On a particular Wednesday, he seemed agitated. As soon as he arrived, he retrieved from his jacket one of these letters faster than usual, shook it in front of our nose and said, with the gravitas of an announcer breaking the hottest news of the century, and it was, "This, my friends, is a letter about the Theory of Relativity."

Solovine then tried to vulgarize for us the theory, using laymen's terms. He was not blind to our ignorance, but he still hoped he had enlightened us some. To state that we didn't grasp what the man was saying is a gross understatement.

As a young student of philosophy in Bern, this intriguing man had applied to study physics with Albert Einstein in response to an ad. The two men struck up a close relationship and Einstein was to say to Solovine a few days after meeting him, "It is not necessary to give you lessons in physics. Let's just discuss the problems we face in physics today. It's far more interesting. Come to me whenever you wish, I'll be pleased to talk to you."

Solovine, the philosopher and mathematician, was fluent in Latin, in ancient Greek and in a dozen other languages including French, German, Italian, Russian, Romanian, and Hungarian. Why did he take up the impossible task of making me fall in love with the dead language? Probably because he loved my father but also because he thrived when faced with impossible challenges.

I'd go twice a week to his small Paris apartment, which was located behind the Montparnasse railroad station. The place was spartan. Solovine was amused by my ignorance and often made fun of it, in an affectionate way. He showed the patience I wish my teachers at the *lycée* had displayed. He passed away in 1958. I still miss him. He did not make me an authority in Latin, but he gave me the basics that would allow me to get my diploma.

He donated his private correspondence with Einstein to Paris' City Hall.

His help allowed me to cruise without major problems through the tenth grade. Then, a major distraction dragged me into a life of crime and degradation.

* * *

It all started in the most innocuous way in the spring of '54. A few African students from the Sorbonne, all children of rich families from Togo, Senegal and the Ivory Coast, were playing poker in the Luxembourg Gardens... of all places. My friend, Claude, joined them on occasions. One afternoon, he asked me to play with him and two others. We used six folding chairs, five for us and one as a table. I was already familiar with the game. One of the players, a young African named Sam, explained to me that they were playing for money, but reassured me that the most I could lose was the equivalent of twenty dollars. I accepted the invite.

Gambling for money was illegal in the Luxembourg Gardens. We would have been arrested if we had been caught exchanging cash. So we devised a system. We played for points, a point for one franc. One of us was assigned to keep the score on paper. When the game was over, we'd settle up in the street outside the gardens.

That day, I won fifteen points and went home with fifteen additional francs in my pocket. I was hooked. From then on, that particular section of the Luxembourg Gardens became my primary residence.

On a particular afternoon, five or six tables of four players each could be spotted through the centenary chestnut trees that dotted the grounds. As the days went by, the sums of money at stake grew higher and higher. By June, a single pot could hold the equivalent of ten thousand dollars. The word got around. The smell of money attracted more kids and a few undesirable characters, among them Corsican gangsters. Because no cash ever passed hands within the boundaries of the Luxembourg Gardens, the sight of these young men playing cards for huge amounts of money appeared anodyne, unnoticed by children playing ball, roller skating or bicycling, by mothers pushing their baby carriages, by lovers necking on benches or by painters trying to capture the beauty of these surroundings on canvas. Who knew that this playground for kids of all ages had been transformed into a high-stakes gambling joint?

I became addicted to the game as if I had taken heroin. My obsession was such that I ended up playing against myself at night, before falling asleep. A deck of cards was always within my reach. Poker got hold of my thoughts, my time, my life and my soul. I lost interest in girls. The more I played, the better I became. It is the risk that turned me on, the risk and the money and the total concentration that was taking me away from my father, from school and from my homework I hated so.

Only fools say they always win at poker. There were some good days, of course; but there were some pretty bad ones as well. I either carried loads of moola in my pockets, or I had to figure out from whom I could bum to feed my habit. I dared asking my father to increase my allowance.

I was an amateur compared to other players. One of them, a slim, dark-skinned, withdrawn young man, had a South American look and the catchy name of an American gumshoe. Max Barnett was a pro. An attractive woman was always seated behind him, watching him play for hours without ever uttering a word. I never saw Max without her. She was glued to his side day and night, from the beginning to the end of every game, no matter how long it lasted. I had no particular affection for Max and I didn't think he had any for me. As a matter of fact, Max had few friends.

I played against him often, but there is one game I will never forget. We were three that day, myself, Max and Crépi, an African built like a hulk. You couldn't help but notice his hands. They were huge. I was winning big time. That didn't make Crépi happy. The more I won, the more aggressive the African became. When my turn came to deal, he grabbed my forehand and tightened his grip around my wrist with such strength that I dropped the stack of cards.

"You're cheating," he jeered. I denied it. He slapped me hard. It felt like an anvil had hit me. Max grabbed his coke bottle, slammed it against a chair and pressed the broken glass against the black man's throat. A few painful seconds passed. We were all frozen. Then Crépi lifted his arms in the air and burst out laughing. We resumed the game as if nothing had happened.

On New Year's Eve of 1954, we started a game at nine. I was playing against Claude, Max and a fourth whose name escapes me. At one in the morning, I was losing almost everything I had. I hung in there, playing it safe, limiting my bluff, waiting for my luck to turn. It did. Little by little I recouped some of my losses. By eight, I had broken even. The four of us were spent. We called it a day, or rather a night. I had played eleven hours straight for nothing, on New Year's night.

Five months later, on a sunny day in the spring of 1955, my father caught me as he was crossing the Luxembourg Gardens. I was too involved in a game to notice him. That evening he entered my room and told me that the sight of me gambling had saddened him. He did not shout, he did not threaten. He asked me to promise him that I'd stop playing poker. I promised and from that moment on, never touched a deck of cards again.

The fifties were turbulent years for the French. Because of its weak constitution, the country had gone through twenty governments from 1946 to 1958, a record only beaten by Italy. That did not put a damper on the Parisians' famous zest for life.

My friendship with Claude, Michel and Bernard had endured. But that spring, I saw Bernard more often. We shared one thing in common. We both loved to dance and we both felt that dancing was the ideal shortcut to sex. So, we met every Thursday afternoon at *Vieux Colombier*, one of the *caves* that were "in" at that time. There were others in Saint-Germain and the Latin Quarter, *Le Club Saint-Germain, La Huchette, Le Club Montpensier*. But Bernard and I preferred *Vieux Colombier* because of the music. It featured Claude Luther, the French clarinetist and the great Sidney Bechet, also a clarinet player from New Orleans. Both played Dixieland Jazz, a swinging, stomping, syncopated beat that made you want to dance.

The *caves* were dark, smoke-filled basements packed with Paris' gilded youth. The band alternated blues and fast tempo pieces. We danced a combination of Jitterbug and Boogie Woogie mixed with a dash of seventeenth century minuet that lent acrobatics an elegant Gallic style. Those who were the best at it often took over the floor and performed like pros under the eyes of envious kids who looked at them with admiration. Sometimes two or three couples performed together in perfect unison.

Bernard and myself were pretty good at it but we preferred the blues. The blues was more conducive to romance. It allowed us to wrap our arms around our female partner, to hold her tight, her face buried in our neck, our pelvis against her pelvis, a close embrace that allowed us to demonstrate how pleased we were to dance with her.

I did not neglect Claude and Michel. On Saturdays, the four of us had dinner at a small bistro on Rue Sainte-Beuve in Montparnasse then would head for a *bal populaire*, a dance hall where tango served the same purpose as the blues.

Summer was around the corner. The great French migration to the sun was about to begin. Paris would soon turn into a ghost town. Summers in France are a reflection of the strength and weakness of the French, their joie de vivre and... their joie de vivre. In France, vacations are and always will be sacrosanct. The French do not work to make money. No, they work so that they can take two weeks off in the winter and four weeks off in the summer. They would lengthen their downtime even more if they could, believing that God brought them on this earth to enjoy life, a philosophy that seems to escape most Americans.

Vacation time in the US is a reflection of the strength and weakness of Americans, their love of money and... their love of money. "The United States," according to John Schmitt of the Center for Economic and Policy Research, "is the only advanced economy in the world that does not guarantee its workers paid vacation." Can anyone imagine New York emptied out of its entire population in August? It is unthinkable. If they had to offer six-week vacations to their employees, corporations and small businesses would go belly up; restaurants, newspaper stands, dry cleaners, bars, movie houses, theaters might as well put their keys under the rug. And how could the average John Doe pay for the mortgage of his house and car if he stopped making money for a month and a half? How could he sustain a standard of living at least equivalent to or, better yet, higher than his neighbor's?

If you'd cut vacation time down to twelve days in France, you'd have another bloody revolution that would make 1789 look like a family feud.

During that particular July, Paris was hot and humid. My mother had fired her servant. We couldn't go on vacation before her replacement showed up. It was going to be another poor farm girl who wanted to escape the boredom of her simple existence, a naïve hick ready to sacrifice everything and anything, including her freedom, for the excitement of living in the big city, unaware of what she was getting into. Oy!

My parents and I were having lunch. The doorbell rang. My mother asked me to see who it was. I walked down the corridor, opened the door and there she stood, tall in her high heels, sexy in a tight raincoat that concealed a tiny waist and a prominent and erect bust. Her face could have been pretty without the heavy makeup. She was in her early twenties.

She asked to see my mother. I picked up her suitcase and took her to the dining room. Her name was Colette. She was our new servant. My mother asked me to accompany her upstairs to her room.

It took me awhile to climb the six stories, hampered by the suitcase that weighed a ton. I was out of breath when we reached our destination. Colette seemed shy. I didn't hear a peep from her. When she took off her raincoat I realized how hot she was. She would have had to be under total anesthesia not to detect my arousal. I was almost eighteen, loaded with testosterone. Suddenly overcome by self-consciousness, I asked her if I could be of further help and started to exit. Then I turned around, grabbed her by the waist and kissed her. We fell on the bed. I almost ripped her blouse, unfastened her bra, fondled and kissed her breasts. She tried to push me away. I pursued my assault with a vengeance. She cried out, "I must go down now. Your mother is waiting for me."

Brought back to reality, I stood up, smiled at her and said, "Later."

She retrieved a handkerchief from her bag and wiped off the bright red lipstick that had smeared the lower part of my face.

Later came sooner. I made love to Colette the moment we were alone. She became my slave. When two, three or four friends of mine would show up at the apartment, she'd cook for them. When I was down, she'd lift my spirits. When I was sick, she'd take care of me. When I was drafted and was sent to Germany, she wrote to me regularly, keeping me abreast of my sick father's condition. In hindsight, I am not proud of the way I treated her. I appreciated her generosity of the heart, but that did not stop me from treating her like a servant. Worse. I had abused my position and used her too often as the object of my desire. I had acted as an arrogant bourgeois, had displayed unacceptable hubris and had been as vain and self-centered as Dorian Gray, Oscar Wilde's character whose name I bear. To this day, I wish I could offer this woman an apology. She was already gone when I returned home from the army almost three years later. My mother told me she had married an Algerian.

My father had done extensive work on my friend's teeth without charging him. As a token of her appreciation, Bernard's mother invited me to spend the summer with her son at their country estate in Chambery, in the Savoie region.

Chambery was too provincial for Bernard and me. Our playground was Aix-les-Bains, a poor man's Riviera stretched along the beautiful *Lac du Bourget*, the largest natural lake in France. It offered water sports during the day and a busy casino at night where we could gamble or dance to Camille Sauvage's music. Camille Sauvage was the French Duke Ellington of the fifties.

Bernard and some of his local friends were having a drink there one evening when I spotted a woman staring at me. She must have been in her mid-forties. She was attractive still. Women aged much earlier then. Her lecherous gaze didn't leave any room for misinterpretation.

I crossed to her table and asked her to dance. She accepted. We tangoed glued to one another. She was holding my hand tightly. When the dance was over, I thanked her. She returned to her friends without saying a word. She appeared torn. Was she married? Did she have children? Once back at her table, she tried to engage in the conversation her friends were having but could not help staring at me.

At one point, I exchanged a few words with Bernard, then turned to her. She was gone. I looked around, checked the back of the room just in time to see her exit on the sly. I stood up and ran after her. She was already out in the street when I caught up with her. "I don't want to lose you, " I said.

"What do you want?"

"I think you like me."

"Really!" she replied with sarcasm.

"All I want is to have a drink with you. Please have a drink with me. Just one drink. Please."

"And then, you'll let me go?"

"I swear!"

We crossed to a little café located at a crossroad and sat at a table. She ordered a coke, and then apologized. She had to go to the ladies room. I waited. The woman was not returning. I knew that something had gone astray. I exited the bistro and spotted her. She was already down the block. Bent on outsmarting her, I took the street parallel to the one she was on. I hurried, reached an intersection, turned left and left again and there she was, walking toward me. She almost fainted when she saw me. "You win," she said, resigned and out of breath.

"Where do you stay?"

"At a hotel, a block away. But you can't come with me."

"Why not?"

"I am a married woman. I don't want to take the risk of being seen with you."

"So?"

"Here is the key to my room. I'll go first. Wait a few minutes. I'm on the second floor. Don't come right away."

"Where's your husband?"

"In Paris."

Half an hour later, I entered her room. She took me in her arms. We kissed. I unbuttoned her blouse and tried to undo the clip of her bra. She stopped me. "Not the bra," she pleaded. "Please, not the bra." I did not insist. Her body was full, well shaped. The few wrinkles that carved her face gave her character and enhanced her sex appeal. Her thighs were not as firm as those of a twenty-year-old, but her skin was soft. Her breasts were the first items that had succumbed to time. She might have taken off her bra if I had been ten years older.

We made love. I came prematurely. She tried to hide her disappointment by displaying tenderness, disarming warmth, motherly care. She asked me questions about my life, about my school, about my parents. "I almost could be your mother, you know," she said.

Out of the blue, she asked, "Do you prefer men?"

Had she made that remark because I had been gentle with her? When I made love to her for the second time, I turned creative, displayed unusual generosity, forgot about my own gratification, tried to please her as much as I could. Maybe her husband was much older than she was; maybe he had gotten fat; maybe he had fallen gravely ill; maybe she did not love him anymore. Whatever the case might have been, I did not want to disappoint her. She had longed to make love to a younger man. She would have felt guilty if I had botched that moment. I was her last fling. I wanted her to return to her family happy, satisfied, free of remorse, her fantasies fulfilled. I could not let her down.

I wasn't a boy anymore.

The Last Carefree Years

The roots of education are bitter, but the fruit is sweet.

—ARISTOTLE

To shield me from temptation and to increase my chances of success, my parents sent me to boarding school in Fountainbleau, forty miles south of Paris. So, in September of 1954, I moved to this charming city, in the heart of a beautiful forest bearing its name and entered *Lycée de Fontainebleau*, an establishment less competitive than *Lycée-Louis-le-Grand*.

As I was getting accustomed to my life as a boarder, France was going through the throes of decolonization. The start of hostilities in Algeria in late 1954 marked the beginning of the end of France's influence in North Africa, just as the disastrous fall of the French army at Dien Bien Phu six months earlier had signified the end of French hegemony in Asia. France was losing its empire and its world influence. Dien Bien Phu set the stage for another devastating conflict that would oppose the forces that had defeated France in Indochina to the United States six years later.

Algeria was divided into three departments under the jurisdiction of the Department of the Interior and was headed by a governor. Its 1947 statute provided for the election of a hundred-and-twenty-member assembly with limited prerogatives. The nine million Muslims that made up Algeria's population could elect the same number of deputies as the one million French citizens residing there. Modern agriculture, the country's main source of revenue besides oil, was in the hands of Europeans. Muslims were practicing an antiquated form of farming that did not produce enough to lift the citizens of this North African nation out of poverty. Europeans were for the most part city folks, workers. They belonged to a middle class that opposed any reform that would grant Muslims greater equality.

Years of unfair representation, of abuses, of blatant racism and of exploitation of the Algerian population by whites resulted in the creation of the FLN, the National Front of Liberation, a revolutionary organization that would mobilize a majority of Muslims against their colonial oppressor.

In the wee hours of the morning of November 1, 1954, guerillas launched several attacks against military installations, communication facilities, public utilities, police precincts, and warehouses throughout Algeria. The Algerian insurrection had begun. It amplified exponentially throughout eight years of a bitter and cruel conflict that ended when France granted independence to the last of its most important colonies.

The French called it a dirty war, *une sale guerre*. In fact, the insurgents in Algeria waged a form of guerilla warfare and terrorism that would spread and flourish in the years to come. Guerilla warfare was not new, but the National Front Liberation Army refined it into an efficient and devastating military art form, as it specialized in hit-and-run tactics, ambushes and night raids, thus avoiding direct contact with superior French firepower. In large cities such as Algiers, Oran or Constantine, it created a perpetual atmosphere of fear and insecurity by randomly placing explosives on the terraces of cafés, in movie houses, in buses, even in schools. Algerian guerillas did not sacrifice their lives like today's suicide bombers do, but they paved the way to a form of warfare that would change the meaning western countries gave to the word victory. It set forth a strategy that would shake the confidence of the world's two super powers in South East Asia, and in the Middle East. In Afghanistan, guerilla warfare helped a comparatively small contingent of insurgents defeat the mighty Soviet Union.

The complex nature of the relationship that existed between Arabs and the white population added an element of cruelty to this conflict. The French who lived in Algeria, the *Pieds-Noirs*, could not understand why their Arab friends, with whom they had gone to school, played soccer and hung out, had turned against them with such acrimony and violence. The two people had a common history. Entire Muslim regiments had fought side by side with the French against the Germans during two world wars.

Many military units made of Algerians who were loyal to France served as auxiliaries in the French army during the Algerian War.

This war that wasn't a war while still being one, affected everyone. The French government hypocritically called it a "public order operation." Who didn't have a brother, a husband, a father, a friend drafted or who was going to be drafted and sent to the Algerian *bled*? As the French got sucked deeper and deeper into this quagmire, public opinion turned. The conflict ended up dividing France, opposing the ones who were against French intervention to those who felt that Algeria had to remain French.

My first and only year at *Lycée de Fontainebleau* ended successfully. I passed the first part of my *baccalauréat*. My parents were so pleased that they suggested I have my eighteenth birthday party at the apartment free of their interference.

Since I was still in boarding school on that April 1, 1955, we postponed the celebration until early July. My parents went on vacation. I had the place to myself.

Thanks to my connections at *Club du Vieux Colombier,* I secured the entire Claude Luther band, a coup that boosted my reputation as a cool and connected dude. The friends I had invited were not the only ones who flocked to Rue Joseph Bara on that warm Saturday evening. The challenge for kids my age was to find out where the good parties were taking place. *Surbooms*—that's how the French called them—were rated according to the number of girls who attended and according to location and affluence. Total strangers always crashed these parties uninvited, anytime, anywhere. They were rarely turned down. They added life to these events and even resurrected a few that had turned moribund.

At one point, the apartment was packed with kids I had never seen before. Joints had not yet been introduced to French teens. I didn't need any. Couples were flirting in the semi-obscurity of the garden; the band was at its best. I had enough booze to fuddle a battalion. All that gave me enough of a high.

At around ten-thirty the doorbell rang. I opened the front door and came face to face with a group of the most gorgeous females I had ever seen. They were ten young gals, tall, elegant, clad in designer clothes and made up like high-society babes.

"Can we come in?" asked one of them.

"Sure," I answered, bewitched, *bedazzled* and bewildered. "But, who are you?"

"The Bluebell Girls."

They were the famous nightclub dancers who were performing at the Lido. Like the Rockettes at Radio City Music Hall, the Bluebell Girls were an impeccably drilled ensemble decked out in feathered headdresses, G-strings and high heels.

Here they stood, in their elegant outfits that contrasted so much with the skimpy costumes they wore on stage. Needless to say, the guys became frantic and went for them, to the utter annoyance of their dates. They all danced with them, but that's as far as it went. At the stroke of midnight, like Cinderellas, my uninvited guests vanished. I caught up with one of them at the doorstep. "Why are you leaving so soon?" I asked, disappointed.

"Miss Kelly's orders. Midnight's our deadline."

She left with a smile and that was that. Margaret Kelly was their iron-fist English matron who always made sure her dancers were well-behaved.

The following year, I flunked the second part of my *baccalauréat* miserably. My parents sent me to *Lycée Pasteur* in Neuilly, on the opposite side of Paris, to repeat my philosophy year.

Amazingly, I took a liking to philosophy. My grades improved. In the third trimester, I was in the top five of my class. I passed the second part of my *baccalauréat* hands down.

The diploma did not mean much in and of itself. What I had learned would fast be forgotten. What remained was an appetite for knowledge, the urge to understand, to analyze, to explore, to question, the need to be informed. All the stuff I forgot—the dates of historical battles, philosophical essays, mathematical equations, laws of physics, Victor Hugo's body of work—made me hungry for more stuff to forget.

I owe it all to my dad.

8

The Calling

Becoming an actor? If it's not a calling,
don't do it. It's so hard.

—SANDRA OH

My mind was made up. I wanted to be an actor. No one could stop me from becoming one. Was this a genuine calling? Was I up to suffering the pangs of rejection for the sake of my art, confident in my talent and in my ability to succeed? Was I ready to face starvation, me, the spoiled little bourgeois whose material needs had always been met? Or was I overtaken by a passing whim, fueled by the need to be loved, admired, revered, adulated, just like Flynn, Stewart, Bogart or Fonda had been?

I was convinced that theater was my vocation. If I did not pursue my dream, I'd regret it the rest of my life. My mother was my role model. Through her, I experienced the thrills of limelight at an early age. My father had great respect and admiration for artists. He just didn't want me to be one. So he tried his best to dissuade me.

He always wanted me to go to medical school so that I could take over his practice. The thought of my becoming an actor terrified him. He kept repeating that my chances of making it in that God-awful profession were close to nil. And I kept telling him that there was nothing else I wanted to do.

He must have mulled over each and every argument he could muster to make me change my mind, each and every way he could think of to stop me from ruining my life. I did not budge. As a last resort, he decided to gamble by seeking the proof that I did not have the stuff it took to pursue this route. He asked his friend Georges Leroy to settle the issue. "If he thinks you have some gift for it, I'll bow out. But if he doesn't, then promise me you'll enter the university." I promised.

Georges Leroy was his patient and close friend. He started his acting career at *La Comédie Française* in 1908, and taught drama at the Paris Conservatory, *Le Conservatoire d'Art Dramatique,* where he trained some of the leading stage and screen actors of the first part of the twentieth century. Georges Leroy was the guru of French theater. There wasn't one performer who at one point of his career hadn't asked for his guidance. The man was *the* authority in all matters of acting, like Stella Adler and Lee Strasberg had been in the United States from the late forties to the late sixties.

When I first met him, *Maître* Georges Leroy was a frail seventy-one-year-old. He epitomized elegance, inside and out. The way he kept his index finger on the side of his lips, his focused gaze when you were talking to him or performing for him, showed how intensely he listened and how much he cared. His piercing eyes revealed an immense perspicacity. His gentle and mischievous smile was more eloquent than words. His criticisms were always subtle and constructive, never hurtful. Young talents as well as people of all walks of life intrigued him. He was a humanist. This man who never talked for the sake of talking, turned loquacious every time he mentioned his pet student Gérard Philippe, the French idol of the fifties.

Leroy was holding my future in his hands. I liked him from day one.

The light that bathed his studio, which was a stone's throw away from the Arc de Triomphe, the carved wooden panels that covered its walls and the paraphernalia spoke of theater. A bust of Molière Leroy kept on his mantelpiece showed his reverence for the seventeenth century playwright.

Our meeting lasted a few minutes. He asked me to study Act I Scene II of *Fantasio*, Alfred de Musset's short play. "Have fun with it," he suggested.

I rushed home and devoured it, once, twice. I read it aloud a third time. I then concentrated on Scene II. I was amazed at how modern this multi-faceted character was. Part dandy, part poet, his bushy hair as untidy as Rimbaud's orphan, Fantasio is stricken by the same melancholy, boredom, *ennui*, spleen, restlessness that consumed Hamlet or Jim Stark, James Dean's character in *Rebel Without a Cause*.

One can give many different interpretations of Fantasio, just like one can interpret Hamlet a thousand different ways. Seen from Georges Leroy's point of view, there was no better material to assess an actor's sensitivity, range and intelligence, to discover raw talent than the one he chose to evaluate me.

I memorized the scene and worked on it for weeks, rehearsing in front of a mirror, reciting both parts in the Luxembourg Gardens, in subways and buses, in the living room, in the kitchen, in the johns, in my sleep. I tried different interpretations, aloof, haunted, angry, sarcastic, jovial, bitter, romantic, naïve. I decided that *I* was Fantasio. I'd offer Georges Leroy every bit of enthusiasm, authenticity, fervor, élan I could draw from my heart. A month after our first meeting, I called him to make an appointment. When I hung up, my heart pounded.

The day of the audition, I took the subway to *Etoile*, at the Arc de Triomphe, and walked to Rue Bayens, rehearsing the dialogue aloud over and over again, making sure I had memorized it well. People in the streets must have thought I was deranged.

As soon as I arrived at his apartment, Georges Leroy told me that he would play the part of Spark. He sat down in front of me in a comfortable armchair and signaled me to start. I took a deep breath and dove into the character head on, putting to good use the colossal stage fright that overtook me to express Fantasio's discontent.

When the ordeal was over, I was drained.

"I will call your father later on. Good luck, young man," Leroy said. He took me to the door and, without further ado, bid me goodbye. My legs were shaky, my shirt was soaked and I had a formidable headache. I walked all the way home like a zombie.

I waited impatiently for my father to return. He was late that evening. He finally arrived, hung his coat in the foyer and walked to his room where he stayed for what seemed an eternity. "So?" I asked the moment he stepped in my room.

"Georges Leroy came to see me late this afternoon." My father reached into his inside pocket, retrieved a letter. "He asked me to give you this."

It was addressed to *Julien Bertheau, de la Comédie Française*. (Julien

Bertheau was one of the most celebrated actors of the illustrious theater.)

> My Dear Friend,
> I have several reasons to take an interest in the young man who just delivered this letter to you. He played the part of Fantasio for me. I don't think I have the right to tell him that he is wrong to consider becoming an actor. Could you put him to work?
>
> Georges Leroy

Tears filled my eyes. My father took my head in his hands and whispered, "Congratulations, Daniel. I am happy for you."

The letter was dated December 15. Christmas of 1956 would be the best of my entire life. I had already received my gift, and what a gift!

In the fall of 1957, I applied to the Sorbonne, a move aimed at reassuring my father. I attended a few courses at the Paris University and quit after a couple of months. Why pursue a BA in French literature since I had been told that I had what it took to become an actor? I wanted to go to drama school. Georges Leroy felt that I was what he called a "modern" and that consequently I should attend a school that suited my dramatic register. Bogart was a "modern" as opposed to Laurence Olivier who was best suited for Shakespeare. In France, more than in Great Britain, the distinction was categorical. You either were a "modern," acting in contemporary plays or in movies, or you were an actor versed in the classics. Few succeeded at being both.

The best school in Paris for a "modern" like me was *Cours Simon*. René Simon founded it in 1925.

During my first days there, I was asked to choose a scene from a play I'd have to perform in front of the entire school. Its name escapes me. Once a week, *Cours Simon* organized an audition in its theater to introduce the newcomers to its students and to directors in search of new talents. I asked a young Pied Noir from Algeria, Gérard Fabiani, to play opposite.

On the afternoon we performed, the place was packed with one of the toughest audiences a young actor could ever confront. These kids were competition.

We acted with all the conviction, heart, pathos we could muster. Yet the end of our performance was met with deadly silence. Gérard and I were convinced that we had tanked. Then a burst of loud and sustained applause shook the walls of this little theater. The students stood up, whistled and clapped, giving us the rock star treatment. We had touched their hearts. All eyes were wet. It was a triumph.

Following that performance, René Simon nourished high hopes for me. At age fifty-nine, he was a bundle of energy. This cheerful and mischievous man was an astute pedagogue who used his experience as an actor and as a teacher to optimize the potential of the young performers who were in his care. He knew the business of acting intimately. He kept repeating that talent was not a guarantee of success and that the more gifted you were the more assiduously you had to hone your skills. He bore no illusion and was aware that only a tiny percentage of his students would reach the top or at the very least would make a living in the acting profession. He pushed hard the ones he thought had the greatest potential while discouraging the young men and women who either were not talented enough or who refused to take acting seriously.

It is not the lack of talent that precipitated my downfall at *Cours Simon*, I was blessed with plenty of it. It was the way I dealt with my responsibilities as an artist. I lacked humility and failed to understand that I had to work hard to acquire a technique that would allow me to become an accomplished actor. Georges Leroy tried to make me understand all this in a letter he sent me on May 6, 1957. "Do not cut corners," he wrote. "An actor needs time to develop his personality. When art and life intermingle, nothing should be hastened."

Leroy had confirmed that I had talent. My first efforts were met with great enthusiasm; I had impressed René Simon, a man who was not easily impressed. So, why work so hard?

It did not take long for this intuitive teacher to realize that I wasn't sufficiently dedicated. I was wasting his time and my talent, and, in his eyes, wasting talent was a capital sin. Simon lost interest in me. Instead of doing voice exercises, instead of exploring, searching, trying different parts, instead of familiarizing myself with the works of Sartre, Camus, Strindberg or Giraudoux, I philandered. Where else could I find the greatest concentration of gorgeous women per square foot other than in a drama school?

Most of us were more attracted to the screen than to the stage. Theater wasn't as glamorous. When we were not studying at *Cours Simon* or drinking coffee at *Le Villars*, a bistro located just across from the school, we were auditioning for small roles. The producer of *Les Tricheurs*, a movie directed by Marcel Carné, the man who had also directed *Les Enfants du Paradis*, gave me my first non-speaking part. Many of my contemporaries were cast in this movie, including Jean-Paul Belmondo and my friend Jacques Charrier, the handsome young man who married Brigitte Bardot in 1959, only to divorce her less than five years later after they had a son.

During that year, I landed several small parts that were shot at *Studio de Joinville*, the largest sound stage outside of Paris. I was willing to take any job I could grab.

An actor friend of mine asked me to replace him for just one performance. He had a date with the woman of his dreams. I did not have the heart to turn him down. He was an extra in *Amphitryon 38*, a three-act comedy by Jean Giraudoux that was running at the *Théâtre des Champs Elysées* on Avenue Montaigne. It starred Jean-Pierre Aumont. My friend explained to me the moves in great detail, as we were having a drink at the terrace of a bistro. It took some nerve to accept doing this without rehearsal.

That evening, I got lost on my way to the dressing rooms. I had never been inside that theater. The woman who was in charge of costumes helped me slip my centurion garb on, unaware that I was a replacement. Luckily they fit. I then waited in the wings for the last scene of the last act. When it was time, a stagehand led me to my first position in total darkness. The curtain went up. I felt queasy; sweat made a mess of my makeup. I once heard Michael Jackson say, "When you know what you're doing, you're not scared on stage." Well, that night, I surely didn't know what I was doing and I was plenty scared. I missed the cue, crossed the stage a little late, picked up the pace, tried to catch up with the other guard, reached my final position downstage and stayed there, motionless, dazzled by the spotlights. I was standing alone in front of Jean -Pierre Aumont, as he ended his final monologue when I should have been behind him, as was the other guard. The curtain fell behind me, leaving me standing at the edge of the stage, by myself, within touch of the spectators seated on the first row of the orchestra. The audience burst out laughing. I wished I could have disappeared.

My father was convinced that I was wasting my time and his money at *Cours Simon*. He wanted me to enter the *Conservatoire d'Art Dramatique de Paris*, the government-sponsored conservatory specialized in the training of actors destined to *Comédie Française*. Leroy and René Simon opposed the idea. They insisted that I was a "modern," but my father chose not to listen to them. He trusted Georges Leroy, but he refused to take his advice. In his eyes, the *Conservatoire* bore more legitimacy than a private drama school. So Georges Leroy gave up reluctantly, even volunteered to help me prepare the entrance exam at his country house in Eygalières, a charming hamlet situated in the heart of the Alpilles, a couple of miles outside of Les Baux de Provence.

On my way to Saint-Raphaël, a resort on the French Riviera where I had been invited to spend to few days by a schoolmate, I stopped at Eygalières. Georges Leroy handed me my homework. I returned to Eygalières on August 25.

The time I spent with the Leroys was blessed. Their house made of local stones was magnificent in its austerity. It was an old twelfth century monastery, with thick stone walls, cool and spacious rooms that transported you to the Middle Ages. It featured a rich and beautifully designed rose garden facing the lower Alps.

Georges Leroy preferred working with me in the morning. He made me try several characters from different plays and decided that Emperor Nero, the lead part of Racine's *Britannicus*, would suit me best. This character's mood swings—he shifts from unbridled anger to sentimentality, to jealousy, to sadism, in the span of a few minutes—is the ideal stuff for a bravura performance, although actors playing the part run the risk of making fools of themselves. To portray a histrionic madman without being melodramatic or even clownish is not an easy task, particularly when you have to do justice to Racine's magnificent poetry, to the rhythm, pace and music of its twelve-syllable verses. Georges Leroy was a master at teaching this type of theater. He had a deep love and admiration for Racine, the greatest respect for the purity of his language, for the perfection of its form.

The four or five hours spent every day with this unique teacher were intense. In a letter he sent my father on September 3, 1958, he wrote, "Daniel left us yesterday at around noon. His friend drove him back to Saint-Raphaël. I have tried to help him the best I could. We worked on two scenes (*Britannicus* and *Fantasio*). It is more and more obvious to me that his best qualities are those of a modern."

Leroy was reminding my father again that the *Conservatoire* was a mistake.

Back in Paris, I resumed honing the scene Georges Leroy had chosen for me. I asked a friend of mine from *Cours Simon* to play Narcisse opposite me. We rehearsed at home, in the Luxembourg Gardens and even on the banks of the Seine at night, near the Pont Napoleon with Notre-Dame in the background, a location so inspiring that I felt as if I owned Paris, just as my character had owned Rome.

The entrance exam took place October 13, 1958, at the *Conservatoire* on Rue du Conservatoire in the ninth arrondissement. Hundreds of contestants were waiting for their turn. My name was called at two o'clock. Dazzled by the powerful projectors that lit the stage, I discerned the blurred contours of a few people in the audience. They were the members of the jury. René Simon was one of them. He'd vote against my admission. I was petrified.

After my performance, I felt defeated. Chances to enter this venerable institution were as slim as they were for anyone trying to enter Juilliard, the New York school for the performing arts. Each year, fifteen young men and fifteen young women are selected by the *Conservatoire* out of 1,200 contenders.

A few days later, I was notified that I had been accepted. I was dumbfounded to find myself in the lucky two point five percent.

The school assigned me to Jean-Louis Barrault's class. A blessing. Barrault was a modern, the only modern teacher in this venerable institution.

Still remembered for his brilliant portrayal of the nineteenth century mime Gaspard Dubreau in Marcel Carné's masterpiece *Les Enfants du Paradis*, he began his career in 1940 at *Comédie Française*. That same year he married the actress Madeleine Renaud with whom he founded the *Renaud-Barrault Theater Company* six years later.

The company gained immense popularity. Barrault had achieved what Todd Haimes had with his Roundabout Theater or David Mamet with his Atlantic Theater Company.

He was a mime, therefore didn't feel that dialogue was necessary to express an emotion. Jean-Louis Barrault the teacher always emphasized the importance of physical expression. He taught us body language, how to walk, move, sit or stand up in ways that would fit the psychological/social/physical makeup of the characters we were playing or, as they say in Hollywood, how to be "in character."

While he did not dismiss the value of drawing upon his own emotions and memories for his own portrayals, he was the opposite of a method actor. He had great stage presence but, in my opinion, acting was not his forte. His greatest achievements were those of a man of the theater. He was a driving force, a coordinator of genius who allowed a great company to thrive and who introduced to the public esoteric playwrights such as Eugene Ionesco, Samuel Beckett, Jean Genet, Jean Giraudoux and Paul Claudel.

Two months after the beginning of the school year, he selected a handful of us to join the *Renaud-Barrault Company*.

In 1958, the Barraults settled at the *Théâtre du Palais Royal*, where Jean-Louis produced two major shows, a five-hour version of Paul Claudel's mystic drama, *Le Soulier de Satin* (The Satin Slipper) and Offenbach's operetta, *La Vie Parisienne* (Parisian Life). He managed to cast all of us in both plays, giving us small parts and more importantly, an invaluable education in all things related to theater.

He could fly off the handle. His rehearsals were intense. Every actor called him Jean-Louis. He hated to be called *Maître* or *Monsieur Barrault*. He was an egalitarian and a boss at the same time. The actors in his company were his buddies, his brothers, his comrades-in-arms, but he still made sure they knew *he* was the man.

The rehearsals of *Le Soulier de Satin* were demanding. For Jean-Louis, the production of a play by Claudel was tantamount to a calling. Introducing this arcane playwright to the public was an act of courage. Barrault did not think that a play by Camille Claudel's younger brother was literature or poetry, but in the author's own words, "the obvious. It was all flesh. It was humanity." *Le Soulier de Satin*, which featured many locations, including the ocean, whales and ships, had been partially inspired by the Kabuki Theater. It had been written while Claudel served as France's ambassador to Japan. It is the story of an impossible love and touches upon the respect and obligations carried by the wedding vows and by a religious marriage ordained by a Catholic priest. Only Jean-Louis could faithfully stage Claudel's "disorder and delirious state of the imagination," to paraphrase the author himself.

The *Théâtre du Palais-Royal* was a cozy theater, situated at the far end of the elegant Palais-Royal gardens, a few yards from the oldest and one of the best Parisian eateries, *Le Grand Véfour*, which we could not afford with the meager salary we received from the company. Instead, we all flocked after the show to the Italian restaurant located opposite the theater to devour delicious pizzas and drink affordable wines.

The old building hadn't changed much since it opened in 1641, after Richelieu ordered its construction four years earlier. It looked old. It smelled old. It felt old. It possessed all the charms of an antique.

Jean-Louis would not have hired me if he didn't like me, but Madeleine Renaud, his wife, protected me, pampered me, encouraged me. For a reason that escapes me, I became her favorite, the *chouchou* of the most influential theater figure of the twentieth century. She stayed in touch with me long after I left the company.

My courses at the *Conservatoire* during the day and my acting job at the *Palais-Royal* in the evening kept me busy. I was productive. The theater had allowed me to meet and often befriend fascinating people. The good life could not go on forever. It never does. In January 1959, I received the letter that most men of my age hoped they would never receive. The French army wanted me. I was drafted.

9
The Army
(1959-1961)

*The average bright young man who is drafted hates the whole
business because an army always tries to eliminate the
individual differences in men.*

—ANDY ROONEY

My mother helped me prepare my suitcase, as I was about to leave the cozy and safe world of Rue Joseph Bara. I was drafted in the infantry and bound for Germany. Would I be sent to Algeria from there? I prayed I wouldn't, but the odds were against me.

De Gaulle had been elected president on September 21, 1958. Following the September 28, 1958 referendum, the French had ratified a new constitution and the creation of the Fifth Republic. In 1959, the "dirty war" in Algeria was in its sixth year. It would take de Gaulle almost four years to end it. Meanwhile, it kept jeopardizing and destroying the lives of thousands of young Frenchmen and Algerians. Few rejoiced when called to duty. I joined the ranks of those who opposed the war. I did not care whether Algeria remained French or not. I was not alone. Quite a few young Frenchmen tried to avoid the draft; many came up with false medical certificates and often pretended to be stricken with phony mental illnesses that could have exempted them from military service. I chose not to play that game.

The alarm clock woke me at four. My parents were already up, worried and sad. I took a fast shower, dressed, gulped a cup of coffee, kissed them goodbye and left. I had to report by six-thirty. I took the subway to some barracks in the twelfth arrondissement where the army registered me and ordered me to change into a military uniform. The one I was given was way too big for me. It made me look like a clown. That didn't boost my morale.

The following day, they transported us to barracks north of Paris and on March 5, 1959, trucked us to *Gare de l'Est*. We were led to a platform at the far end of the railroad station and found ourselves walking between rows of soldiers in battle dress, armed with small machine guns. Our throats tightened. What a shock! We did not expect such a reception committee. The army had taken these precautions to avoid the slightest chance of rebellion. There had been ominous antecedents. On September 11, 1955, soldiers at *Gare de Lyon*, another Paris railroad station, had refused to board the train that was going to take them to Marseilles, where they would be shipped to Algeria. They were entrained by force. As soon as they departed, they pulled the alarm signal every nine hundred feet. They were disembarked and sent to Algeria by plane.

Discontent had spread since that incident. By 1959, it had divided the French. A majority favored France's withdrawal from Algeria. Several factors brought about that reversal. One, and not the least of them, was the disclosure that the French army tortured civilians. It dragged the country into a bitter national debate. A book published in 1958 entitled *La Question*, confirmed what many suspected. The practice of torture by the French army was routine. Its author, Henri Alleg, had himself been tortured in Algiers. It was from jail that he wrote a condemnation of this violation of human rights and of the Geneva Convention. The Bush Administration would be criticized for similar exactions in Iraq almost half a century later, triggering the same outrage in the US many French citizens felt in the late fifties.

Most intellectuals and artists opposed the war. A manifesto entitled *Manifeste des 121*, named after the number of signatories, demanded that the government grant its citizens the right to insubordination against the war. It was signed by prominent personalities such as François Truffaut, Jean-Paul Sartre, Simone de Beauvoir, Simone Signoret, Nathalie Sarraute, Françoise Sagan and Alain Resnais. The French were angry.

So were we. Wasn't it odd for draftees who were about to do their duty and who ran the chance of being wounded or killed in action, to be escorted by armed guards, like criminals? They made us feel as if we were the enemy.

* * *

We left the station in the wee hours and crossed the German border by one in the morning the following day. The army had given priority to all civilian trains along the way. It had taken us sixteen hours to cover approximately two hundred miles.

When we arrived in Radolfzell-am-Bodensee in southern Germany, a town located at the western end of Lake Constance, we boarded trucks in the middle of the night. It was close to four in the morning when we reached our final destination.

The hard reality of the moment and of the harshness of the place hit us with unexpected brutality. Our faces slapped by the bitter wind of March, we stood in the middle of a gigantic tar-covered yard lit with powerful spotlights and flanked by small barracks. The sight was eerie, threatening. It felt as if we had been beamed into a WWII movie. Officers barked orders. We fell in and stood at attention. A deep depression overcame me.

The place had been the home to a Waffen-SS infantry battalion. According to reliable sources, the SS soldiers who trained there received a bonus for being exposed to the dampness and the cold of the area, which was surrounded by marshlands. No bonus for us.

How ironic. Here I was, the Jewish boy who had escaped the Nazis and who now was about to receive basic military training where my old enemies had also received basic military training to eradicate me. Talk about divine coincidence.

I did not see myself leading men in combat in a war I morally opposed. During the two months I spent in Radolfzell, I faked pain whenever we exercised, complaining that an old fracture of my kneecap had not healed. I also made sure not to excel at the firing range even though I was a decent marksman. As a consequence, the army took me off the list of those who were eligible to attend officer school. I remained a private, thus enduring for a while longer the pettiness and the demeaning affronts privates suffer from small ranking officers.

The news of my father's failing health made matters worse. He had been diagnosed with multiple sclerosis. His speech and his ability to walk had been hampered. His hypertension was reaching dangerous levels.

* * *

Early June, the army transferred me to the Signal Corps in Freiburg, a quaint and prosperous city in the south of Germany, on the western edge of the Black Forest. Freiburg was renowned for its old university and for its medieval cathedral. I was taught how to read and send messages in Morse code. Being a fast learner, it took me two weeks to decipher speedy messages. My life took a turn for the better.

Meanwhile, my father used his connections to get me a better posting. A general who was one of his patients intervened in high places. On a gorgeous spring afternoon, as I was busy sending and receiving messages during military exercises in a village that was miles away from Freiburg, I intercepted a communication addressed to my superiors. Private Daniel Dorian was to return to the barracks ASAP. A jeep and a chauffeur were put at my disposal. I was driven back to Freiburg where I was told that I had been transferred to the Press Service of the army. I had to pack my gear and leave on the double. I took the train to Baden-Baden that same day.

10

Was it Luck?

Control your fate or somebody else will.
—HEINRICH VON PIERER, FORMER CEO OF SIEMENS

I had just escaped boredom and hardship and I was about to spend the next few months with the crème de la crème in Baden-Baden, the headquarters of the French Forces in Germany. Luxurious hotels and a magnificent casino, "the most beautiful in the world," according to Marlene Dietrich, earned this spa town the reputation of being Germany's Monte Carlo.

I reported to headquarters late in the afternoon in full uniform, carrying a heavy pack over my shoulder. The guards told me where to go. On my way, I saluted a few colonels and dozens of generals. I had never saluted so many generals in such a short period of time. I might have saved a lot of arm lifting if my right hand had been affixed to my forehead all the way to my final destination.

The office had the feel of a newsroom. Several young men were beating the keys of their typewriters behind their desks. When I stepped in, they interrupted what they were doing and introduced themselves. Before being drafted, all of them had been working for French media outfits such as *Le Figaro*, *Le Monde*, *France-Soir* or *Radio Luxembourg*. It was past five o'clock in the evening. The officer in charge had already left. My future colleagues were also about to call it a day, but before turning in, they made a point of giving me two major pieces of advice.

"Rule number one. Get rid of your uniform. Tomorrow, one of us will take you to town where you'll buy civilian clothes.

"Rule number two. Never, we repeat, never ever report to the roll call. If you do, you'll have to bunk in the barracks. Tomorrow we will find you a room to rent in town."

Wasn't failing to report to the morning roll call a serious offense tantamount to desertion? And wasn't desertion punishable by death in time of war? My fears amused them. They had all done it and they had never been caught.

"And where will I sleep tonight?" I asked.

"In the captain's office," they answered.

"In the...? Are you sure?"

"If you report to the corporal downstairs, we're all fucked," they retorted. "So please do as we say. For everyone's sake." They took me to the captain's office, gave me a blanket and bid me goodnight. I was exhausted. I undressed, wrapped myself in the blanket, curled in a leather armchair and fell asleep.

The following morning, someone shook me hard. "Dorian, Dorian, wake up!" I opened an eye.

"The captain's on his way."

Panicked, I jumped, folded the blanket, put on my shirt, my pants and my shoes, slipped into my jacket as fast as I could and started buttoning it when the captain stepped in. I stood at attention, saluted him, my jacket half unbuttoned and my uncombed hair sticking out, straight up in the air. "Private Dorian *à votre service, mon Capitaine*."

"At ease, Dorian, at ease. Welcome to the Press Service."

The man was in his early forties, slim, elegant in his gabardine uniform. He was Captain Gérard de Castelnau, the grandson of General de Castelnau, the World War I hero who, as Commander of the Second Army, had been partly responsible for an aggressive French strategy at the start of *La Grande Guerre*.

My captain had been transferred to the Press Service after having served in Algeria in intelligence (*Deuxième Bureau*). The Algerian National Front of Liberation had put a high price on his head. During a military operation, a grenade had exploded in his right hand. Instead of saluting me, he shook my hand with his left one and smiled. He knew I had spent the night in his office.

The Press Service published *5/5 Forces Françaises*, a monthly magazine geared to the servicemen of the three branches of the army. It had advertising just like any regular magazine and could be bought for one franc twenty-five at newspaper stands. The main purpose of this sleek publication, which offered military reportages and features on various subjects ranging from architecture, cars, wines, culture or education, was to inform and motivate the men fighting in Algeria.

The morning following my arrival, someone took me to town where I bought two pairs of trousers, shirts, socks, a tie, a jacket and a sweater. I'd wear my uniform while working within the compounds of the headquarters and change into my civilian clothes when in town.

Becoming a journalist overnight was challenging. I had to compete with guys who had graduated from schools for journalism and who already had some experience. For me journalism was a first. The captain understood. He first assigned me to the entertainment section, because of my theater background. So I wrote film reviews and articles on French entertainment. The first movie I was asked to critique was *Gunfight at OK Corral,* starring Burt Lancaster and Kirk Douglas.

A month later, de Castlenau asked me if I was interested in writing a piece on French police and in particular on the vice squad in Paris. He sent me there on a mission and requested the authorities to grant me full access to the famous *Quai des Orfèvres,* Paris' police headquarters. I spent five nights accompanying a lieutenant on his rounds of shady bars and seedy nude shows in Pigalle.

During my brief stay in Baden-Baden, I traveled more than a dozen times to Paris and throughout Germany, covering stories that had very little to do with the military. I was even asked to write a piece on the Paris opera première of *Carmen.*

We spent Christmas, my first in the army, in the newsroom. We dressed a nice pine tree that was freshly cut from the Black Forest. The magazine's art director and his team designed sets that transformed the place into a Paris nightclub. The civilians working with us brought their wives. I danced with Francine, the captain's secretary. She was cute, had great legs and a warm smile.

The following week, de Castelnau sent me on a mission to Paris. He allowed me to take Francine along. The both of us spent a lovely weekend at the Terrass Hotel, above the Montmartre cemetery, courtesy of the Press Service of the French Army. From our balcony we had a bird's eye view of the entire city. The set up could not have been more romantic. Francine would brighten the remaining days of my stay in Baden-Baden.

It took eight months for the army to bust me. They found out that I lived in town and that I had avoided the morning roll call. They did not put me in front of a firing squad. They just threw me into the brig.

My stay in the military prison could have been worse. My jailers were draftees, like me. They tried to make me as comfortable as they could. They even asked me if I wanted the services of a prostitute to break the solitude of my cell. I declined.

Eight days later, I was informed that I had been transferred to a combat unit near Miliana, a town located in a mountainous region south of Algiers, one of the most dangerous spots in Algeria. Gaby Othon-Friez, an old friend of mine who was the famous painter's widow, asked a general to intervene in my favor. She had learned that the army had a theater company made of draftees. She felt it would be an ideal posting for me. The request was denied.

The following day, dressed in full uniform, I took the train for Trier, a German city close to Luxembourg. It was home to the First Armored Division. From there, I would be sent to Marseilles and then shipped to Algiers.

The barracks in Trier were spotless. Huge hangars featured wooden floorboards polished to such a high luster that they mirrored the tanks that were parked on them.

I was taken to a dormitory that housed a dozen other draftees. We were told that we would leave Trier for Marseilles within forty-eight hours. The next morning, a corporal woke us up with the traditional bark, *"Debout là d'dans!"* (Let's go!) The young man in the bunk next to me did not budge. The corporal grabbed his cover and his sheet and pulled them off, exposing his body. It was covered with a nasty red rash. The poor fellow had the measles. The army quarantined the entire room. Algeria would have to wait.

The end of the quarantine that had lasted three weeks brought me back to reality. On May 30, 1960, a handful of us were sent to Marseilles where we reported to the authorities. We were told that our ship was scheduled to leave for Algiers in four days and were asked to report six hours before departure. I decided to go to Cassis, a little fishing village near Marseilles known for its quaint streets, its old fountains and its fine bistros. I rented a room in an inexpensive hotel and spent three idyllic days sun bathing at the local beaches and gorging myself with *bouillabaisse*, the famous local fish stew.

On the fourth day, I boarded the *El Djazair*, an old ship that took me across the Mediterranean. I traveled with soldiers from the Foreign Legion and their mascot, a goat that stunk up the entire lower level where we were confined.

I had avoided the gruesome life of an infantryman. Could I finagle my way out of an ominous situation one more time or was I left to face an uncertain and dangerous destiny? Things didn't bode well for me.

11

Algeria, an Adventure

*If Moslems and Christians had paid attention to me, I would
have stopped their quarrels. They would have become
brothers, externally and internally.*

—SULTAN ABD EL-KADER

Seen from the sea, Algiers was dazzling. The white city was shining in
the sunrise light of June 1, 1960. We berthed very early in the
morning in front of a military transit base where I was assigned a
bunker. I was told that a train would take me to Meliana the following
morning.

The place looked dark, old and grim. It must have been a jail once. At
seven, the officer on duty granted me a leave. I would have to report back by
eighteen hundred hours. I left the compound dressed in my heavy winter
uniform. My objective was to find the colonel in charge of the personnel
department that managed the military theater company. The officer who
had signed my leave advised me to check a military base in town where, he
assured me, I could find my man. I was so bent on locating the colonel that
I did not pay much attention to the sights and sounds of the bustling city,
to its mixed crowd of Arabs and Europeans, to the men in their *djellabas*, to
the women wearing *hijabs*, their faces hidden behind veils or to the cries of
the muezzins.

Forty-five minutes later, I stood at the entrance of the military base I
had been advised to check out. I flashed my ID to the guards. A second
lieutenant informed me that Colonel Daviron was not stationed there. He
suggested that I try another base where the man had been sighted a couple

of months ago. It was nine. The sun had risen. The temperature had already reached ninety-five degrees. Sweat was oozing through my shirt. When I reached that second base, I was told that the colonel had been transferred to another location.

I searched for this man all day, walking miles and miles, going from base to base. As the sun started to set, I grew increasingly discouraged. Hot, thirsty, hungry and exhausted, I was about to give up but decided against all wisdom to try one more location. When I got to it, it was almost five o'clock. Some corporal confirmed that Colonel Daviron—that was his name— was working out of a villa in the back hills. It would take me forty-five minutes to reach it. I looked at my watch and realized that I'd never get back to the transit base by six. To press on and to continue my hunt for the elusive colonel would make me a deserter. The alternative wasn't much more appealing. No way was I going to be used as cannon fodder and get killed in some isolated outpost. I summoned the little strength and courage left in me and decided to climb the hills of Algiers.

It was almost six o'clock when I reached a villa named *Oued El Kilaï*, home of a government service in charge of the training of the Algerian youth. The military theater company called GAC for *Groupe d'Action Culturelle*, Cultural Action Group, was part of its operation.

When Colonel Daviron's secretary told her boss I wanted to see him, he ordered her to let me in. I stepped in and saluted. "Am I glad to see you, Dorian," said the colonel. "We're in desperate need of actors."

I mentioned to him that my deadline had expired. He picked up the phone, called the transit base and asked to speak to its commanding officer. "*Mon Commandant*? Colonel Daviron to inform you that Headquarters has approved private Dorian's transfer to the GAC."

He hung up, wrote a brief letter and handed it to me. "It's settled," he said. "Go back to the base. Give this to the officer on duty. I'll send someone to pick you up tomorrow. Welcome to the GAC."

The following morning, I was told that two men were waiting for me. I grabbed my bag and headed toward the reception area. Two young Arabs in T-shirts and jeans were standing in the hallway. They welcomed me with a big smile. One of them said, "Coming?"

We exited the place and crossed to a Renault pick-up truck. The two young men introduced themselves. The short and bulky one was Metref.

He was bold and resembled a Mongolian. The other one was Messaoudi, tall, handsome, with dark hair. They were both Kabyles. In the pick-up, Metref turned to me, "You gotta get rid of the uniform. Let's go and buy you a pair of jeans."

I wound up in jail the last time someone asked me to get rid of my uniform. Messaoudi was driving. He started the vehicle and floored it. I turned back for a last peek at the base. I sighed with relief as I saw it fade and disappear.

We arrived at the foot of the casbah, Arabic for citadel, a maze of dark and narrow lanes, dead-end alleys and gleaming white houses that earned the city the nickname *La Blanche.* This hillside quarter of Algiers that climbs in steps from the sea was built on the ruins of the Roman city of Icosium.

The moment we passed through one of its multiple arched entrance gates, we found ourselves immersed in a thick crowd of veiled women, rambunctious children and men of all ages dressed in their multi-colored *djellabas*, some leading overloaded donkeys by the bridle. No European could be found in this all-Arabic spot. Yet no one paid attention to the incongruous sight of this crazy French soldier in uniform. Overwhelmed by this ocean of humanity, I could have turned claustrophobic. Instead, I felt ecstatic. The symphony of fragrances emanating from the spices and the olives displayed in wooden barrels, the abundance of food, clothes, pottery, rugs, silver, jewels, the incessant and chaotic movement of people, the energy and the very dynamics of this esoteric corner of the world dazzled me. I loved the Casbah of Algiers, the first of many casbahs I'd later visit in Algerian, Tunisian and Moroccan cities.

My two companions never let me out of their sight. The excitement of it all had dulled my sense of reality. We were in the heart of enemy territory. This huge labyrinth had played a central role during the conflict as the epicenter of the rebellion. It had been the FLN's safe haven from which it planned and executed terrorist attacks against the French. *The Battle of Algiers*, the Italian movie released in 1966 and shot in the Casbah, gives an accurate feel of the place, as I experienced it. It tells the story of the beginnings of the Algerian Revolution. It recounts the creation and organization of revolutionary cells, the door to door combat that opposed the French paratroopers led by General Massu to the FLN guerilla, the search and the hunt through the maze of narrow streets for enemy combatants—a term not yet in usage then—the interrogations of Arabs by the paratroopers, the use of the *gegène*, the nickname given to the hand-operated generator that was connected to a prisoner's balls.

The year was 1960 and there I was, teasing a potential enemy in my French army uniform, walking the most dangerous streets of Algeria, maybe of the entire world. Anybody could have stabbed me with impunity in that thick crowd. I could have disappeared without a trace. No wonder my newly found friends insisted I shed my uniform.

I bought a pair of jeans and a light shirt in the first store we could find. Metref handed my uniform to the storeowner and asked him to burn it.

Very few Caucasians can brag to have been in the midst of Algiers' Casbah at the height of the Franco-Algerian conflict.

We left the Algerian capital late morning and drove east along the coast. Our final destination was Dellys, the GAC's Mediterranean base. Messaoudi asked me if I was hungry. We stopped at the first village we encountered, stepped out of the truck and entered a primitive butcher shop on the side of the road. Inside hung the carcasses of sheep that were hidden by clouds of black flies. Blood stains covered the cement floor. The shop was filthy. There were a couple of tables and a few primitive chairs in the rear. Where the hell had they taken me? No way was I going to eat in this dive. We sat down. Metref and Messaoudi ordered in Arabic. A few minutes later the butcher brought a platter filled with lamb and chicken brochettes. I picked one up and took a cautious bite. The spicy meat was delicious. The combination of cumin and salt gave it an exotic taste. We ate everything the butcher threw at us.

12

Theater and War
(A Psychological Weapon)

A half-hour later, we arrived at the GAC's headquarters, just outside of Dellys. We stepped out of the vehicle and crossed to a two-story villa located by the sea on a few acres of land. Made of concrete, the mansion was built in a pseudo Paladio style, with tall columns, Venetian balconies and balustrades punctuated with giant sculpted lions. A garden that led to cliffs overlooked the Mediterranean, along a rugged coast sprinkled with rocky islets. It must have been the residence of rich colonists before being requisitioned by the army. Its warm architectural style clashed with the impersonal and cold feel of cement. The inside included a huge lobby where rehearsals were conducted during inclement weather. The bedrooms, transformed into dormitories for three or four, were on the second floor.

Raymond Hermantier showed up an hour after us. He was a tall man, bulky, with the face of a Roman centurion. The GAC was his creation, his baby. He was thirty-six years old when I first met him.

World War II had interrupted his dream of becoming an actor. At age seventeen, he joined the French Underground movement. Wounded by a machine gun, he lost the use of his right hand. Interestingly, the two men who helped me most during my time in the army had both lost the use of one of their hands. What a coincidence. After the war, General de Gaulle decorated Hermantier for his courage and his sacrifices. As an actor/director, Raymond made a name for himself when he staged a French adaptation of Shakespeare's *Julius Caesar* at the Nîmes Theater Festival.

He possessed the generosity, honesty, righteousness and resilience of a

Templar, qualities he would apply to his Algerian project. The North African conflict touched him profoundly. He was disturbed by the chasm that divided the Arab and the European communities so brutally. He considered this confrontation of two people who had lived side by side for so many years to be fratricidal. He was convinced that theater could heal the wounds of war and could be the ultimate unifier. He conceived a plan that would satisfy two needs. Being a patriot, he aimed first at bringing culture, entertainment and therefore relief to the combatants who were stationed in the remote pitons of the Atlas Mountains, in the *djebels*, in the high plateaus and in the desert. His other goal was to bring French culture to the entire Algerian population by having classics translated in Arabic and played in Arabic by Arab actors.

The army would have scratched the project if Hermantier didn't have Albert Camus' benediction and more importantly, the support of André Malraux, who was then de Gaulle's Minister of Information. In fact, Hermantier always carried a letter from Malraux addressed "To Whom It May Concern." It stated, "Give this man everything he needs."

As a result, he was given the unconditional backing of the high command in Algiers.

He transformed the Dellys villa into a theater factory, with its own set, make-up and costume departments, its thirty to forty actors and a newspaper called *Actes*, penned by professional writers. The most prominent of them was Claude-Henri Rocquet, who became an important French playwright and poet. The Caucasian men working there were for the most part draftees recruited from the three branches of the armed forces. The Arabic actors came from all corners of Algeria. Metref, for instance, had joined the FLN at the beginning of the rebellion and had been caught and tortured by the French army. He had been *pacified*, a euphemism used by French politicians and the army that meant that he had been "persuaded" to betray his cause. The women were all volunteers who felt that the GAC offered them the possibility to hone their skills while serving their country under difficult but also fascinating circumstances. Some came from France. A few were *Pieds-Noirs* from Algiers, Oran or Constantine.

When I arrived in Dellys, the company was about to start rehearsing Molière's *Le Malade Imaginaire* (*The Imaginary Invalid*), a comedy about a cantankerous hypochondriac. In another corner of the garden, Messaoudi, Metref and a handful of natives turned actors were rehearsing the Arabic version of another play by Molière, *L'Avare* (*The Miser*). When Hermantier felt we were ready, he sent us on tour to Kabylia. We took to the road early July 1960.

The convoy consisted of two army trucks, one for our transportation, the other equipped with a foldable stage. It also carried our sets and costumes. We traveled all day and arrived at our destinations in the late afternoon. The actors unfolded and prepped the stage themselves, to the surprise of the soldiers for whom we were about to perform. These fighting men, most of them from modest backgrounds, could only imagine showbiz people as privileged creatures wallowing in a life of glamour, luxury and sex, incapable or unwilling to handle a screwdriver. The sight of actors hammering a nail, sawing a piece of wood, lowering the panels of our stage, installing spotlights, carrying heavy sets took them aback. Hermantier wanted it that way. The theater he had envisioned was a theater for the people by the people, a democratic, egalitarian theater that rejected the star system. He did not want prima donnas in his GAC. And yet, there were some. How could that have been avoided, the notion of equality being so anathema to most actors?

We had an early dinner at the officers' mess and then headed to makeshift dressing rooms, wherever we could apply our makeup and put on our costumes, inside or outside the barracks. After the performance, we answered questions from the audience and then struck the stage. This process took us two to three hours. When we were done, the officers often invited us for drinks. We were not the main cause of their solicitude. The women were. They hadn't seen one for months. Their presence was bliss for them. We weren't in bed before one or two o'clock in the morning. The early hours of the following day were spent scouting for suitable locations for the show destined to the local population. Most of the time it was an open field, a hill or a village plaza. The sets and props used for these performances were a couple of screens we placed on promontories, a mic on a stand and a few loudspeakers.

While we were working on these rudimentary elements, an army vehicle equipped with a PA system was patrolling the streets of the village inviting the people to the show. The potential spectators were women, children and old men. The young men had gone underground, hiding in the nearby mountains.

The women were suspicious. Why would they trust the soldiers whose mission, after all, was to capture or kill their sons, husbands, brothers, cousins or uncles who were fighting them with everything they had? Many had been the victims of the army's brutality. They were not volunteering to attend the show just because the army asked them to. They had to be corralled and coerced.

Soldiers were not always available to help us gather an audience. A few shows had to be canceled for lack of spectators. We had our good days, but we also had our horrendous ones. In the journal I kept, I wrote,

"7/8/60 – The women did not show up."

"7/18/60 – Our show is sabotaged, probably by FLN sympathizers. Someone spread the rumor that we gathered the women for one purpose only, to have them dance in front of the men."

War had destroyed their land. They were poor, hungry, but always proud. How could I have been insensitive to their plight, to their fears, to their misery? I decided to gather a small contingent of volunteers among GAC members and go door to door in each village. We'd bring along bread, milk, aspirin, sodas, whatever we could lay our hands on, just to show these women that we meant no harm, that we respected them, that we were honored to have them as our guests at the performance. Metref and Messaoudi volunteered their services with enthusiasm. A young Kabyle woman by the name of Rabea joined us. Our door-to-door visits became routine but they were not without danger. We were roaming these villages, walking through narrow and isolated alleys without protection, without military escort. It would have defeated the purpose to be accompanied by armed men, so we always ran the risk of being ambushed and killed.

Safety concerns never entered our minds. We were just too involved in what we were doing. I later wondered. How did we escape these excursions unharmed, not only in the villages, but also on the road? Our convoy crossed so many dangerous areas, a few of them in the hands of the enemy.

During my fourteen-month stay in Algeria, only once were we fired upon and I'm still not sure our attackers intended to do us harm. We had performed *Le Malade Imaginaire* in one of those high pitons, in the heart of the Atlas Mountains. The army outpost where we set up our stage was sitting, like an eagle's nest, on a narrow plateau surrounded by higher peaks. Servicemen and the few Kabyles who could understand and appreciate Molière were in attendance. The spotlights made the actors easy targets.

At the end of the performance, the audience applauded. The entire cast gathered on stage, bowed, when the insurgents opened fire on us. The shots came from higher up. We all hit the ground and took cover behind whatever we could find. Our soldiers returned the fire. This exchange lasted for what seemed an eternity. The curving light produced by tracer bullets in the night made it impossible to determine the origin of the fire. When an officer realized that the enemy had long gone and that his men were shooting at rocks, he ordered a ceasefire. No one was hurt. We wondered why. These insurgents could not have been such bad shots. They had decided to enjoy the performance. From their elevated position, they had a better view of the stage than our audience. They had waited for the play to end before opening fire on us, not with the intention of killing us, but just to let us know they were there. If they had intended to kill us, they could have done it easily.

The fact that we did not suffer casualties raised questions. Hermantier, according to some rumors, had made a deal with the insurgency. We suspected he had contacts within the FLN. Before creating the GAC, he is said to have interviewed Colonel Amirouche, a prominent Kabyle rebel. The rebel might have influenced the way Hermantier perceived the future of France's relationship with Algeria, and particularly with Kabylia.

I shared Hermantier's fondness for Kabylia. To this day, I miss the unmatched beauty of its land, of its lush mountains and of its picturesque, gravity-defying villages nested on their crests. I miss the warmth and hospitality of its people, the smiles of the women who showed so much strength in the face of adversity. I loved the way the natives greet each other, a hand on the heart, a gesture warmer and seemingly more genuine than our impersonal "how are you?"

During our tour of Kabylia, we covered close to twenty-five hundred miles, visited seventy-three small towns and villages and gave three hundred and fifty performances, some more successful than others. We had a few setbacks. The draftees' reactions were not always positive. Loud interruptions, total indifference, soldiers leaving in the middle of a show often torpedoed our good will. In this all-male environment, our actresses were sometimes part of the problem. Their bras and panties were once stolen by horny soldiers and hung at the mast of their garrison.

In Tindouf, the home of the Foreign Legion, a tragedy was averted. It is to this God-forsaken corner of Africa that unruly legionnaires were sent to expiate their crimes. Located in the heart of the Sahara Desert, at the Mauritanian and Moroccan borders, Tindouf was a paradise for desert lovers like me. It was hell on earth for legionnaires. Punishments for those who refused to submit to the Legion's draconian discipline were harsh. The day before we arrived, a young man accused of attempting to kill his captain had been buried in the sand up to his neck, his head exposed to the merciless sun of the Sahara, a bowl of water in front of his nose.

During its tour of the Deep South, the GAC was about to perform for these men that society had forgotten a contemporary comedy by Marcel Achard entitled *Voulez-Vous Jouer Avec Moâ*. The play featured three characters: two males and one female. During the performance, which took place under a tent, a lieutenant uncovered a terrible plot. Half a dozen legionnaires had planned to kidnap and to rape after the show, not the girl mind you, but one of the two male actors.

13

The Loss

He who has gone, so we but cherish his memory, abides with
us, more potent, nay, more present than the living man.
—ANTOINE DE SAINT-EXUPÉRY

After the Kabylia tour, the army granted me a leave. I flew back home. My father's condition had deteriorated. He was emaciated and struggled to put a sentence together. To see him like that saddened me. As I was saying goodbye, on the last day of my short stay, he held me in his arms, "I will not see you again, Daniel. My God! What will become of you?"

These discouraging words were the last I'd hear from him.

Hermantier wanted *Le Malade* to tour the Algiers district. He asked me to direct it with a brand new cast. Directing was not for me. I lacked the patience and maybe an overall vision, a distinctive style, but I understood the mechanics of comedy. Comedy is as precise as mathematics. It's all in the timing. Pace and rhythm were the two elements that obsessed me the most as a director. It paid off, but while I had not failed, the laughter each performance generated was more a measure of the actors' talent than mine. The man who played the lead felt that my directing style was heavy handed and didn't give enough slack to his creativity. He might have been right.

We toured the *Algerois* department in November of 1960. The Algiers district was made of flat farmlands in the north and rocky and arid landscapes in the haut plateau. It was in November. The nights were frigid.

Sometimes we had to bunk in unheated rooms. Often the damp and penetrating cold kept us awake all night.

On the grim morning of December 2, 1960, I received a phone call from Hermantier. My father was near death. Someone took a picture of a young actress and me, a few minutes after I heard the news. Shot in black and white in the style of French photographer Robert Doisneau, the photo captures the sorrow that overcame me.

Hermantier arranged for my immediate transfer to Algiers and for my air travel to Paris. The following day, I arrived at my apartment late in the evening. My mother took me in her arms and held me tight for a few minutes. As I passed by her bedroom, I heard groans. When we entered the living room, Mom explained that my father had tried to hold on as long as he could, in the hope of seeing me for the last time, before falling into a coma a couple of hours before my arrival.

She then told me that a priest had showed up at the apartment the night before and asked to see my father. She let him know in no uncertain terms that her husband was not up to it. The priest didn't take no for an answer. He tried to bypass her. She stood in front of him. He pushed her aside, bee-lined to my father's bedroom, closed the door and stayed with him the better part of an hour. I assume that the proselytizer gave my dad the last rites, indifferent to the fact that he had stolen the soul of a Jew and, furthermore, of a staunch atheist. For the man of cloth, the end justified the means.

My mother asked me if I wanted to see my father. In an act of pure cowardice, I pretended that I was too tired. I would in the morning, I said. I had never experienced death from so close. Society, my upbringing had not prepared me to confront the end of life. In the world I lived in, death was never spoken of, rarely dealt with... taboo. I wasn't prepared to witness it. That evening, I eluded it like a terrified child. Yet, I was twenty-three and had twenty-one months of army life under my belt. I should have shown more guts.

At around two, physically and emotionally exhausted, I fell into a deep sleep on a sofa in the living room. Early, the following morning, my mother woke me up with a gentle kiss. Dad had passed away. I felt guilty not to have gone to see him when he was still breathing.

The moment I had dreaded for so long had arrived, but its impact had been softened. The prospect of my father's demise had kept me awake for so many nights, for so many months. Now that he was dead the anxiety that had filled my heart was gone. I almost felt relieved. The only thing that remained was a numbing sense of loss.

Dad was cremated, according to his wishes, at the famous Paris cemetery, *Père Lachaise*.

14

From Stage to Chronicle

In Dellys, four actors were rehearsing Marcel Achard's play, *Voulez-Vous Jouer Avec Moâ*, under the direction of Pierre-Alain Jolivet, French composer André Jolivet's son. Hermantier wanted to tour the Sahara Desert with it. He asked me to be part of that new venture, not as an actor but as an observer and journalist. On December 17, he wrote to me, "I have learned with great sadness of the death of your father. I know that in spite of your sorrow, you have courageously rejoined the GAC. I thank you for it. Our country is being put to the test. Let's fight to try to save our honor. The Sahara tour will help you find yourself again. Study the strange humanity of Tindouf and write a comprehensive article for *Actes*. Be strong. Raymond Hermantier."

I welcomed the offer with enthusiasm.

We first flew to Hassi-Messaoud in an old DC-3. Hassi-Messaoud, Arabic for Blessed Well, was home to an oil field in the middle of eastern Algeria. It earned such a favorable name because it had been an old waterhole surrounded by a dry sandy desert in the *Grand Erg Oriental* of the Sahara (Great Eastern Sand Sea).

When we arrived at the site, the very first plant of what was to grow into a major oil and gas-generating complex had just been built. It would produce an estimated four hundred thousand barrels a day. The huge potential that Hassi-Messaoud represented was another reason why France was so reluctant to lose Algeria, having no oil of its own.

Multicolored pipes and flares, a few rigs hung with arc lights for around-the-clock production, and a cluster of what looked like lengthy and ugly warehouses with curved roofs made of corrugated metal stood a few yards from the huddled Bedouin encampments outside the security fence, a reminder of what the place must have been like before oil was discovered. The contrast between the exterior and the interior of these unsightly buildings was startling. Inside them lay a rich, sensuous Huxleyan world cooled by a powerful and silent air-conditioning system, furnished with ultra-thick carpets and avant-garde furniture, lit by expensive chandeliers, its walls adorned with beautiful tapestries and paintings. Oil people did not mind this blatant ostentation. They flaunted it with a total lack of decency in this war-torn country.

We had given a performance for the oil company's entire personnel the night before. In gratitude, we were invited to celebrate New Year's Eve in their midst. The festivities started with a special New Year's Eve supper in one of the buildings that had been made into a high-end restaurant. Champagne, vintage wines and all the aperitifs you could imagine flowed freely. Fresh oysters, foie gras, caviar, pheasants, cheese, elaborate desserts and freshly baked *baguettes* had been shipped from France that same day on a Caravelle jet chartered for the occasion. At midnight, everyone moved to an amphitheater. There, we were treated to a Folies-Bergères show that had also been flown from Paris. Money spoke.

These treats rekindled our spirits and prepared us to move on to places bearing exotic names: Colomb-Bechard, Adrar, Ouargla, Ghardaïa, Lagouat, Fort Flatters, where we performed for the *Bat' d'Af* (African Battalion), otherwise called *Les Joyeux* (the Happy Ones).

Hermantier's decision to send me to the Sahara paid off. The articles I wrote were published in *5/5* and in *Le Bled*, the two publications I had written for while in Germany, as well as in two French newspapers, *Combat* and *Le Figaro*.

Charles de Gaulle's return to power in 1958 was supposed to ensure Algeria's continued occupation. However, the general shifted progressively in favor of Algerian independence. It can be asserted that the French army was victorious on the ground, but that France had lost the political battle. The Algerians responded overwhelmingly in favor of independence in a vote ordered by de Gaulle. The French government was about to recognize the FLN as the political representative of the Algerian people. It had started serious peace negotiations with it. The *Pied Noir* population felt betrayed, as did certain elements of the armed forces.

I had gone on a mission to Algiers and had spent the night in the barracks at Point Carré, one of its suburbs. The following morning, on April 21, 1961, I woke up at six-thirty and took a walk in the yard. The sun was not quite up yet. The silence of dawn was broken by the grinding sound of tracked vehicles. A column of armored trucks mounted with machine guns headed by a jeep entered the compound. In the jeep sat four men in camouflaged battledress, a chauffeur and three high-ranking officers.

They were the 1ˢᵗ REP, the Foreign Legion paratroopers, an elite corps that had seen action and had distinguished itself in Indochina and in Egypt during the Suez Canal crisis.

A few months earlier, we had performed for them in Zeralda, their operations base located thirteen miles outside of Algiers. Their post was pristine inside and out. The main road that led to it was flanked on both sides by a row of majestic eucalyptus trees. The men from the 1ˢᵗ REP had paved it with quaint cobblestones they had stolen here and there. Thieving for the benefit of the corps was an old Foreign Legion tradition. They also had painted their barracks anew. The men took pride in maintaining the lush lawns and the rose bushes that bordered the alleys. The place had the look of a private club.

A captain had welcomed us and had taken us to the mess, where he introduced us to the corps' high-ranking officers. Following a delicious lunch, we toured the military complex. At one point, we stopped at the front steps of a small building.

"Our brothel," the captain explained. "It's open to privates in the afternoon, to non-commissioned officers from seven to nine-thirty and to officers from nine-thirty to midnight." He went on explaining, "The girls are clean. They have regular medical check ups and have one day off. They're quite happy here. We treat them like ladies. When we mount an operation in the Jebel Mountains, we take a few of them along. It releases the tension and helps our fighting boys. Please follow me."

We passed through the main entrance and faced a long corridor with five doors on each side. The captain opened the first one to the left. A young woman, in bed with a man, interrupted whatever she was doing and waved, "*Bonjour mon Capitaine.*" Her john did not go as far as to stand at attention, but he saluted. He must have been a private, given the time of day. The captain shut the door, moved on and opened the next one, interrupting another couple's quality time.

The tidiness of the place, the warm welcome of these tough soldiers impressed us. They were the fiercest combatants the French army had in its ranks, and the luckiest.

And here stood their leaders, a few feet from me.

As I approached the jeep, I recognized the colonel who was in the back seat. We had met during our visit to Zeralda. The man sitting next to him might very well have been his commanding officer, Hélie Denoix de Saint-Marc. I crossed to the colonel. He recognized me as well. "What are you doing here, *mon Colonel*?" I asked.

"We came to take Algiers," he replied.

And so they had. The night before, Maurice Challe, a retired general who had been in charge of the French forces in Algeria, had met with Commandant de Saint-Marc to ask him to participate in a coup to take over Algiers. Three other generals, Edmond Jouhaud, André Zeller and Raoul Salan, had been part of it.

Helie Denoix de Saint-Marc was the son of a President of the Bar in Bordeaux. He had fought in the Underground in 1941, had been deported to Buchenwald when he was twenty and had been liberated, half-dead. He had gone through three tours of duty in Indochina and had been assigned to the Algerian Djebel in 1955. At thirty-five, he had earned thirteen medals including the French Legion of Honor. The man was a legend. He had the full respect of the press for always telling the truth within the constraints of what he was allowed to reveal. Historians wonder why this hero allowed himself to be dragged into such a foolish enterprise.

The mutineers had taken over the radio and television building. In the wee hours of the morning of April 22, they announced that they controlled the entire Algerian territory, including the Sahara Desert. Their goal was to overthrow de Gaulle's government, to insure that Algeria would remain French and to establish a military junta. Their first order of the day was to rally the support of draftees that composed eighty percent of the armed forces. They failed. Most of us opposed the war that had extended our tour of duty to three years. We wanted to go home.

The first evening of the coup, Hermantier harangued his people in the Dellys villa, as Robespierre would have done during the French Revolution. He exhorted them to resist the mutiny and to save France's honor. Dear Raymond had histrionic tendencies. It all came from a good place. He was a patriot after all. Meanwhile, all airports in Paris were closed down for fear that *les paras*, the paratroopers, would attempt a landing and take over the capital.

Convinced that de Gaulle would send troops to quell the revolt and defeat the coup, Hermantier ordered his actors and technicians to spread out a huge French flag on the roof of the villa and to wave flashlights to help guide the forces faithful to the legitimate government in the eventuality of a landing. They never came.

That night, everyone grabbed their *PM*s, short for *pistolets mitrailleurs*, the weapon of choice used by the infantry. As incredible as it may seem, we were armed. When we joined the GAC, we had been given these semi-automatic Sten guns that most of us kept under our pillows in case of an attack. Such an attack was improbable. Dellys was known to be an R&R hub for high-ranking insurgents.

Claude-Henri Rocquet, the GAC's resident poet, took position at the gates and stood guard all night, his *PM* hanging across his chest. I am not sure how this bard would have reacted had he been under attack.

All draftees, from privates to non-commissioned officers, sabotaged the coup by any means at their disposal. Many put army vehicles out of commission by pouring sugar in their tanks, thus hampering the movements of colonels and generals. Others took over ammunition depots, denying their commanding officers access to weapons. Still others refused to send vital communications.

The mutinous generals, who had grown desperate and powerless, broadcasted hourly news bulletins promising us that they would reduce the length of our tour of duty more and more as time went by. No one fell for it, *au contraire.*

Tuesday, April 25, four days after the start of the coup, the government recaptured Algiers radio. The "bunch of retired generals," as de Gaulle called them, had been defeated. Hélie de Saint Marc and Maurice Challe handed themselves over to the authorities.

That same day in Zeralda, the 1ˢᵗ REP was dissolved. Resigned, its men sang Edith Piaf's "Non, Je Ne Regrette Rien." A few hours before giving himself up, de Saint Marc, in battledress, bareheaded, had crossed to the guardroom to meet dozens of journalists who had tried to negotiate their entrance into the premises with an uncompromising legionnaire. Roadblocks were set up everywhere; helicopters were hovering low over the military complex, and armored cars were stationed at every intersection. Police surrounded the barracks. De Saint Marc, drawn and exhausted, said to the press, "We are not Nazis. Write it; tell it. Spread the word. Please."

All the theater in the world would not have prevented Algeria from becoming independent. The insurgency had been on the side of history. Our work though might have convinced some Algerians that France wasn't all bad. It might have made up, in a small and ephemeral way, for the abuses and the injustices perpetrated by the metropole. Its benefits wouldn't last as long as the ugly and sterile *gendarmeries* (police stations) France had built in every Algerian town and village, the only relics of a one hundred and thirty-two-year occupation. I had two more months to serve before what the Brits call my demob.

In the Caravelle that flew me back to Paris, on June 23, 1961, I harbored ambivalent feelings. I had lived a great adventure. I had learned a thing or two and I had been busy doing stuff that I loved. I was happy to return home but the prospect of losing all that and of starting anew scared me.

15

Last Days on Old Soil

There is nothing like returning to a place that remains unchanged to find the ways in which you yourself have altered.
—NELSON MANDELA

hree months prior to my demobilization, my actor friend Henri Crémieux tried to prepare me for what awaited me upon my return. "I understand that you still have a few weeks to go," he wrote to me. "I also understand that you will be disoriented when you hit the pavement in Paris. Friendships, the necessary courage and a bit of philosophical attitude will help you face disappointments."

He was right on all counts. I was twenty-four with no job in sight. The transition from busy to idle was painful. I had lost my father. The prospect of living with my mother did not appeal to me. The old apartment in Paris felt just that, old. Yet, I had nowhere else to go. I was free, but had no use for my freedom. Summer was not the best time to return. Everyone had sun and beaches on their minds.

A fellow actor, with whom I had spent most of my stay in Algeria, had been demobilized around the same time. He too was disoriented like most men who had returned from their tour of duty in Algeria. He needed a soul mate. So did I. We became inseparable. His name was Bernard.

He had sartorial elegance. He was a Beau Brummel, always dapper, always impeccably groomed. When shopping for clothes, he was the most discriminate, choosing garments that not only were well cut but that had his kind of cut. He never purchased a jacket, a shirt, a sweater that would betray his vision of how he wanted to look. He was the dark-blue, double-breasted-blazer, gray-flannel-pants, striped-shirts, assorted-tie type of guy. That was the trademark he never deviated from, in an anal sort of way. He would stop in front of a mirror, pick up a lock of hair and take hours rearranging it, a grimace on his face, as if the act had been a painful do-or-die task. He was not vain for vanity's sake. He put a high value on his physical appearance, which is what actors do. His aim was to project the image of a debonair.

The man's uprightness was matched by his tendency to argue for argument's sake. He was a misanthrope of sort and surrounded himself exclusively with people who made him feel comfortable. He had his vulnerabilities and his sensitivities. He was prone to anxiety. Human suffering always touched him; beauty and talent exalted him; stupidity, cruelty and vulgarity repelled him. He was as generous as the rest of his family. I enjoyed his company. I valued his friendship.

We were not rich but had plenty of free time on our hands. We filled it with good food, wine and women, mainly women. We'd lay a wager. The tossing of a coin would first determine who'd be assigned the left or the right side of the Avenue des Champs-Elysées. The winner of this stupid bet would be the one who'd succeed in dating the most women he could cruise in a day. That July, we went up and down the avenue day in day out, from Monday to Sunday, from morning to night, entering each and every store that bordered our side of the avenue, picking up saleswomen, patrons, managers, pedestrians, young ones, not so young ones, tall, short, skinny, chubby, blondes, brunettes, redheads. We were good looking, we had chutzpah and we knew how to spin a woman a yarn. We ended up scoring big time, but we also had our share of painful and sometimes embarrassing rejections. Our impressive tally included the good, the bad, the occasional sublime, and the ugly, lots of uglies. Quantity took precedence over quality.

We roamed the eighth arrondissement during the day, Montparnasse at night. A dive by the name of *Chez Adrien* became our other hunting ground. The seedy bar, located on Rue Vavin, catered to call girls and go-go dancers who performed in the nearby cabarets. Monsieur Adrien, a shady character, owned the smoky joint. He might have been a pusher or a pimp. He was short, bulky and always wore pinstriped suits, black shirts and white ties, like the true Corsican gangster he was. He loved us. We were bringing a touch of class to his operation. He put us in a category apart and always justified the affection he felt for us by saying, in his inimitable Corsican accent, "Because you, my friends, you are artists." He had an unconditional admiration for actors.

The front bell rang. I was having lunch with my mother at the apartment. Colette, the servant, had left the year before. August had just started. I headed to the door, opened it and faced five strangers standing at the doorstep, each carrying a suitcase. I did a double take and recognized them from photographs. They were my grandmother Fanny, her daughter Zica, her son-in-law Fritz and their two children, Annie and Peter. My Romanian family I had never met and to which I had been indifferent for years, stood before me. We fell into each other's arms.

Until that moment, they had been names mentioned by my parents and relegated in the back of my mind. My aloofness toward them had always hurt my father's feelings.

Zica and Fritz had succeeded in escaping communist Romania, not without hardship and sacrifices. They were living in Bucharest in a two-bedroom apartment. They were fortunate. In normal circumstances, a flat of that size would have housed two other families. Life under communism was constricted. The children could not tell anyone that their parents were listening to foreign broadcasts. Listening to foreign broadcasts carried harsh punishment. Everybody spied on everybody else. Anti-Semitism was rampant.

Fritz owned an interior decorating business and Zica was a lawyer. They both had yearned to leave Romania for Israel since the late forties. A window of opportunity opened in 1950. They applied for a visa. They sold everything they owned to raise enough money to pay for the trip and to survive the first weeks of their stay in Israel. Their application was denied. They would have to remain in Romania for another ten years. In 1960, another window of opportunity opened. When they reapplied, they were warned against telling friends, family or neighbors that they were leaving the country. If they did, their visa would be denied. Each of them was restricted to one piece of luggage per person that did not exceed eighty pounds. Their jewelry had to be left behind, their photo albums had to be burnt. Written material of any kind could not be taken out of the country.

In 1961, Zica and her family first traveled to Paris where they stayed a few days. Before leaving for Israel, they took a huge salami my mother had kept for them and their life savings, nine hundred dollars, which Zica had entrusted to my oldest friend, Claude, when he attended the fourth World Youth Festival in Bucharest in 1953.

My grandmother Fanny died one year after her arrival in the Promised Land at age eighty-six.

I had been raised as an only child. We were a family of three and for me a family of three was not a real family, particularly in comparison to our Catholic neighbors who each had four to six children and thirty to forty aunts, cousins and nephews.

It was nice to realize that I had a family after all. To my surprise they grew on me. My grandmother Fanny was energetic, knowledgeable, sharp, funny and unusually alert for her age. And Zica? How could anyone not love her? She was as beautiful as she appeared in early photographs. She oozed kindness and generosity and she always apologized. She apologized for loving you too much, for not loving you enough, she apologized for not having given you an expensive enough gift; she apologized for breathing.

During their short layover in Paris, Fritz asked his children, Annie and Peter, where they wanted to live. Would they rather settle in the French capital or in Israel? They opted for the latter. In hindsight, who can say that their choice was the wisest and served their best interest? Given the reality of Israel's geo-political context, I have my doubts.

Thirty years later, Annie's husband, Sorel, confided in me that he had advised his own two children to leave Israel. They turned him down.

16

The Break that Broke Me

*I have friends that are much better actors than I am that had
to quit the business because they couldn't survive the auditions
or the rejections, or people just didn't realize how
good they were.*

—ROBERT ENGLUND

During the winter of 1961, the first since our return from Algeria,
my friend Bernard and I went through our share of auditions. We
auditioned for plays; we auditioned for movies; we auditioned for
teleplays. And in the process, we learned how to handle the pains of
rejection. Or did we?

The break all actors dream of came late November when I was asked
to participate in a television show entitled *L'Ecole des Vedettes*, literally
translated *The School of Stars*, a French *American Idol* of sorts. It featured
stage and movie stars chosen to perform opposite newcomers. It was not
only a springboard for young actors. Johnny Hallyday, the famous French
rocker, was discovered after he performed in it in 1960.

Its producer offered me the chance to play Dmitri in a scene from *The
Brothers Karamazov* by Dostoyevsky, with Magali Noël in the role of
Grushenka. Magali was a top name then. Born in 1932 —she was five years
older than I—she emigrated from Turkey to Paris and starred in several
films directed by Frederico Fellini. She then worked with the likes of Costa
Gavras, Jean Renoir and Jules Dassin. She had already performed in more
than thirty movies when she was asked to play opposite me.

The prospect of acting with Magali terrified me. How would I fare next to this movie idol? Would I live up to the director's expectations? Would I have the strength to execute the acrobatic Russian dance that the scene required?

I had caught the flu the day prior to my performance and was running a temperature of one hundred and two degrees. I'd have canceled my appearance if Magali hadn't called that evening to cheer me up. Her warm voice on the phone soothed me; her affection and her concern comforted me. She had restored my self-confidence.

Dmitri, the most turbulent of the three brothers, is headstrong, reckless and passionate. He lives a life torn between sin and redemption. He is a physical man, a sensualist, a party animal who is on the brink of murdering his father as they both fight over Grushenka. Actors love these characters.

The morning of the shoot, I was still feverish. We taped the entire scene without interruption. I had given it all I had. I was drained but happy to have gone through it without a glitch. As was required in the script, I had taken Magali Noël in my arms and had kissed her with all the passion Dmitri could muster. It would have been a great experience had I not felt guilty about passing my germs on to her.

The program was aired two weeks later. The press praised my work. I had interpreted Dmitri, wrote *Le Figaro*, the way Dostoyevsky would have imagined him to be. I couldn't have received a better compliment. This would launch my career; the telephone wouldn't stop ringing.

It remained silent. So, I called dozens of production companies, directors and agents. To no avail. I was demoralized.

17

The End of a Chapter
(Jeannie)

A true encounter, a decisive encounter is
something that feels like destiny.
—TAHAR BEN JELLOUN, MOROCCAN POET

T he atheist in me says she was God sent.

She was a Swiss-born painter whom my father and I had met during his visits of young artists organized by the *Société des Amateurs d'Art*. Her name was Jeannie Borel. When we reunited at a cocktail party in the winter of January 1962, we took to each other right away. She was thirty-four, nine years my elder. She had no financial backing, no safety net to fall back onto. Fending for herself had matured her into a strong woman. I had still a boy's mentality. She was making a living from the sale of her works. It was not easy for a thirty-four-year-old woman to survive in Paris, let alone a female painter. Yet, Jeannie got through.

She was not a figurative painter. She had a passion for stringed instruments and gave abstract renditions of them that possessed an aura of sophistication. They exuded an undeniable romanticism underneath the dispersed curvatures of tailpieces and bellies, the straight lines of pegs and strings that suggested a cello here, a violin there. Her watercolors and oils had strength, character, a bit of mysticism and refreshing originality. I loved her art.

Jeannie was her own toughest critic, dissatisfied with her work, questioning it, deconstructing it, seeking new shapes, new forms. These incessant explorations, this constant search for perfection were the mark of a true artist.

Her struggle to make ends meet had hardened her. She had few illusions and expected very little from people. That did not put a damper on her generosity. She knew how to give to friends and lovers alike. And when she gave, she gave her all. When she loved, a painting, a song, a movie, a novel or a man, she loved with every inch of her body. She was intellectually savvy but relied on her instinct. Though capable of meticulous and balanced analysis, she preferred to trust her first impressions. She had an unquenchable zest for life. She prized each and every second she breathed.

The two-bedroom apartment she rented on Rue Raynouard, a stone's throw from the Eiffel Tower, became our love nest. It was not one of those cluttered, old and dusty artist studios associated with starving painters. Her place was on the top floor of a bourgeois building, located in an upscale neighborhood.

She made love the way she painted, with a blend of sensitivity and gusto. We lived happily together. She had already achieved something. I was a "nobody," broke and obsessed with myself, a state of mind not uncommon for an actor. She became my crutch, my light beam. Without her support, I would have drowned.

As early as January 1962, I felt that I had to do something to salvage my life. I could not remain idle another day, another minute. My talent had remained undiscovered. I had hit a wall of rejection. Asking my mother to give me pocket money had become unbearably embarrassing. I could not even pay the restaurant bill whenever Jeannie and I decided to eat out. At twenty-five, I was too dependent on others. This could not go on. I began to fantasize about escape. Marius, Marcel Pagnol's character, had abandoned his native Marseilles to navigate far away oceans on a merchant marine ship, running out on Fanny, the woman he loved. I too ached to get away. I too was prepared to desert the woman I loved.

I felt like a wild beast pacing in his cage, trying to find a breach through which I could break free. It hurt Jeannie to see me hurt. One night, she and I went to see *West Side Story*. When we returned to her apartment, I exclaimed, "I want to go to New York," without realizing the meaning of what I had just said. A genuine *cri de cœur*. The actors' skills and their professionalism, Leonard Bernstein's vibrant, sensual, alternatively graceful and powerful score had galvanized me into shaking off the rut I was in. The musical was a catalyst that brought to the surface the restlessness and disillusionment that had already been building up in me for a while. I could see myself dancing in the eerie streets of New York's Barrio, beautifully photographed by Daniel Fapp. New York was where I had to go; New York was my escape. New York became my obsession.

Jeannie decided to help. She had a friend in Manhattan who owned a drama school located inside the Carnegie Hall building. It was called The Senior Dramatic Workshop. Jeannie asked him if I could attend. He told her by return mail that I was welcome to come study in his school.

I applied for a student visa at the American Embassy. I had to raise enough money to pay for my trip. A friend of my mother knew an executive at Radio Luxembourg, one of France's largest broadcasting networks. Jean Carlier, the station's News Director, agreed to see me. I leveled with him and explained to him that the reason I wanted a job was to earn enough money to pay for my trip to the United States. "I like that," he said. "Have you any experience in journalism?" I told him about my work at the press service of the armed forces. He must have found the reference pretty thin. "How about working at the news desk?" he asked.

"If you think I can handle it…" I answered, flabbergasted.

"Okay. You start tomorrow on the midnight to eight o'clock shift."

"And what will I have to do?"

"The news, Mr. Dorian. The news, every hour on the hour."

Jean Carlier was the first person after Jeannie to lend me a hand since my return from Algeria. He also was the first to take my dream seriously, while my parents' friends reacted to my decision to emigrate with sarcasm. "What will you find over there you can't find here?" they nagged.

The following evening, I showed up for work at eleven. Two young journalists who were going to be my co-anchors taught me how to retrieve data from the news wires and how to write short news bulletins. Being concise was not easy. It required expertise. In hindsight, I must have been crazy to take a job I knew nothing about. I'd repeat that sort of stunt twenty years later.

I had so much to learn and very little time to learn it. I had to tackle domestic and international news: January 16, military coup in the Dominican Republic; January 29, deferment of the Geneva Conference on disarmament; February 7, US embargo against Cuba; March 7, beginning of negotiations with the FLN; March 14, resumption of the Geneva Conference without France; March 18, the Evian Accords granting independence to Algeria. I was thrilled.

I read as many newspapers and magazines as I could lay my hands on. Early evening, I hung out at *Le Dôme* or *La Coupole* until ten-thirty. I then went to work. The following morning, I headed to my mother's apartment or to Jeannie's. I had breakfast, went to bed and woke up at around four in the afternoon to start all over again. As Henry Miller put it, "One of the things to guard against when you work nights is not to break your schedule; if you don't get to bed before the birds begin to screech, it's useless to go to bed at all." I heard the birds twitter a few times and, indeed, didn't bother going to bed. I became exhausted.

At around midnight, May 31, 1962, I retrieved an Agence France-Presse wire stating that Adolph Eichmann, the Nazi, had just been executed by hanging at a prison in Ramla, Israel, after having been found guilty of crimes against humanity. I don't know what got into me. I disregarded the information. The following morning, Jean Carlier called me in his office. He was beside himself, but didn't fire me. He should have, but he didn't. I stayed at the desk of Radio Luxembourg two more months, until I received my student visa.

My departure date for the United States was scheduled for September, out of Rotterdam, Holland. I bought the cheapest ticket I could find from Holland America Lines for $190. It was a fortune for me then.

Sometime in August, I attended a party given by friends with whom I had gone to school at *Ecole Alsacienne*. There I confided in a young woman I just met that I was about to leave for the United States. She happened to have a cousin who had just done that. His name was Michel Auder. Could he put me up for a few days, I asked? She wrote to him. He answered that he would. I had found a place in New York where I could crash.

I had been lucky. The only glitch is that I was abandoning my mother. She knew that she would be left to live by herself in an apartment full of memories and far too big for her. Yet, she gave me her unconditional support and never overwhelmed me with the sorrow that filled her heart.

My friends, Claude, Michel and Bernard were not particularly pleased to see me go either, but they also supported me. Jeannie kept her composure. She, who had fallen in love with me, had done what she deemed to be the ultimate sacrifice at the time. She gave me up.

Very early on that Monday morning, September 17, 1962, I kissed my mother goodbye. My friends accompanied me to *Gare du Nord*, the railroad station north of Paris. I caught a train bound for Rotterdam, where my ship was anchored. I was carrying with me a heavy suitcase.

As the train started to move, I waved to Claude, Michel and Bernard. After they disappeared from view, I returned to my seat, more exhilarated than apprehensive, more hopeful than sad. I had taken hold of my destiny. I was in control, maybe for the first time in my life. I felt no regrets, no fear. I was headed toward the unknown, with a few dollars in my pocket, but rich in expectations. I did not know what was in store for me but I was determined not to look back. It never occurred to me that I'd ever return to France had my American experience turned sour. I was about to start Act II of my life.

The Crossing

18

Suspended Between Today and Tomorrow

You must live in the present, launch yourself on every wave,
find your eternity in each moment.
—HENRY DAVID THOREAU

I boarded the *Groote Beer* in Rotterdam. Formerly named the *SS Costa Rica Victory*, the *Groote Beer* was an improved version of the famed *Liberty* ships built to transport troops toward the end of World War II. In 1951, she was rebuilt for general passenger use, mainly shipping emigrants from Rotterdam to New York. In 1961, its accommodations were vastly improved. The *Groote Beer* was revamped and upgraded to a genuine Tourist Class status.

She was not the *SS Queen Mary*, nor the *SS Normandie*. She did not feature swimming pools, gourmet restaurants, glamorous shows or casinos. She was definitely low-scale. My single cabin pompously referred to as a room—I was assigned to Room 121—was a closet that accommodated a narrow berth. It would have to do. At least the ship was sea worthy. I would have been spared great discomfort had she been equipped with state-of-the-art stabilizers, like most ocean liners are today, but she wasn't.

I was on deck when we left Rotterdam at two o'clock on a sunny afternoon. As I saw the city, then the coast, fade away, I reflected on the past and mused about the future. Here I stood, like a newborn with his entire life yet to be lived.

It might have been easier to turn my back on France if I had been the son of destitute parents, or if I had to escape oppression, starvation or discrimination, all good reasons to seek refuge in a land of opportunity. But I was not destitute, nor was I oppressed. I came from an affluent family and had been raised in a free country.

I could have entered a lucrative profession, buried in the bliss of a comfortable status quo. I could have been a well-to-do oral surgeon—my father's hope—married to a well-to-do wife, surrounded by a couple of well-mannered children, going to work everyday from nine to six, eloping to visit a mistress or two and spending my Sundays in bed, listening to Mozart on the radio. It was not meant to be, and I am glad it wasn't.

My academic achievements were few and my attempts at conquering the stage had been unsuccessful. That alone did not explain my decision to leave my birthplace, to give up a way of life, to abandon my mother, my friends and the woman who loved me.

All that was French did not agree with me anymore.

The French accuse America of being obsessed with political correctness. But in the France I was leaving behind, almost everything had to be correct: fashion, taste, gastronomy, education. If you did not have your *baccalauréat,* you were a slacker. If you did not dress according to the trends of the moment, you were ridiculed. If you started a meal with salad or cheese, you were deemed uncivilized. If you did not furnish your apartment within the norms of what the French call *le bon goût*, you were ostracized.

Academic achievements remained the only successes the French approved and recognized. Any risk taking was met with deep skepticism. They rejected the very same entrepreneurship that built America. To spurn the comfort that children born out of bourgeoisie inherit almost automatically was seen as a cardinal sin. I had become an outcast. In the eyes of those who were close to me, my decision to emigrate was nothing less than a crime of lèse-majesté.

My fellow countrymen were out of sync with the times we lived in. Their way of thinking was anachronistic. "The French are stricken by a deep sickness," De Gaulle said. "They refuse to understand that the era in which they live requires from them a huge effort to adapt."

I'd be remiss not to admit that my failures were also the cause of my desertion. I had no other choice but to move forward. I had to reinvent myself. I had to settle in a land where no one would hold my past mistakes against me. I had to find a country that welcomed any man or woman determined to work his or her way up. I needed a place where mobility was not only possible, but also encouraged. The United States fit the bill.

I was resolute, ready to tackle any task at hand, even the most menial. I needed to do something with myself even if it meant waiting on tables, an activity considered degrading in France for a young man *de bonne famille*.

September was hurricane season. The first one hit us a day after our departure. The passengers were told to stay in their cabins. I chose to remain on deck and decided to move toward the bow. I wanted to witness nature's fury from up close. The heavy swell gave the impression that the ocean had given birth to millions of white sheep that were popping in and out of the surface, haphazardly, as far as the eye could see. I was mesmerized, hypnotized. The ship would stay suspended on the crest of a thirty-foot wave for a brief instant, before diving into its trough. It heaved and surged, shoved around by the raging waters, like a match bobbing up and down an overflowed gutter. Whiplashing spume blinded me. I had difficulty standing. Lightning pierced the dark, ominous sky in short intervals. If I had been found there, I would have been confined to my quarters for the duration of the trip. But I was alone. Not one soul was on deck.

That "Titanic" moment made me forget that I was seasick. Once I reached my cabin, I threw up everything I had in my stomach.

It was mid-afternoon when I emerged on the third day. I went to the bar and asked to be served a chamomile tea and a slice of bread. A man seated on a stool was sipping a martini. He was in his mid-thirties. We talked. He was an American who had been sent to France and to the Netherlands on a job. He could not wait to get back to New York. I asked him why. He was craving a hamburger, he said, a nice juicy burger with tons of French fries and ketchup. I looked at him as if he was a Martian. He had been to France and he still longed for a hamburger? The man was nuts.

It took me a while to empathize with him. A few months later, I had my first all-American burger at Macy's. It was beyond delicious, a confession any true Frenchman would deny, even under torture. As soon as

I took the first bite, I thought of my traveling companion. Craving a hamburger, I realized, was my first step toward Americanization. Hot dogs would come next.

I befriended two people during the trip: a young Frenchman by the name of Gérard, and a young American lady who was returning to New York after a year spent studying at the Sorbonne. Gérard was a bit younger than I was. His father, who owned a button factory near Paris, wanted his son to be a trainee in the United States. Gérard was a typical *fils à papa*, spoiled rotten, with a caustic sense of humor.

The girl was a sort of Joan Baez, tall, dark-haired, sweet and shy. She was about my age. She loved France and was not happy to return to the United States. We flirted in between hurricanes. I tried to make love to her. She pretended that she was a virgin, a suspicious claim for a twenty-five year-old. She became hysterical when I tried to slide my hands in-between her legs. I did not insist. Later on, she asked me if she could see me again. Go figure! I gave her the phone number of the man who had offered me his hospitality. She gave me hers.

We weathered two more hurricanes. The last one turned out to be so scary that we all stayed in our cabins. Some folks were praying on their knees. The crossing took nine days, an unusually long time.

The ocean was smooth on that Tuesday, September 26. The sun was shining. I got dressed and climbed on deck, impatient to catch the sight of land. By mid-morning a bold edge underlined the horizon. The United States of America was within reach. I felt a warm rush throughout my body.

When we sailed past the Statue of Liberty, the passengers of the *Groote Beer* exhaled a sigh of relief. The crossing had been arduous, at times terrifying. We docked in Hoboken, New Jersey.

Milly in Paris Opera program

Lundi 8 Novembre, à 20 h. 45 - 13ᵉ Représentation
(Le Spectacle se terminera vers 23 h. 50)

L'AIGLON

Drame musical en 5 Actes
Poème d'Edmond ROSTAND
Adapté par M. Henri CAIN

Musique de MM. Arthur HONNEGGER
et Jacques IBERT

Costumes et Décors d'après les maquettes de
M. Pedro PRUNA

Décors exécutés par M. MOULENE
Projections de M. Ernst KLAUSZ

•

Frantz, Duc
de Reichs'adt Mmes Fanny HELDY
Thérèse
de Lorget. . Renée MAHÉ
Marie-Louise. . Annita VOLFER
La Comtesse
de Camérata. . Milly MORERE
Fanny Essler. . Odette RICQUIER
Une Marquise . LAFON
Isabelle . . . . Mlle LUMIERE

•

Chef d'Orchestre : M. François RUHLMANN

(Voir suite de la distribution page suivante)

Les Papiers à lettres G.L.
créent les teintes à la mode
Cette grande marque est une garantie
de Qualité et de Goût

The pass granted my father by German and French authorities

St. Priest, the schoolyard

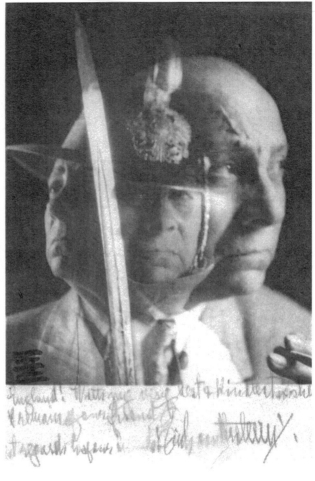

Postcard from Eric von Stroheim

Maurice Siegel admiring my catch   *At the Saturn V launch pad, still a work in progress*

With a tender Nelson Rockefeller at the Metropolitan Museum

Marlon Brando and beauty

Partying with Trini Lopez

Deejaying with Joe O'Brien

Tête-à-tête with Sammy

With Alfred Hitchcock

Flirting with Irina Demick under Darryl Zanuck's watchful eye

Interviewing Tippi Hedren   *With Petula Clark and Joe O'Brien*

Photo courtesy JP Laffont

Hugging a police van during the riots in Newark

Electronic passes to the 1968 Democratic Convention

Inside a Miami police car after assault

A man's errors are his portals of discovery.

—JAMES JOYCE

The New Continent

19

Days of Discovery

The voyage of discovery is not in seeking new
landscapes but in having new eyes.
—Marcel Proust

My first steps on American soil were wobbly and hesitant. The streets, the trees, the buildings were pitching and yawing, rolling and swaying. It felt as if the ground was giving way beneath me. It took my body a few days to get used to terra firma.

Gérard's new boss was waiting for him past customs. He offered me a ride to New York. We boarded a Continental limo and took off for Manhattan. Gérard had a room reserved at the Martinique, a cheap hotel located on Thirty-second Street, right off Broadway. When we reached our destination, no one proposed to take me to where I was going. So, I picked up my heavy suitcase and walked west. I asked the first person I bumped into where the subway was. I could not afford a cab. I took the local downtown with the confidence of a true New Yorker and got off at Cooper Union.

226 East Sixth Street was an old, decrepit, four-story building similar to the tenements featured in *West Side Story*. It stood next to a meat-packaging factory. The overflowing garbage cans, the greasy and loose newspaper pages sent whirling in the air by a strong September wind and the foul smell of rotten flesh would have repulsed anyone accustomed to the beauty and neatness of Paris.

My mind was not into esthetics. I had nowhere else to go, no one to call for assistance and I was exhausted. I was praying that my host was home waiting for me. I rang the buzzer, heard a click and pushed the front door, relieved.

The lobby was dark, narrow and filthy. I walked up to the second floor, reached Michel Auder's apartment and knocked at the door. No answer. I knocked again. The door opened revealing a young Adonis. As my eyes adapted to the semi-obscurity, I discerned long, curly hair framing a sweet, almost angelic face that could have belonged to Lord Byron. I scanned down and realized that the man standing in front of me was stark naked, uninhibited by a hard-on that he flaunted unabashedly. Did I say flaunt? Maybe his was a deliberate act, the man's way of saying to me, "Take me as I am. If you don't, Bud, go fuck yourself."

"Daniel?" He motioned me to come in.

I stepped in, dragging my suitcase with me. The studio was small and narrow, furnished with two beds. The one against the wall, on the left, was empty. On the one to the right lay a skeletal teenager, also in the buff. She must have been eighteen tops. No hello, no smile, no salute, just a frown on her face. She was not pleased to see me. "Guess which is your bed?" my host asked sarcastically. I crossed to the one on the left, while Michel resumed his love making, as if I had not been there.

This was the first day of the rest of my life in the United States.

I felt at home in Manhattan from day one. "One belongs to New York instantly," wrote Thomas Wolfe, "one belongs to it as much in five minutes as in five years."

I perceived New York and Paris as being on the opposite poles of the esthetic spectrum. Paris was black and white, sometimes sepia. New York was all 'technicolor.' The symphony of reds, yellows, oranges and blues scattered all over awnings, store signs, taxis, advertisements and buses, the obscene display of neon, the cacophony of sounds, of fashions and of architectures, the diversity of skin colors, of clothes, of hairdos enchanted me.

I had traded a clean, well-proportioned, harmonious metropolis for chaos, noise, filth and pollution. I had gone from order to shambles, from beauty to ugliness. It was worth it. Paris was disciplined. New York was all over the place, never static, always on the move, like Brownian motion, like me. I had in fact left a museum for a city of sweat and blood, filled with excesses and originality, fueled by creativity, talent and ambition, turned on by greed and sex. Yes, I almost forgot to mention it: New York was the sexiest city on the planet. "New York has a trip-hammer vitality which drives you insane with restlessness if you have no inner stabilizer," wrote Henry Miller. Paris possessed external beauty. New York shined from within.

That first immersion, on that first day of my life in Manhattan, started an addiction I wouldn't be able to shake for years. On that morning, I could have paraphrased Kennedy by shouting, *"Ich bin ein New Yorker."*

The Lower East Side was a village unlike any other. It had traditionally been an immigrant, working class neighborhood, one of the oldest in the city, where Germans were once the majority.

In the late eighteen hundreds, more Germans lived in *Kleindeutschland* (Little Germany) than in Berlin. At one point in its history, the Lower East Side became a place of Jewish beginnings in contemporary American Jewish culture. Then Italians, Poles, Ukrainians and a few Puerto Ricans took over. If New York City was a "melting pot," the East Village was the first recipient of this rich and diverse affluence.

For a boy accustomed to living in an all-white country, with a common history—Algerians had not migrated to France yet—this incredible diversity was refreshing. You could hear people speak Russian, Italian, Polish, Yiddish, even Hebrew all around you. And if you were hungry you could choose between a pastrami sandwich, kreplach, borscht, pierogi, a goulash, spaghetti and meatballs, or a *steak au poivre* within a few feet from where you stood. Where else could that be possible?

Once I had familiarized myself with the Lower East Side, I dared to transgress its boundaries. I ventured as far as Times Square. This was years before Mayor Rudy Giuliani's clean up. Forty-second Street was still a dirty, seedy, sometimes dangerous no-man's land, swarming with prostitutes, pimps, stinky hobos, pickpockets, pushers and drug addicts. The place, "still known as the deuce," as a *New York Times* film critic once put it, "and lined with movie palaces playing the best and worst in trash cinema," was brightly lit by a profusion of tacky neon on top of a myriad of canopies.

Theaters were playing double features. I adored watching two movies in a row. It reminded me of the good times I had in England when I was a teen. French cinemas never offered double features. In London, they always did. A second movie meant the prolongation of an ephemeral pleasure, but not twice the satisfaction, particularly when it was not as good as the first one, which was often the case. I didn't care. Two were still better than one.

So, I went to the movies on Forty-second Street by myself. I went at eight in the evening and did not return home before one.

One morning after, I woke up itchy. The more I scratched, the more I itched. When I checked myself in the bathroom I discovered a colony of lice crawling under my armpits. I dashed to the first drug store, purchased an insecticide, hurried back to my apartment and applied the ointment all over my body. When it turned into powder, I brushed myself off sending small and hideous wingless insects to the floor. A half hour later, a mound of dead lice had amassed at my feet. That's the sort of thing you can expect when you explore. In Africa it's leeches. On Forty-second Street it was lice. The horrendous experience did not dampen my enthusiasm for New York.

When I returned home from my explorations one day, I found Michel packing. His girlfriend was lying on their bed, somber. "What's going on?" I asked.

"Michel has been deported," the girl whined. "I'm taking him to the airport. Wanna come?"

My roommate had been working illegally. Someone at the office, a begrudged employee or some jealous woman, had squealed on him to the Immigration Bureau. The authorities had given him a forty-eight hour reprieve. His time was up.

The three of us drove in an old Bug to Idlewild Airport in silence. The girlfriend and I bade Michel goodbye. As we headed back to the city, she turned to me and said, matter-of-factly, "The rent's due end of next week... Ninety bucks."

She dropped me in front of 226 East Sixth Street. I never saw her again.

At last I was on my own, free and broke. It was cause for celebration. Up until that moment, I had fed myself with cans of Heinz pork n' beans, seasoned with a dash of oil and vinegar, my way of gallicizing this poor people's fare. So, I decided to indulge. I rushed to a coffee shop on Eighth Street, bought half a cooked chicken, half a pound of potato salad, a pickle and a beer and had a ball.

I loved Eighth Street. It had its own personality. It was alive. I was too. Life is contagious.

That evening a thought crossed my mind just before I fell into Morpheus' arms. How was I going to pay the goddamn rent? Ninety dollars was a lot of dough.

My first order of the day was to register at Saul Colin's Senior Dramatic Workshop in the Carnegie Hall building on Fifty-seventh Street. Saul Colin was in his early sixties. His authoritarian appearance hid great generosity. This Romanian Jew who spoke English and French with a charming accent, was always courteous, always ready to help.

A film and theater agent, he had bought the school from Erwin Piscator's wife, Maria. Piscator was a German expatriate stage director who had signed an agreement in 1938 with Alvin Johnson, the President of the New School for Social Research in New York, to found a drama and acting school. The Dramatic Workshop started its operation in January 1940 with a handful of students. Following World War II, the GI Bill led to a massive student increase at the Workshop, making it one of the largest drama schools in America. When he returned to his native Germany, Erwin Piscator entrusted the school to his wife. Bea Arthur, Harry Belafonte, Marlon Brando, Tony Curtis, Walter Matthau, Rod Steiger, Elaine Stritch and Tennessee Williams were its most illustrious alumni.

By the time I joined it the school had lost its glitter and its reputation. Colin did not have the talent or the ability of a Strasberg, whom he tried to imitate. I hadn't anything to learn from him that Jean-Louis Barrault hadn't taught me.

I was tempted to play hooky, but I did not want to hurt Mr. Colin's feelings. If he had not opened the doors of his workshop to me, I would not have been able to come to New York. He also showed generous flexibility when it came to payments. I would be eternally grateful to him.

The classes were scheduled in the morning and early in the afternoon. It left me ample time to search for something else to do. I needed to earn some money.

*   *   *

The first man I decided to call for guidance was the French television correspondent in the United States. Jacques Sallebert was a handsome, tall, self-assured man, well groomed, on the side of arrogance. He was one of the pioneers who started the first televised news programs in 1949.

He advised me to check out the Cultural Services of the French Embassy. That's where I met Huguette, a native of Brittany endowed with a sharp intelligence, wit and limitless generosity. This Ph.D. in math headed FACSEA, short for French American Cultural Services & Educational Aid, a non-profit organization that produced audiovisual material for American schools and universities.

She jump-started my life in the United States by giving me my first job. And what a job! I had to tape record poetry and French literature classics for colleges and universities, thus giving me the opportunity to make a little money doing something I loved.

My recordings were occasionally praised. I once received a letter from Sister Agnes Virginia, a nun who taught at Brentwood College, in Long Island. "I was in ecstasy after I heard your reading of Paul Claudel's *Magnificat*," she wrote. "Really, you must have the soul of a poet to be able to read Paul Claudel in such a way."

The letter strengthened my self-confidence and helped me face the future.

At the end of February 1963, the French Embassy asked me if I was interested in working on a project with René Lagraine Eiffel. René Eiffel, grandson of Gustave Eiffel, the structural engineer who gave us the Eiffel Tower, needed someone to translate the speech he had been invited to deliver at the inauguration of Unisphere.

Designed by a landscape architect, Unisphere was a gift from the United States Steel Corporation to the city of New York. This one hundred forty feet-high, seven hundred thousand pound structure was destined to be the symbol of the 1964 World's Fair, just as the Eiffel Tower had been the symbol of the 1889 Paris International Expo. For USS Steel, inviting René Eiffel was a PR coup that would add prestige to the whole enterprise.

René Eiffel was in his early sixties when I met him. He took a liking to me. He not only asked me to translate his speech into English, he also sought my input. To my surprise, he insisted I accompany him to the inauguration ceremony. He wanted me to deliver the English translation at the podium, following his presentation.

It was agreed that we would meet in the lobby of the Waldorf Astoria, where he was staying. From there, a limousine took us to the future site of Unisphere in Flushing, Queens. A cold and steady rain was falling on the city that morning of Wednesday March 6, 1963.

When we entered the model room, the media and dignitaries had already arrived. Cameras were directed at the podium. Richard Patterson, the city's Chief of Protocol introduced Thomas Deegan, the Chairman of the Executive Committee. Then, Mayor Robert Wagner spoke, followed by Roger Blough, the Chairman of the Board of USS Steel Corporation. Mr. Blough introduced René Eiffel, who crossed to the podium and gave his short address in French. It was met with total silence. No one had understood a word of the speech.

I stepped to the microphone and delivered the English translation with authority. I even turned nostalgic and emotional when I read aloud the paragraph related to Gustave Eiffel. "If he could see us from above," Eiffel's grandson had written, "you can be sure he would feel richly rewarded by this commemorative ceremony held by the compatriots of his old friend Edison." Everyone applauded.

As soon as I was finished, Robert Moses, the "master builder" of mid-twentieth century New York City, crossed to Eiffel and shook his hand, giving me the cold shoulder. He offered to drive Eiffel back to New York in his limo. Being the gentleman he was, Eiffel insisted I accompany him. No one in the limo spoke to me. When we reached First Avenue, Moses asked the chauffeur to pull over, extended his arm over my knees, opened the back door and said, "Goodbye, sir."

He must have been pissed off that the audience had applauded me instead of René Eiffel. Eiffel did not seem to mind. The following day, he sent me a signed book on the history of the Eiffel Tower to thank me for my collaboration. It was his way of saying "Unisphere will never make it as big as my great grandfather's masterpiece."

Unisphere never became the landmark Moses had hoped it would be.

I decided to teach French to make ends meet. I purchased a one-time spot in *France-Amérique*, New York's French newspaper, and advertised private lessons at a competitive price. I wound up making a few bucks teaching the language of Molière to all kinds of people scattered throughout the city. Most were well to do. One of them wasn't. She lived below Fourteenth Street, on Avenue B, one of Manhattan's most dysfunctional neighborhoods.

The woman lived in a depressing lower-middle class project house located a couple of blocks from Tompkins Square, otherwise known as "Needle Park." The area was crawling with pushers and drug addicts who bought heroin and shot it right there.

The apartment was on the tenth floor. I rang the bell. A large black woman endowed with a huge bust and a derrière no less impressive opened the door. She was in her mid-thirties. "Dan?" she inquired. "Oh! I'm so glad you could come. Hey Lee, come meet my French teach." An obese white man showed up, shook my hand and left.

I gave French lessons to that woman twice a week. "Could we both sit on the sofa?" she simpered one afternoon, pretending that her chair was uncomfortable. She moved next to me. She had over-sprayed herself with cheap perfume. As I was going through the conjugation of a French verb, she squeezed my hand. Her advances became more and more targeted. She took off her blouse and unfastened her bra faster than I could bat an eye. The incongruity of the moment, and the sight of so much flesh overwhelmed me. Miraculously, I succeeded in breaking the embrace and ran out of her apartment as fast as I could. In hindsight, maybe I should have let the seductress have her way. I might have learned a thing or two in the process. On the other hand, I would have run the risk of an unpleasant confrontation with her overweight hubby.

The money I earned with my French lessons paid for part of my basic expenses, but didn't allow me to indulge in decent restaurants. I was willing to shed all that was French in me, but not my love for good food. Fast food was out of the question. If I wanted to eat well, I had to cook. I had never touched a frying pan but I had observed my mother prepare scrumptious dishes. I was ready and willing to put my shoulder to the wheel, but when I found out how expensive steaks and lamb chops were, I realized that I had to look for additional sources of revenue if I wanted to upgrade my quality of life.

Jacques Sallebert had also given me the phone number of a young woman, who, he said, knew everyone in New York. Her name was Jacqueline. I was not the first newcomer who had knocked at her door for leads and advice. She was a one-woman welcoming committee for newly arrived Frenchmen in distress. She asked me if I'd like to have dinner with her and proposed we meet at a midtown French restaurant called *Henry IV*. It was one of these upscale eateries that were way out of reach for me then.

The woman was already seated when I arrived. She was *bon chic bon genre*, a Chanel type of gal. The haughtiness and snootiness she displayed when she spoke bordered on caricature. The French would have accused her of being a *Marie-Chantale*, the nickname they gave to snobbish women.

When the waiter brought the two espressos we had ordered at the end of a delicious meal, I wondered, not without apprehension, when my gracious hostess would ask for the bill. How could she not realize that I was poor?

She talked non-stop and asked me questions about my life. The fear that I'd be stuck with the check tightened my throat. It dawned on me that I was in for it. Women did not even go Dutch in the sixties.

The waiter who had grown impatient crossed to our table, delicately placing an elegant silver plate in front of me, in the middle of which lay a little piece of paper. Gosh, that little piece of paper lost in the middle of this large silverware looked so threatening. I mustered the courage to take a fast peek and saw the total amount. Oh, my God! I first wondered if I should level with that stranger. Instead, I decided to fake it. I reached for my inside pocket, acted contrite and said, "Silly of me. I think I have forgotten my wallet."

My dinner guest did not budge as I continued to search frantically for the wallet I knew wasn't there. I took a deep breath and brought myself to saying, "I'll be right back. It'll only take a few minutes."

I rushed out of the restaurant and ran downtown, covering forty-four blocks at a record speed. I entered my apartment, grabbed all the money I possessed, dashed out and took a cab back. I was still short of breath and soaked with sweat when I reached our table. Jacqueline welcomed me with a big smile of relief. She wore expensive clothes, but she might not have been as comfortable as she tried to appear. I paid the bill, kissed the lady goodbye and returned home. When I lay down on my bed, I was satiated but broke and exhausted. It was going to be pork 'n' beans for a bit longer.

An unexpected phone call interrupted my solitude. The young lady I had met on the ship invited me to her place for Thanksgiving. She lived at the London Terrace Gardens, off Twenty-third Street, in Chelsea. We were already in November.

This huge apartment complex with its red brick façade, its maze of corridors and its swimming pool was conceived and developed in the late twenties by Henry Mandel, the Donald Trump of the time. In 1930, the year it was completed, London Terrace was considered the largest apartment building in the world with its one thousand six hundred and sixty-five units.

My young friend lived in a one-bedroom apartment. I expected a crowd. She had cooked a whole turkey for the two of us. We had a few drinks, went swimming downstairs—an attendant lent me a swimsuit—and returned to the apartment just in time to eat the bird and all its accouterments: cranberry sauce, sweet potatoes, brussels sprouts et al. I did not have a penny, but life was good. Later in the evening, the girl turned flirtatious. She gave me the opportunity to be profoundly thankful.

The relationship did not endure but Thanksgiving became my favorite holiday.

20

Swan Song
(My Last Acting Days)

I wanted to give acting one last chance. A friend of my mother had handed me a letter of recommendation addressed to Molly Picon, the famous star in Yiddish theater and film. Miss Picon, who was in her sixties then, advised me to go see Stella Adler, the American actress and drama teacher who founded the Stella Adler Conservatory in New York in 1949. She became a method teacher after having seen the Russian actor/director Constantin Stanislavski and his Moscow Art Theater perform, when they toured the US. She embraced the Stanislavski Method and joined the Group Theater founded by Harold Clurman, Lee Strasberg and Cheryl Crawford. She coached Marlon Brando, Robert De Niro, Martin Sheen and Warren Beatty to name a few.

After I told her that I had been a student at the Paris Conservatory and a member of the Jean-Louis Barrault Company, she asked me if I'd be interested in attending Lee Strasberg's classes at the Actors Studio. I knew that America's best talents were honing their skills there, and the Studio's members were all consummate actors who had already made a name for themselves. The thought of rubbing elbows with the likes of Karl Malden, Paul Newman, Lee J. Cobb or Geraldine Page terrified me. Adler said it would be a sobering experience I'd benefit from.

I became an observer at the Studio thanks to her intervention and to Strasberg's generosity. The fact that I was French helped. Talent had nothing to do with it.

The classes were held on Thursday and Saturday mornings in an old converted church on West Forty-fourth Street. I had been given a pass to the temple of American theater and an opportunity to see its high priest officiate.

Lee Strasberg was seated at the center of the front row with his second wife Paula at his side. What a lesson in humility to see these Hollywood stars behave like attentive students, these prima donnas who never raised an eyebrow when given their bottom line by the teacher who had earned their trust. Lee could be harsh, biting at times. Not everybody liked him. Brando wrote these scathing words about him in his autobiography, *Brando, Songs My Mother Taught Me.* "After I had some success, Lee Strasberg tried to take credit for teaching me how to act. He never taught me anything... He tried to project himself as an acting oracle and guru. Some people worship him. But I never knew why."

The two of them might have had a falling-out or might have been incompatible. Besides, Brando might not have been comfortable with Strasberg. He revered Stella Adler. Who knows? Most actors felt differently. According to James Dean's biographer, the idol referred to the Studio, in a 1952 letter to his family, as "the greatest school of the theater. Very few get into it. It is the best thing that can happen to an actor." "The Actors Studio meant so much in my life," once stated Al Pacino.

Strasberg was a master at digging out and pulling to the surface a quality, an emotion an actor did not suspect he had in him or at revealing options his students did not know were available to them. He helped actors delve deep into their inner selves, an introspective process that allowed them to identify a palette of feelings they could recall and use at will as they needed them.

Being surrounded by so much talent had a stifling effect on me. American actors were perfectionists, so were dancers and musicians, something that could not always be said about their French counterparts. Yves Montand told me, in an interview I conducted with him in the sixties on top of the Pan Am Building, where he was shooting *On a Clear Day You Can See Forever* with Barbra Streisand, "What struck me is the work ethic of the musicians I recorded with. You arrive at the studio. You start chatting with this one and that one for a few minutes. Then comes a sort of Master of Ceremonies. He claps his hands and immediately after that, the musicians refrain from talking. No one opens his mouth for the next fifty minutes. We rehearse. These people have the sense of collectivity, of a job well done."

My old boss Jean-Louis Barrault had his own take concerning these breaks imposed by Equity, the actors' union. "Something is physically and mentally trying," he said. "It's what they call the break, the ten-minute break every fifty minutes. Imagine you are with a beautiful woman and you must pause every fifty minutes." (It's actually eighty minutes) "It's nerve wracking. It saps your drive."

Lee's daughter, Susan, asked me to do a scene with her. I felt I was out of my league. Performing in front of such an audience was out of the question. When I confessed to my mother that I had turned down Susan Strasberg, she had a fit. She called me long distance and asked, "Why on earth didn't you do it? You have to be daring, Daniel. In this business you have to be daring." I did not possess her chutzpah.

I mentioned to Susan that I was considering touring the universities with a French poetry recital. She encouraged me to go ahead with it.

I had recorded many poems at FACSEA, but to put together a recital was a whole different thing. It had to have a theme. Was I going to focus on the Middle Ages, on the seventeenth century, on the romantics, or would I tackle the moderns exclusively? A French actor had recorded an album entitled *De Villon à Prévert* in the fifties. The idea of covering six centuries of French poetry and of introducing to a young audience so many styles, moods and genres appealed to me. I stole the idea and selected twenty-five poems from the fifteenth to the twentieth century for their dramatic values. I was not going to just recite them standing still in front of a microphone. No, I planned on bringing them to life as if each of them was a short play.

I opened with *La Ballade des Pendus* by François Villon, who in this particular piece borrows the voice of a man who has just been hung in public. Villon wrote the poem awaiting his own execution. I followed with works by Pierre Ronsard, the sixteenth century "Prince of Poets." The first part ended with a few fables by Jean de La Fontaine. They featured animal characters that each bore a human trait: the lion symbolized power, the fox trickery, the donkey weakness, the peacock vanity. They lent themselves to a performance à la Commedia dell' Arte. The second part of the recital was dedicated to the moderns. It included works by Baudelaire, Paul Fort, Charles Cros and Louis Aragon. The recital ended with Prévert's masterpiece *Barbara*.

I gave my first recital in New York at NYU's *Maison Française*, a beautiful building located at 16 Washington Mews. The small auditorium was packed with students, teachers, a couple of friends from the Actors Studio and reviewers.

The write-ups were better than I expected. *France-Amérique*, the French newspaper in New York, wrote, "Poetry has too rarely a place of honor. Its return to center stage and the audience's enthusiasm and reactions to every bit of nuance has showed how much joy Polymnie's reappearance has brought us. What a great servant this daughter of Zeus has found in the young performer. He laughs, he cries with the ardor and the sincerity of a true artist."

The English poet Robert Graves once said during an interview he granted to BBC-TV in 1962, "There's no money in poetry, but then there's no poetry in money." The latter might be true, but not the former. My recitals helped me earn a significant income. I often performed three to four times a week and was paid between eighty and two hundred dollars per show, nifty sums then. My new earnings boosted my standard of living and far exceeded the limited amount of money the bearer of a student visa was allowed to earn.

In the winter of 1963, Charles Boyer, the movie star, who appeared in more than eighty films between 1920 and 1976, asked me one day, to replace him. He had made the commitment to narrate Sergei Prokofiev's fanciful musical tale, *Peter and the Wolf*, at Carnegie Hall. He either could not make it or did not feel like doing it. Jacques Sallebert had introduced him to me. Boyer liked me. He was nice but reserved. He had seen it all and was a bit jaded and caustic.

Sensing my reluctance, I remember him trying to sell me the bill of goods with the charm that made his fame. "It's nothing, Daniel," I recall him saying. "All you have to do is read the copy. Anybody could do it."

"Ladies and gentlemen, the part played by Charles Boyer will be interpreted tonight by Daniel Dorian." Seriously!

He insisted. He even called me a few times to ask me if I had changed my mind. I mustered the courage to turn him down.

21

Intermezzo

Those who know nothing of foreign
languages know nothing of their own.
—JOHANN WOLFGANG VON GOETHE

I loved my life in Manhattan, but my struggle for survival had worn me down. I needed a break. In the spring of 1963, Huguette informed me that the National Defense Language Institute needed foreign natives to help high school teachers of foreign languages improve their skills. The University of Kentucky in Lexington had an opening for a French-born coach. The idea of spending the summer outside of Manhattan appealed to me. I signed on.

I would never have had this opportunity had it not been for the Cold War. The launch of the Sputnik satellite by the Soviet Union on October 4, 1957, shook American belief that the US was superior in math and science to all other countries. If the Russians were capable of such technological feats, it was reasoned, it meant that they turned out brilliant technocrats and consequently, that their academic level was equal, if not superior to that of the United States. In the context of the Cold War, such an edge was unacceptable. The US. Congress reacted by signing into law the National Defense Education Act (NDEA) on September 2, 1958.

The act was designed to fulfill two purposes: to provide the country with specific defense personnel and to increase student enrollment in colleges and universities through financial assistance, primarily through the National Defense Student Loan Program.

The teaching of foreign languages was historically linked to national defense. It all started on the eve of American involvement in World War II, when the US army established a secret school to teach the Japanese language at the San Francisco Presidio. Half a century later, on January 6, 2006, President Bush announced a wide-ranging plan to enhance the foreign language skills of American students within the framework of a national security language proposal, which the president described as a "broad-gauged initiative that deals with the defense of the country, the diplomacy of the country, the intelligence to defend our country..." Today's priority would be to motivate young people to take up Arabic to better prepare the country in its struggle against terrorism.

The eight-week program in Lexington started on June 17, and ended on August 9, 1963. Classes were held on the sprawling campus of the university. There was a huge difference between giving private lessons to a handful of rich New Yorkers and teaching a class of forty-eight students on a daily basis. Moreover, these students were teachers. I was not. Some were in their fifties. They taught French at high schools in twenty-one states, from California to Virginia, from Connecticut to North Carolina, from Georgia to Missouri. I had to do my homework to avoid being perceived as an amateur. It took me a few sleepless nights to ready my courses and quite a bit of imagination and creativity to keep my adult pupils interested.

From the moment I introduced myself, I sensed their genuine desire to learn. They all had a myriad of questions about Paris, about the French. Their curiosity made me feel good, but it did not take me long to discover the depth of their ignorance. Most of them could not put a French sentence together.

"Americans who travel abroad for the first time are often shocked to discover that, despite all the progress that has been made in the last thirty years, many foreign people still speak in foreign languages," wrote Dave Barry, the humorous columnist. They indeed do, but most Parisians speak English as well. When it comes to foreign languages, Europeans have an edge. Foreign languages are an integral part of the French academic curriculum, as important as math, physics or literature. I suspect that today many Chinese make a point of learning English. So, why did Americans lag so far behind?

My students' shortcomings were, in my opinion, the result of decades of isolationism that can be traced to the late eighteenth, early nineteenth century. Thomas Paine is credited in instilling the first non-interventionist ideas in the American body politic. In his 1796 farewell address, George Washington warned against foreign influence. And it was Thomas Jefferson who coined the expression "entangling alliances," as he extended Washington's ideas in his inaugural address of March 4, 1801.

During most of its history, this country objected to foreign interference in any shape or form and refused to participate in foreign conflicts, thus isolating itself while asserting its self-sufficiency. The US involvement in World War I and World War II marked a victory over the non-interventionists, among them the America First Committee, during the Second World War, who felt that both conflicts were fought by other nations for their own purposes, and posed inevitable threats to Constitutional liberties. According to Averell Harriman, "Roosevelt was the one who had the vision to change the policy of the US from isolationism to world leadership."

Meanwhile, average Americans remained reluctant to open up to the rest of the world, in spite of this about-face at the top. Even today, many, from the deep south to mid-America, show appalling indifference toward anything foreign, often unaware that most products they buy at their local supermarkets, from strawberries to toilet paper, are imports from foreign countries. If they knew, they'd be hard-pressed to pinpoint these countries on a map. It would be interesting to find out how many Americans know where Iraq is located, even among those who favored military intervention there. As a matter of fact, according to *Newsweek*, sixty-three percent of young Americans can't find Iraq on a map. Nine out of ten can't find Afghanistan, even if you give them the advantage of a map limited to Asia.

"What the United States does best," wrote Carlos Fuentes, the Mexican novelist, "is to understand itself. What it does worst is to understand others." The 1958 best seller entitled *The Ugly American*, a book that described the United States' losing struggle against communism because of innate arrogance and ignorance of the local culture, illustrated this disregard and often contempt for all things foreign.

"My one thought is to get out of New York," wrote Henry Miller, "to experience something genuinely American." The environment at the University of Kentucky could not have been more genuinely American. It revealed an America that in some respects was similar to the one the French could have extrapolated by just observing the GIs who had come to liberate them, but also an America so different in many other ways.

The French had fallen in love with the tall, easy-going cowboys who not only gave them back their freedom but who also showered them with cigarettes and chocolate bars. They had been seduced and disarmed by these cool, handsome, gum-chewing young men, whose ways contrasted so much with their aloofness and their Gallic formality. But they also were humiliated by their generosity. So, they belittled them and looked upon them as if they were *des grands enfants*, big, irresponsible kids. It was their condescending way of saying, "we're amused by your naiveté and immaturity, but don't you dare think that you're smarter than we are just because you've liberated us." To call Americans big kids made the French feel better about themselves and gave them a false sense of superiority.

In Lexington, breaks, luncheons, dinners and evenings were spent exchanging platitudes, discussing minutia. My dear French teachers wallowed in the mundane at a time when clean-cut American boys had already been sent to die in Vietnam, a fact they might or might not have been aware of at the early stage of the conflict. More and more draftees were shipped everyday to Saigon to fight. President Johnson would soon start his escalation of the war, yet no one at the university ever alluded to, let alone debated, this horrible conflict. My adult students were more concerned about Joe Namath's knee injury or Steve Sloan's performance than about Eisenhower's Domino Theory. They were far from realizing that the conflict in Southeast Asia would soon wash away their naiveté and their free and easy attitude like a tsunami, and that it would mature them faster than they had during the two centuries of their country's young existence. Vietnam had not yet shattered their consciousness and innocence. Things would change, but at that time, the pursuit of happiness was all that mattered.

My teachers were not concerned with the great issues that affected the US at the time, therefore did not shed much light on their country's weaknesses. I had heard more about America's pitfalls and blunders in Paris bistros than in Lexington coffee shops, but whatever negative opinions the French had of America and Americans paled compared to Hollywood's. The movies I rushed to see in the fifties and early sixties could have dissuaded me from immigrating. Gregory Peck as Philip Schuyler revealed the nasty anti-Semitism that prevailed in America in Elia Kazan's *Gentleman's Agreement*. Gregory Peck again, but this time as Atticus Finch, exposed prevalent racism in the South in Robert Mulligan's *To Kill a Mockingbird*. Jimmy Stewart as Jefferson Smith fought corruption in Congress in Frank Capra's *Mr. Smith Goes to Washington* and Spencer Tracy as Henry Drummond confronted bigotry, ignorance and backwardness in Stanley Kramer's *Inherit the Wind*.

No Hollywood movie could have helped me realize as clearly as my new friends had that I had immigrated to a country that was different from the one I had just left. My students made me feel like a foreigner for the first time since my arrival in the United States. They were not antagonistic. *Au contraire*. In fact, I had rarely encountered so gregarious a people. They also were refreshingly direct. They possessed the type of straightforwardness that saves time and avoids ambiguity. They lacked manners, but at least you knew where you stood. They were not always worldly, but it was refreshing for me to break bread with men and women who were not as jaded and judgmental as the French. But to have a meaningful relationship with any of them, even to exchange deep personal thoughts was elusive. Prudishness came in the way of openness. Their brand of puritanism was different from that of the Brits. It was not as stern but it always materialized in one form or another. I could talk about sex with men of my age for instance, but not as graphically or jokingly as I would have with their French counterparts, or even with African-Americans.

I'd also realized in time that there was a part of America that espoused ideologies, philosophies and dogmas that were anathema to what I believed in, that even were repugnant to me. I never would have settled in Mississippi, North Carolina or Oklahoma where a man could be sentenced to ten years in jail for sodomy or in Florida where oral sex or kissing your wife's breasts was illegal. As an American living in the twenty-first century, I still wish that my country had not been ruled by an unforgiving sexual inquisition, eager to pillory a president for his denial of his amorous escapades but willing to forgive the lies of another concerning the existence of WMDs.

It dawned on me very early on that I had not emigrated to one America, but to two Americas: the enlightened America and the benighted

America, the violent America and the peaceful America, the America of evolutionism and the America of creationism, the smart, sophisticated, ingenious America and the America of ignorance and bigotry, the urban America and the rural America, the modern America and the antiquated America, two distinct worlds that occasionally clash but that, most of the time, coexist on a parallel course.

By mid-July, I received an offer from the University of Indiana. They needed a full-time French teacher. Teaching was not my vocation. I was not going to bury myself in Bloomington, Fort Wayne, South Bend or even Indianapolis. I longed to go back to New York and its buzz. "I think you know that when an American stays away from New York too long," wrote the novelist Sherwood Anderson, "something happens to him. Perhaps he becomes a little provincial, a little dead and afraid." I wasn't going to let that happen to me.

I sensed I did not have what it took to become a successful actor. I just wanted to do stuff. What type of stuff? I had no clue. What I knew for sure was that I missed the excitement of the city. I had my fill of clean haircuts, fresh air and softball.

A week before I left the University of Kentucky, I purchased a used Simca from a car lot with the few dollars I had earned. It was my first car, a cute machine, with the stick shift on the steering post, not on the floor. It had decent pick-up. While I drove it all the way to New York, I soon realized that road signs in America were not as accurate as they were in France. When I first transferred from one highway to another, I chose west instead of east and drove two hundred miles before realizing that I was headed in the wrong direction. If you wanted to go places in America, you better know your east, west, north and south.

First Take on American Women

*I have no hesitation in saying that although the American
woman never leaves her domestic sphere and is in some respect
very independent within it, nowhere does she enjoy a higher
station. And if anyone asks me what I think the chief cause of
the extraordinary prosperity and growing power of this
nation, I should answer that it is due to the
superiority of their women.*

—ALEXIS DE TOCQUEVILLE

My cousin Sophie suggested I call one of her friends who lived in Manhattan. "His name is Jim Smith," she said. "I don't have his phone number, but you can look him up in the telephone book. He is a very resourceful man. Maybe he can help you."

When I returned to New York, I let my fingers do the search. The number of J. Smiths listed was staggering. So, I lifted my index in the air, closed my eyes, let it fall haphazardly somewhere on the Smith, J. column and dialed the corresponding number. A male voice answered. "Hello."

"Mister Smith?"

"Yes."

"Jim Smith?

"I'm afraid you got the wrong Smith."

"Sorry."

"It's okay." (Pause) "Hey, you wouldn't be French by any chance? I detect an accent."

"I am."

"Well, I'm not the guy you're looking for but a good friend of mine, how shall I put it, is... partial to French men, if you know what I mean. I'm sure she'd love to meet you. Interested?"

"Is she pretty?"

"I think she is. Her name is Joan. She's Irish... and divorced. Here's her number. Good luck."

I waited a day before calling. I had nothing to lose. I dialed. A woman answered. "Joan?" I asked.

"Yes."

"My name is Daniel Dorian."

"Oh yes, the Frenchman. Jonathan said you'd call. Are you a Parisian?"

"Yes."

"Ha!" (Pause) "What brings you to our city?"

I explained the best I could. The woman had a sensuous voice. My curiosity was peaked. I wondered how old she was, what she looked like.

"Have you ever had a blind date?" she asked.

"No."

"It's an interesting experience, full of surprises. Willing to take a gamble?"

"Why not."

"I never invite men to my place on a first date. How about dinner? You choose the restaurant. I'm a redhead and I'll be holding a copy of *Harper's Bazaar*."

I met Joan at P.J. Clarke's on Fifty-fifth Street and Third Avenue. It was the only decent place I could afford. I arrived first. The pub was packed and noisy. The crowd was so thick that you could barely move, not ideal for a first time rendezvous. It was eight-thirty. She was already half an hour late. I waited some more. She showed up at nine.

She had *un certain je ne sais quoi*. She was wearing glasses and was at least eight to ten years my senior. She looked happy to see me, judging by the smile she threw at me when I introduced myself.

I had slipped a few dollars in Frank's palm. This bulky, short and bossy little fellow was one of the two maîtres d at P.J.'s. If he liked you and your tip, he'd seat you as soon as he could. If he didn't, well... good luck. He'd make you wait for hours. He enjoyed his moments of power.

That evening, Frank was in a generous mood. He gave us a table in the back, far from the brouhaha. I ordered my two favorites, a red caviar soup, a

P.J.'s specialty, and a steak tartare. Joan ordered a spinach salad.

She was smart, warm and had a good sense of humor. She confirmed that she was divorced and told me that she had a little girl who was in her mother's care. Like hundreds of other women who lived in the Big City, she was lonely. Life for a single woman was not easy in Manhattan. "You meet so many creeps," she sighed. "They're either gay, married or they're trash. You seem to be a nice young man. I hope you're not married."

After dinner, she asked me to take her back to her place, on Thirteenth Street between Sixth and Seventh Avenue.

The cabbie stopped in front of one of the charming brownstones that lined this elegant block. We got out. I accompanied Joan to her doorstep and kissed her, secretly hoping that she would ask me in. "I like you," she said. "But I never go to bed on the first night. Never. I have to prepare myself for it, physically and mentally, you understand? We will make love the next time we see each other. Okay?"

"How about tomorrow?"

"Tomorrow's fine with me. Show up at around seven. I'll prepare dinner."

She turned around, opened her door and disappeared inside, leaving me a little perplexed.

A French woman would have displayed coyness and charm before finding an elegant out. If she had been attracted to me and did not want to give in on the first date, she would have waited for me to ask her for another date. Better yet, she would have subtly led me to doing it.

Joan didn't think that opening her legs on the second night might be construed by me as less promiscuous than opening them on the first one. No, she telegraphed an obvious message: no man was going to force a decision on her. She was in charge. She was not going to give me access to her bed that evening, no matter how strongly she wanted to. She had made that decision way before we met. That was her modus operandi, her way of saying to a man, "Beware. The weaker sex is not the one you think."

I arrived at her brownstone at seven-thirty sharp the day after our first meeting. Should I have been late in order to cover up my eagerness? Or could my punctuality have played in my favor and been construed as flattery? Either way, Joan had made up her mind.

I opened an iron gate and went down a few steps to reach the entrance door. The ground floors in these brownstones were located below street level. Joan welcomed me with a sexy kiss. She had prepared a steak and potato dinner, a treat I could not have afforded, and had opened a bottle of mediocre French Bordeaux. She had purchased the two huge aged rib eyes at Jefferson Market, one of the best butchers in New York City at the time. The meat melted in the mouth.

After dinner, Joan grabbed my hand and led me upstairs.

When we reached her bedroom, she pulled my jacket off me and unbuttoned my shirt. I started to unbutton her blouse. "Be patient," she ordered.

She crossed to her bathroom. I finished undressing and slid under her covers. The king bed was soft and cozy. I must have waited a good fifteen minutes. She was probably putting her diaphragm in place and sprinkling herself with a sexy perfume. She reappeared, naked. Her body was a cross between a Rubens and a Jean Gabriel Domergue. She had generous breasts, a flat belly and firm buttocks. She had sprayed herself with Chanel No. 5.

Offering herself to me so easily did not mean that she was easy. "Easy," said Nancy Linn-Desmond, the author, "is an adjective used to describe a woman who has the sexual morals of a man."

Joan was in charge of her life and a control freak. She decided whether we would go out or dine at home, whether we would have sex that night or which movie we would go see. She was bossy, overpowering and at times motherly, which was fine by me.

I yearned for affection and for the warmth of a home. Her brownstone became a haven, her body my refuge, not only sexually but emotionally as well. It comforted me as I struggled for survival, with no family and no friends.

Joan loved to turn me on. It empowered her to arouse a young man. She once told me that her husband's boyish attitude and his chauvinism were the principal causes of her divorce. Following an unsuccessful marriage, she vowed not to be in a position of inferiority again. She therefore decided to act as if she was on an equal footing with men. She indeed carried in her the seeds of feminism.

* * *

Our affair lasted a few weeks, until the day she decided to pay me a visit at my Sixth Street studio. When she entered, she let go a condescending, "How charming!" The bohemia might have startled her, but it also turned her on.

We made love on my narrow bed. I sensed that she was uptight, unsettled. When we were through, she turned to me. "I've grown attached to you, you know," she said with gravitas. "Do you love me?"

"I'm very fond of you, Joan."

"Do you love me?"

"I enjoy being with you."

She turned her back on me abruptly. "I cannot go on like this any longer. I need a commitment from you, Daniel," she whispered.

"What sort of commitment?"

"Marriage."

I was almost ten years younger than she was. I barely made a living, my future was filled with question marks, and she wanted me to marry her?
The woman was insane. Her anger covered up a weakness. I had caught her at a vulnerable moment in her life. She was divorced, lonely, already in her late thirties. The fear of aging alone had put her in a position of weakness. She had dropped her guard and had become vulnerable.

I jumped out of bed, crossed to the sink, splattered my face with cold water then turned to her. "Joan, I'm not ready for marriage. I don't even know what I am going to do tomorrow. Besides, I'm broke."

"I have enough money for the two of us."

"I'm not that kind of guy, Joan. I'm not ready to tie the knot, with or without money."

Joan probably thought she had me in the palm of her hand. She got off the bed, got dressed and left without saying a word. I never saw her again.

23

Back to Journalism

S omeone had suggested I check out Voice of America (VOA), a government-sponsored broadcasting system always on the lookout for French-speaking journalists. When I applied for a job, they asked me to fill out a long and detailed form and they took my fingerprints.

In 1962, VOA was operating under The United States Information Agency (USIA), a government organization created to "support US foreign policy and national interests abroad." Twenty years earlier, VOA began broadcasting programs in Europe, North Africa, Japan and the South Pacific under the Office of War Information Agency. Its main objective was to broadcast American propaganda on shortwave radio frequencies, but not exclusively directed at countries hostile to the United States, such as the Soviet Union, the Eastern block, Communist China and Cuba. It broadcast in forty-seven languages, including French.

Many questioned its credibility, even its raison d'être. That did not stop Congress from allocating significant budgets to its operation year after year. USIA's headquarters were in Washington, DC. VOA also had a New York branch located at 250 West Fifty-seventh Street.

When I visited VOA in November 1962, Jacques Bablon was in charge of its French-speaking broadcasts produced for Europe. Kenneth Watson handled the programs destined for Africa. Both were interested in me but could not use my services until I was given full clearance.

The Soviet Union and the United States were at each other's throats then, trying to outdo each other with rhetoric and propaganda, spying on each other, deploying strategic conventional forces, escalating their nuclear arms race and regularly exchanging threats of annihilation. Hysteria no longer led to the construction of atomic shelters throughout these United States as it had in the fifties, but tensions were still pretty high. Paranoia ruled.

The last major incident in the Cold War concerned the status of Berlin in post-World War II Germany. A year before my arrival in New York, thousands had emigrated from East Germany to West Germany, a "brain drain" the Communists did not tolerate. In June 1961, the Soviet Union issued an ultimatum demanding the withdrawal of Allied Forces from West Berlin. The request was turned down. As a consequence, East Germany erected a barbed-wire barrier that would be expanded through construction into the Berlin Wall.

In this geo-political context, no one was allowed to work for the federal government, even as a freelancer, without being subjected to a thorough background investigation.

A few weeks after I submitted my job application, I took a short trip to Paris. In a moment of nostalgia, I went to visit the building where I had spent my youth. My gregarious concierge barely said hello to me, displaying a behavior so at odds with her customary persona that I decided to corner her the following day.

"I don't know if I should tell you, *Monsieur Dorian*." She took a deep breath and made sure no one was eavesdropping. "Two detectives came to see me and asked if you were a Communist." She paused, looked around a second time. "They also asked if you were..." she whispered, "...a homosexual."

The FBI had given her the third degree. They had made sure I had no Communist affiliations and that I was not, nor had ever been a homosexual, which in their eyes was as serious an offense as being a Commie. They also questioned many of my friends, neighbors and teachers from the schools I had attended. This investigative process took six months.

Once I received my "Full Back Clearance" in March 1963, I started freelancing for Voice of America, producing features on lifestyle, entertainment, social events and French-related topics.

At the end of March 1963, headquarters requested that VOA cover Hassan II's visit to the United States. Ken Watson asked me to interview the King of Morocco on his way to New York. It was the monarch's first official trip to America since his coronation. Hassan II had traveled by ship and was still at sea, a few miles off the coast. Voice of America had commissioned a US Navy helicopter that landed me on the deck of his ship. A man from his entourage took me below deck to a spacious and elegant living room. "The king will join you shortly," he said solemnly.

I waited a few minutes. The king entered alone, without press secretary or bodyguard. I stood up and bowed. Dressed in a dark suit, he crossed to me, shook my hand and said, in French, "*Monsieur Dorian, je vous en prie, asseyez-vous.*" (Mr. Dorian, please take a seat) His people had briefed him. I was nonetheless impressed. The king knew my name. He sat on a sofa, across from me.

He was thirty-three years old and had only been king for two years. He was already a powerful sovereign, but the March 1963 elections in his country did not turn out in his favor. It had eroded the support he had acquired with the success of his December 1962 referendum, which had guaranteed him a new constitution that would reinforce his power while reaffirming Morocco's choice of a multi-party system.

Algeria's independence appeared to be a potential threat to his monarchy. The FLN supported the Moroccan left. It is also during that month of March that Algerian and Moroccan forces began a border war, following Morocco's claim to stretches of southern and western Algeria that had been under its sovereignty before the French gained control of the area in the nineteenth century.

The king's trip to the United States was timely. It would take him away from his domestic headaches and boost his prestige at home. He was going to be welcomed in Washington D.C. with great pomp and ceremony by John F. Kennedy, one of the most popular American presidents in history, an occasion that would demonstrate to his people how solid his relationship was with the most powerful country on earth. This is why the king's people had given VOA the green light for this interview, which was going to be aired on short waves in Morocco.

The king was reserved but friendly. He first warned me that he would not give his answers in French. Since he was on an official visit, he was under the obligation to use his mother tongue. Therefore, he would answer my questions in Arabic. It is not easy to conduct an interview and to ask follow-up questions if you do not understand the answers. I did not speak Arabic. I dared interrupt the monarch a couple of times and asked him to translate what he had just said. He obliged. The encounter lasted twenty minutes. I had been in a tête-à-tête with a king for almost half an hour.

The more stories I produced, the more money I made. Washington approached me to translate and voice their television specials as well as their documentaries. This activity turned out to be quite lucrative. Poverty was now behind me.

Harlem on my Mind

It is said that Jews own New York,
the Irish manage it and Negroes enjoy it.
—NEW YORK, PAUL MORAND

uring my first months in New York, Harlem never left my mind. French tourists adored going to Harlem. Women were drawn to the black ghetto by the music, whether it was jazz or gospel, men by black women and by the music.

Someone I met at the office of the French Broadcasting System introduced me to this part of the world like no other could have. His name was Pierre Dominique Gaisseau, a forty-year-old French journalist famous for having produced *The Sky Above, The Mud Below,* an Oscar winning documentary on his expedition to Dutch New Guinea.

Besides being an excellent reporter, always in search of poignant and unusual stories, Pierre Dominique was what the French call a *baroudeur,* an adventurer who had been around, a man fired up by curiosity and danger. He had been a saboteur, parachuted behind German lines during World War II and had often defied death in Vietnam, where he accompanied one of the last combat units. When he was filming in Biafra with artist Larry Rivers, he was captured and sentenced to death by a drunken officer because he was French. He managed to convince that officer to let him go free while up against a tree, with rifles aimed at his heart. He died in 1997 of a heart attack, as he was preparing to paraglide from the Alps. He was seventy-four years old.

He had the detachment of a poker player. Adventure was written all over his craggy face. He bore the calm and fatalism of men who confront danger with impassivity. He was quick, daring and a consummate pro.

When I met him, Pierre Dominique was producing and directing a documentary on minorities. It was called *Only One New York*. He allowed me to accompany him to his shoots, giving me the opportunity to discover the city from a unique angle.

He was about to film a segment on Puerto Rican gangs the day I joined his crew. We drove in his station wagon to El Barrio or Spanish Harlem, a Manhattan neighborhood located in the Upper East Side and parked on One Hundred Seventeenth Street between Lexington Avenue and Third Avenue. Two cops were patrolling the block, one watching the other's back. The moment Pierre Dominique turned the motor off, one of them crossed to the station wagon and signaled him to lower his window. There appeared from nowhere a young Puerto Rican in his early twenties, elegantly dressed in a suit, shirt and tie. He approached the man in uniform and whispered to him, "They're okay." The cop nodded and walked away. Puerto Rican gangs were as territorial as wolves. God help you if you transgressed.

The Hispanic Beau Brummel greeted us with a big, wide grin, hugged Pierre Dominique and motioned us to follow him. We entered a four-story brownstone, reached a narrow staircase, walked all the way up to the top floor and found ourselves on the flat roof of the building where half a dozen gang members awaited us. They were young and well-mannered. The brownstone was their headquarters. We noticed that they all wore sweaters of different colors, one on top of another. They explained that it was their way of evading their pursuers, be they cops or members of other gangs. On the run, they'd just shed a sweater, exposing one of a different shape and color, enough to confuse their assailants.

When we reached the opposite side of the roof, our hosts pointed at a police car parked down below. The gang leader asked Pierre Dominique if he would be interested in filming his buddies stoning it. My friend would have given anything to capture such a scene, but he declined. He was not crazy.

One evening, Pierre-Dominique took me to Brooklyn where he had a date with American Indians he had filmed earlier in the day working on top of a skyscraper in construction. Because they were not prone to vertigo, Indians were ideal for these high-risk jobs. They could walk on narrow steel beams six hundred feet high as assuredly as if they were strolling down Fifth Avenue.

They were Iroquois, specifically Mohawks from the Kahnawake reservation near Montreal. They had fallen into that profession by happenstance. In 1886, a Canadian company was building a railroad bridge over the Saint Lawrence River near the reservation. The company hired a number of Mohawks as day laborers and found out that these Indians climbed on the ironwork without any apparent fear of heights. The Mohawks branched out from bridges into general steel construction.

Were they unafraid of heights? Their employers thought so. But one night, a few Indians under the influence confessed to us that they were scared shitless while iron hopping and that they did not want to admit it because it was against the tribe's ethics. That might explain why most of them were addicted to the bottle.

They allowed Pierre Dominique to film them only after he had downed a full glass of scotch. He had to gulp down a glass of scotch filled to the brim for a twenty-second sequence, another for another twenty-second take. Watching Pierre Dominique getting drunk in the line of duty became the Indians' favorite form of entertainment. Pierre Dominique didn't like scotch, but he felt he had no choice if he wanted to get the good stuff. By two a.m. he could barely move. His crew members had to carry him to the station wagon, semi-conscious.

Capturing a Chinese New Year in Chinatown, a Hasidic wedding, a fashion show in an Abyssinian church, voodoo rituals, Oktoberfest in Brooklyn, an Irish celebration on Saint Patrick's Day, Japanese Buddhists celebrating the Festival of Flowers, Gypsies in Coney Island, Armenians in Queens, a Ukrainian wedding, Russian Orthodox, Greeks celebrating their Independence Day, an Italian fiesta downtown was Pierre Dominique's way of expressing his awe and love for the city. I shared his feelings.

The narration of *Only One New York* over shots of modern skyscrapers built of glass at the beginning of the documentary conjures up easier times. "People who expect bombs to fall do not build a city of glass. A city of glass," the narrator goes on saying, "is like a declaration of peace." Pierre Dominique did not live long enough to witness the destruction of the Twin Towers by terrorists on September 11, 2001. The builders of these skyscrapers would never have imagined, forty years earlier, that foreign aggressors would attack and destroy their daring but vulnerable architectural masterpieces.

Pierre Dominique's black girlfriend, Ellen Faison, was a tall and slim beauty, with big green eyes, a Greek nose, symmetrical features and a silky soft ebony skin. She moved with the grace and ease of a panther.

Ellen was modeling for her mother who was a designer in Harlem. At times, she also freelanced for Jacques Kaplan, the glamorous furrier on Fifth Avenue. Jacques loved to dress beautiful black women in mink, astrakhan, chinchilla or leopard. The movement against the use of animal furs had not yet peaked.

Ellen's fifty year-old mother was typical of many black women of that era, abrasive, controlling, direct, tough as nails. She was without a doubt the head of the Faison family and its breadwinner. God would have mercy on you if you crossed her. Her husband was a weak man she used as a gofer and chauffeur.

The fashion studio, where I wound up spending most of my time, was located on One Hundred Twenty-fifth Street near Fifth Avenue. Mrs. Faison organized shows unlike any other. They featured gorgeous black models as well as children, older men and even chubby women. The black designer's approach to marketing did not exclusively focus on "the beautiful people" but aimed at appealing to everyone, the tall, the short, the skinny, the fat, the old and the young. It was inclusive.

Blacks had few inhibitions, were not ashamed of their love of sex, made fun of it and of themselves and adored dancing and having a good time. They possessed a profound *joie de vivre*. I loved hanging out with them, even though the racial divide was widening every day. Discontent was just about to peak in the sixties. Harlem was not safe for white folks. Blacks tolerated me because I was French.

In return, the French adored them and their music and they knew it. Josephine Baker, who had gone into exile to Paris, was the first black

American to be idolized by them. So were and still are many expatriate jazzmen, as the Kanye West and Jay-Z song entitled "Niggas in Paris" attests.

The French empathized so much with black Americans that they readily condemned racial discrimination in America while failing to denounce their own. They sided with American blacks when riots erupted in large American cities in 1967 and 1968 but had no qualms about abusing the Africans and Muslims that had immigrated to France from their former colonies. They showed as much hatred and contempt for *les Beurs*, the derogatory moniker they still use today to describe Algerians, as many Americans had for their "niggers" in the sixties.

In 2009, the French supported Obama unconditionally and praised America for its boldness, but would they ever elevate a French-Algerian candidate to the presidency?

I had not yet found the black woman of my dreams. I compensated with music, not a difficult task in the world Mecca of jazz and gospel music. I used to listen to gospel music on the radio live from a church in Harlem, The Faith Temple of God in Christ, located at the corner of One Hundred Forty-seventh Street and Amsterdam Avenue, at the top of Sugar Hill. It conducted a service at ten o'clock on Sunday nights. I decided to pay a visit to this black House of the Lord.

The choir's passion, energy, power and rhythm was contagious. The audience was as much part of the entertainment as the singers. Blacks display such theatrics when they express faith. The hand clapping, the swaying in unison from right to left, from left to right, the adoring calls to Jesus, the lamentations, the exhortations, the "Oh Lords!" were so catching. The high octaves reached by the leads sent shivers down my spine. Following that experience, I, the atheist, made a point of going to church every Sunday without fail.

Faith Temple was founded in the fall of 1948. It had a membership of thirty under the leadership of Dr. Alvin A. Childs when it settled in Imperial Elks Hall on One Hundred Twenty-ninth Street. In the summer of 1949, Dr. Childs brought a huge circus tent from Chicago and erected it at One Hundred and Twenty-fourth Street and Saint Nicholas Avenue, where people gathered by the thousands nightly for eight weeks. The church then leased quarters at 236 West One Hundred Sixteenth Street and moved to its permanent home, settling in the old Lido Theater.

Faith Temple became a growing Pentecostal Church with over three thousand members, still under the leadership of Bishop Childs who had been given the unofficial title of Mayor of Harlem. He was an important figure among blacks.

When Malcolm X was assassinated in February 1965, none of Harlem's cathedrals would open their doors for his funeral. Bishop Childs dared to allow the black militant's slim body, riddled with bullet holes in the chest, to be rolled into Faith Temple. Thousands of people lined the streets as hundreds squeezed into the six hundred-seat church, where actor Ossie Davis delivered the eulogy.

After a few visits, I introduced myself to the bishop. His welcome was reserved at first. He warmed up when I told him that I was French and encouraged me to bring along my European friends. The moment I did, the news spread by word of mouth. Many of the people I had taken uptown boasted that they had ventured into the heart of Harlem to listen to authentic gospel music, like veterans recalling their acts of bravery with pride.

Baron Sigismund von Braun became a regular visitor once I introduced him to the church. He was West Germany's Permanent United Nations Observer—The Federal Republic of Germany and the German Democratic Republic (East Germany) would not be admitted to the UN as permanent members until 1973. In gratitude, he often invited me to dinner at his midtown brownstone on East Sixty-fifth Street and later on, when I turned correspondent, shared with me the latest UN gossip as well as his outlook on the Middle East, the war in Vietnam, nuclear disarmament, East-West relations and Germany's efforts to reunify, often handing me scoops that made me look good with my editors. I spent hours discussing with 'Siggy'—that's what the press called him—the headlines of the day, sometimes until the wee hours of the morning. I was fond of the ambassador, of his carved face and bushy eyebrows. He was quite Germanic in many ways, but had a kindness and a generosity that were only matched by his acute sense of humor and his vitality.

His daughter Christina was nineteen then. She was studying at New

York University. We began to flirt. She was not pretty but her smarts made you forget her physical flaws. The few kisses we exchanged cemented our friendship and fulfilled some of her fantasies.

Her father was recalled to the mother country in 1968. The whole family moved back to Germany. Christina went on to do bigger and better things.

In 2009, this woman whose uncle, Wernher von Braun, had been a member of the Nazi Party and an ex-commissioned SS officer, co-founded the *Kollegium of Jewish Studies* at Humboldt University in Berlin. The *Kollegium* was a network of scholars interested in Jewish life in Germany and in the interdependence of Jewish and non-Jewish culture. Such achievement speaks volumes of my old girlfriend's character and humanism.

My innocent tryst with Christina had been enriching, but I still fantasized about a hot affair, not with a Germanic blonde with blue eyes, but with my concept of the "ideal black woman." It was one of these uncontrollable yearnings I had to satisfy no matter what.

25

Jo-Ann
(From Swing to the Blues)

Love is like a war, easy to begin. Hard to end!
—ANCIENT PROVERB

Her name was Jo-Ann. She was twenty. I was twenty-six. To repeat the words Harry Reid, the Senate Majority Leader, once used to describe President Barack Obama, she was a "light-skinned African-American." In other words, she was a mulatto, a café au lait. There is no politically correct way of describing that particular skin shade in America. You'll always offend somebody trying, whatever words you use.

She was slim, possessed great legs, long, delicate hands, a tiny waist, a disarming smile and a twinkle in her eyes. Every part of her body breathed natural elegance.

When I first laid my eyes on her, at the Faison's in Harlem, I knew I had found my "ideal black woman."

My courting was short. We introduced ourselves to each other, took a cab to my apartment and made love, furiously, madly, passionately. Complete harmony crowned our first sexual encounter. The texture of her skin, the softness of her lips, her smell, the way her body awakened to my caresses, the grace of her abandon, the depth of her ecstasy made me forget where I was, who I was, the time of day, the year we lived in.

Seeking the ideal black woman might have been preferential, but it was not prejudicial, just a bias toward, not against. I had not been raised as a racist. I wasn't colorblind either. I just liked black, and that made me a pariah.

As Sidney Poitier says in the now classic *Guess Who's Coming To Dinner,* "After all, a lot of people are going to think we are a shocking pair." There weren't many inter-racial couples in the US in the sixties. Miscegenation was repulsive to many Americans and that didn't make our lives easy. We were denied entrance to parties; restaurants refused to serve us or made us wait endlessly for a table. We were the undesirables, wherever we'd go. We got used to it. We were so much into each other that we did not care.

After our first night of love making, Jo-Ann asked me to accompany her home. She lived with her grandmother in the Bronx, off Willis Avenue, in one of these gray, depressing public housing units, in an all-black neighborhood. Her mother, who was a salesperson at *Macy's,* either could not afford to take care of her or had sidestepped her responsibilities. I never knew which.

In the courtyard leading to her grandmother's building, teenagers were playing basketball. Others were hanging out, listening to the sounds of the Jive Five, Marvin Gaye and the Temptations blasting on their boomboxes. Old folks were just enjoying the warm evening.

The moment they spotted me holding hands with "one of theirs" everyone interrupted whatever they were doing. Rancor filled the air.

Jo-Ann's grandmother made a face when she laid eyes on me for the first time. She must have wondered what in the world a white man was doing in her apartment. She was working as a maid then, cleaning white folks' dirt, as she often put it. Her mother, Jo-Ann's great grandmother, had been a slave who had transmitted her fear and her aversion of whites to her daughter who had passed it on to Jo-Ann's mom. And that's where it stopped. Jo-Ann belonged to a generation of blacks who were the first to break from that heritage of hatred. She felt emancipated and wanted to assimilate. It wasn't until a year later that President Lyndon B. Johnson would sign the Civil Rights Act into law on July 2, 1964.

Relations between whites and blacks were tense in 1963. A series of incidents that year marked the beginnings of a long struggle for race equality: Martin Luther King's arrest in Birmingham Alabama following a non-violent demonstration, Medgar Evers' assassination, the Civil Rights

March in Washington, D.C., a bomb that exploded in the Sixteenth Street Baptist Church in Birmingham, Alabama that killed four young girls who were in church for Sunday school.

It was only a matter of time before racial violence would spread north. Blacks were not relegated to the back of the bus in New York, but segregation and inequality might have been even more pernicious above the Mason-Dixon Line, where ghettos were as isolated from the rest of the country as they were in the Land of Dixie. Los Angeles, Chicago, Detroit, Washington, New York were powder kegs waiting to explode.

For Jo-Ann, to insist that black did not make a difference, for her to turn a blind eye to prejudice and to expect to be treated as an equal, was an act of exceptional courage in that noxious environment.

My early experiences in Harlem were not tainted by violence. We, as an interracial couple, often suffered rejection, but our lives had never been in jeopardy. My black friends knew I sympathized with their plight. I felt secure among them.

An incident was about to shake that certitude. It happened in March 1964, when Malcolm X returned from his trip to Mecca. He was at that time the most polarizing black leader in America.

At age thirty-nine, he had travelled to Jeddah, in Saudi Arabia, where he completed the Hajj as a state guest of Prince Faisal, making the seven circuits around the Kaaba, drinking from the Zamzam Well and running between the hills of Safah and Marwah seven times, rituals followed by millions of Islamic pilgrims.

Upon his return, he declared that the trip to Mecca had changed his perspective on race and had led him to reappraise white America. He had seen white skin Muslims in Jeddah and had concluded that not all whites were evil.

He decided to share his revised philosophy with the people of Harlem. He scheduled an appearance at a large auditorium, around One Hundred Twenty-fifth Street.

A friend who was freelancing for Radio Luxembourg asked me if I'd like to accompany him to that event. I jumped at the occasion.

Hundreds of blacks were on line waiting to enter the auditorium when we arrived. My friend and I went to the box office, showed our IDs and explained that we were affiliated with the French media. The people in charge let us in. We were the only journalists in attendance; in fact we were the only two whites in this all-black crowd. They gave us the best seats in the house, center row, in the middle of the orchestra.

The room filled up fast. Malcolm X's bodyguards were positioned at regular intervals around the auditorium, at the ready, poised to react to the slightest disturbance. They were young, tall and powerfully built. They wore short haircuts, identical black suits, white shirts and black ties. All of them, we were told, were karate experts.

Malcolm's appearance on stage was met with hysteria. In their eyes, he was the only one who dared standing up to whitey. He had become an icon more adulated than a rock star. He personified black power. He was black power.

The man was imposing. He stood six feet three inches tall and weighed about a hundred and eighty pounds. One writer once described him as "mesmerizingly handsome and always spotlessly well-groomed." Blacks either revered him or feared him. Many whites wished him dead.

This high school dropout used the English language like a surgeon would a scalpel, incisively. We were smitten by his charm and uncomfortable when his anger surfaced. Malcolm was hypnotic.

He concluded his speech with words I will never forget. "Do not buy guns. Guns are illegal," he first whispered. Then he paused and added, in a higher pitch that sounded like the hiss of a poisonous snake, "Buy shotguns. Shotguns are LEGAL." This inflammatory exhortation sent shivers down my spine. It brought the audience to the boiling point.

Once Malcolm left the stage, the blacks in our immediate vicinity took sudden notice of our presence. Hate in that theater had thickened like a dense fog. We were in imminent danger. I motioned my friend to pick up his gear and to get out. Several men blocked our escape. They were coming at us from both sides of our orchestra row. We had nowhere to go. Were we going to fall, like sacrificial lambs?

Malcolm X's bodyguards dispersed the crowd, pushing anyone who was in their way. Then, they formed a human fence around us, allowing us to escape. They escorted us outside of the auditorium and hailed a cab for us. It had been a close call. These men, and by extension Malcolm X, had saved our hides.

I don't know how I would have controlled my resentment if my ancestors had been enslaved and lynched, if I had been forced to travel in the back of the bus, if I had been beaten by police, if dogs had been used against me, if I had been denied the right to vote. Non-violence requires an unimaginable amount of restraint in the face of abuse.

If I had been the victim of such brutal discrimination, would I have sided with Martin Luther King Jr. or with Malcolm X who felt that the only way for blacks to achieve equality was to revolt and fight?

Who should claim responsibility for the social and political advancement of blacks, the moderates or the extremists? King or Malcolm? It is impossible to dismiss the impact the 1967 and 1968 race riots had on the process. At the same time, the ultimate success, in earlier years, of the Montgomery bus boycott had made King a national hero. His *Letter from Birmingham Jail* had inspired a growing national civil rights movement.

King had created an awareness without which the struggle for equality might have been delayed for years, even decades. But his influence had diminished by 1967. The black population at large had lost faith in non-violence.

There was a time for non-violence in America and there was a time for revolt. The time for revolt arrived four years later, and I'd be there to witness it all, from one of the best seats in the house.

I had outgrown the studio at 226 East Sixth Street. I could now afford a bigger pad. I found a cute one-bedroom apartment at 342 East Nineteenth Street, in a brownstone that was converted into furnished apartments.

The place was not spacious. The kitchen, if you could have called it that, was just a stove and a mini fridge tucked against the wall, in the back of the living room. The adjacent bedroom was tiny.

The first thing I did was to set up the stereo I had found on the curb, in front of my building on Sixth Street, put away my personal belongings and lay down on the bed for a few minutes. I then stood up, crossed to the living room, sat on an ugly armchair, so excited to be in a room that did not have a bed. I crossed back to the bedroom and moved again to the living room while the stereo was blasting Dakota Staton's "Broadway" over and over again.

The buzzer woke me at six one morning. A couple of minutes later, someone timidly knocked at the door. I opened. Jo-Ann was standing there, holding a suitcase in her hand, tears rolling down her cheeks. She had had a terrible altercation with her grandmother over me the night before. In her grandmother's eyes, she had betrayed her black sisters and brothers by dating a white man.

Jo-Ann moved in with me, putting a temporary end to my life as a single. She was a secretary for Metropolitan Life but aspired to becoming a jazz singer. She was working during the day. I was busy day and night.

I had landed a freelance job with Radio Luxembourg, the same outfit that had hired me in Paris. The deejay of a daily jazz program had asked me to interview American musicians. So, for a period of time, I roamed the jazz clubs of the city, often taking Jo-Ann with me, to her utter delight.

One night, I caught Charles Mingus rehearsing at the Five Spot Café, at Cooper Square, in the Bowery. When I arrived he was already dabbing at the bass, alone. The technician who came with me set up the sound equipment, positioned his mics, tested the sound levels. As soon as he was done, I signaled him to push the recording button. A couple of minutes later, the drummer showed up and accompanied Mingus. Then came the flutist. He too jumped into the act. Thirty seconds later, the trumpeter, the saxophonist and the tenor saxophonist stepped in one by one and joined the others. The sextet was now in full swing. The progression from one player to six had been awesome. The drummer was Dannie Richmond, the flutist Eric Dolphy, the sax Jaki Byard, the trumpeter Johnny Coles and the tenor saxophonist Clifford Jordan.

During the interview that followed, I called "The Angry Man of Jazz" Charlie instead of Charles. He interrupted me and said to me, half serious, half joking, "Hey man, don't call me Charlie. Charlie's the name of a horse."

Jo-Ann had a few gigs booked in small clubs in the Village. She had swing; her voice was smooth and velvety but, in my opinion, had failed to develop a style of her own. That being said, having a jazz singer as a girlfriend was cool.

When we were not busy, we loved to go out. One of our favorite hangouts was Small's Paradise at One Hundred and Thirty-fifth and Seventh Avenue. The place was jumping on Saturday nights.

Small's was one of the "Big Three" nightclubs in Harlem along with the Cotton Club and Connie's Inn. In the thirties and forties, it was drawing the rich and famous. As race relations deteriorated and as crime rose in Harlem, fewer whites ventured uptown. By the early sixties, the crowd at Small's was exclusively black.

That didn't stop me from taking a few white friends there. I had kept in touch with Gérard, the Frenchman I had met on the ship that brought me to the US. His girlfriend was Martine Alphand, the niece of Hervé Alphand, the French Ambassador who had become famous for having dared serve a peasant stew, a *pot-au-feu*, to John and Jackie Kennedy when they first dined at the Ambassador's residence in Washington. Martine had a first cousin, Rémi, who later became my daughter's godfather. They were way out of my league. They belonged to the gilded youth. I was far less fortunate than they were.

Rémi wanted to listen to jazz and had invited along Martine and his roommate, Didier, who was a trainee at a financial institution downtown. The young man belonged to an old upper bourgeois family of devout Catholics from Lille. He was WASPier than the WASPs, stiffer than a corpse. We decided to go to Small's.

Our entrance did not remain unnoticed. We were the only whites in the joint. When a waiter took us to our table, across the spacious room, all heads turned toward us. My friends were so thrilled that they did not even realize how much attention we had drawn.

The energy and sensuality of the place were contagious. I asked Jo-Ann to dance with me. Rémi later remarked that I moved with the grace of an elephant in the midst of these natural hoofers. Few whites could compete with blacks on the dance floor.

Didier, who had the demeanor of a New England puritan, stood up, crossed the room, reached a table of six, stopped in front of an attractive young woman, bowed and asked her to dance with the decorum of a Prussian officer. The young lady had never been approached with such formality.

I looked at Jo-Ann, alarmed. Was Didier's move bold or suicidal? The blacks seated at that table were startled, to say the least, but they remained cool.

The young lady smiled at our fearless Casanova, stood up and followed him to the dance floor. Our anxiety grew, as their embrace got tighter. Our eyes shifted back and forth, from them to the black men who shared the young lady's table. We all felt ill at ease.

When the music came to an end. I tried to locate Didier and his belle. They had vanished. I thought for a moment that they had gone to refresh themselves. I waited a few more minutes, but after awhile had to face the facts, the two had flown the coop. It was late. We decided to go back home, reluctantly. We were concerned.

The following day, I called Rémi and asked him if Didier had returned. He had not. He was beside himself. I felt bad. After all, I was the one who had taken them to Small's. Anything could have happened. For all I knew, Didier's body could be lying in a gutter somewhere in Harlem.

The young man from Lille reemerged the following day, a big smile across his face. He had accompanied the young woman to her place. They had stayed in bed for two nights and one day. The experience had given our Wall Street trainee a new outlook on life. It had morphed him into a much more relaxed and lovable individual.

Jo-Ann and I lived moments of extreme happiness interrupted at times by feuds, some more intense than others. We loved as passionately as we fought. She was an independent woman, maybe too independent for my taste. I was a spoiled brat. The worst was bound to happen.

After a severe falling-out, she packed and moved back to her grandmother's, leaving me lost, empty, depressed. She called me a few days later. The moment I picked up the phone, I sensed that something had gone awry. She remained silent for a good fifteen seconds, then whispered my name, "Daniel..." She was sobbing. "I'm scared..." She paused. "I'm losing a lot of blood." She paused again. "Please come."

"I'll be right there."

I hung up, rushed out, jumped in my car and drove to the Bronx like a madman. I feared that she had slit her wrists. When I reached her grandmother's housing complex I spotted an ambulance parked in front of the building. I ran inside, took the elevator. The door to her apartment was opened. I barged in and collided with a paramedic rolling a stretcher with Jo-Ann lying on it. She looked pale, distraught and in pain. Behind the stretcher stood her grandmother in tears. I hugged the wall, making way for them. "Stay with me. Don't leave," Jo-Ann said when she saw me.

The paramedic carried her to the elevator.

I ran down the stairs and reached the ground floor as the paramedic was already sliding the stretcher into the ambulance. I rushed to my car, turned the motor on and burnt rubber trying to tailgate the ambulance as it took off with its sirens on.

When I entered the hospital lobby, Jo-Ann's grandmother was already filling out the admittance papers at the admission desk. I waited until she was done and asked, "Can you tell me what's going on?

"As if you didn't know!"

I learned later that she had discovered her granddaughter in a pool of blood, on the bathroom floor. Jo-Ann had found out that she was pregnant and had tried to induce a miscarriage by herself, causing her to hemorrhage. The thought that I could have been a father did not cross my mind then. I only worried about Jo-Ann's well being.

I stayed in the waiting room all night, inquiring about my girlfriend's status. The following morning, they allowed me to see her.

The second I entered her room, her grandmother, who was at her side, stood up and walked out. I crossed to Jo-Ann, took her hand, told her that I was sorry, that everything was going to be okay, that I loved her and that she should move back to the apartment as soon as she could. She burst into tears. I stayed with her until she fell asleep.

I left her room, walked by her grandmother who was standing outside the door. As I hurried down the corridor, she hissed, "You know I hate your guts, don't you, boy?"

I turned around and met the old woman's eyes. They were no longer filled with hatred. She then murmured, "But I gotta admit, you behaved like a gent."

I never saw her again. A few days later, Jo-Ann was back in our nest.

* * *

I had to fly to Paris on business. Jo-Ann assured me that she would take care of the apartment. I missed her the moment I landed at Orly.

My mother who knew my attraction to black women and who was aware of Jo-Ann's existence, had written me a letter before I left New York, in which she advised, "Don't be seen with beautiful black women. If you go out with Negroes, you'll be burnt. Think of your future." I was shocked. She had always condemned racism, but in that instance, her protective instincts got the best of her and stifled her basic convictions.

Being so far away from the woman I loved made me long for her. I felt the irresistible impulse to go back. On the second day of my stay, I picked up the phone and called Jo-Ann. She sounded so happy to hear from me. "Do you miss me?" she asked.

"I want to marry you."

"You what?"

"I WANT TO MARRY YOU."

"You're crazy!"

"I mean it."

"You do?"

I cut my stay short and told my mother that I had to go back for professional reasons. The following morning, I was boarding an Air France plane that would fly me back to my sweetheart.

At JFK, I took a cab to Nineteenth Street, paid the fare, ran up the stairs as Jo-Ann was rushing down. We met midway and fell in each other's arms. We kissed as if we had been separated for years, a long, interminable kiss. I entered the apartment. My heart stopped. During my short absence, Jo-Ann had redecorated the place in the style of her grandmother's. She had clogged it with huge, invading green plants that she must have moved in the moment I left for Europe. The walls were covered with cheap and tacky drawings. A white sheepskin rug was standing out like a stain in the middle of the living room. To top it all, a fat cat was lounging on my armchair. This unexpected interior-decorating job was, I thought, a harbinger of things to come. What an eye opener. Had the real Jo-Ann surfaced? She was no longer the cool, hip jazz singer, the elegant, cosmopolitan young woman I had fallen in love with, but an ordinary little girl from the Bronx whose culture, or lack thereof, was miles apart from mine. She didn't realize it, but she had handed me the excuse to evade the challenges of being married to a black woman, at a time when such a union was condemned by society.

Jo-Ann felt my disappointment. We broke the heavy silence with small talk, but something had snapped inside me. I'd never mention the word marriage to her again.

Jo-Ann had landed a gig at the Village Vanguard. She usually came home late, after her performance. One night, she did not return and the cat was gone.

I waited for her 'til morning and spent the day curled in my armchair, prostrated, plunged in a daze. When evening came, I shook off my torpor and decided to go find her at the Vanguard. I was going to persuade her to return home. I crossed to the bar, ordered one scotch after another, as I waited for the end of her performance. I headed for her dressing room the second she left the stage.

She was wiping off her makeup in front of her mirror. A black man was standing at her side. Jo-Ann introduced him to me as her agent. His name was Monte Kay. He was the impresario who represented Herbie Mann, Stan Getz, Sonny Rollins, The Modern Jazz Quartet and Flip Wilson, the black comedian who was popular in the sixties.

Jo-Ann did not want me to make a scene in front of Mr. Kay. She pulled me outside.

It was past two o'clock when we reached Washington Square. We sat on a public bench and remained silent for a while. Tears cascaded down my cheeks. Jo-Ann put her arms around me, in the vain attempt to comfort me. I realized that I had lost her. She had decided to move on. I, on the other hand, was left with a terrible guilt. I had dashed my girlfriend's hopes too soon after having raised them. My sudden change of mind had not been racist in nature. Or had it been? Whatever the case was, it was construed as such. Its impact would have been less significant if Jo-Ann had been white. But she was a black woman who had trusted a white man, and this white man had betrayed that trust.

Several months later, I learned that Jo-Ann and Monte had moved to Los Angeles. The last time I saw her was on the small screen in 1976. She had a small part in an episode of "Hawaii Five-O."

26

Showbiz

Then I just moved into being a DJ when
that turned into the hottest thing.

—JAM MASTER JAY

Many visitors who came from France for the first time asked me to help them find their way in the city. Jacques Garnier was one of them.

He was the producer of one of the most popular hit parade radio programs in France. The broadcast, entitled *Balzac 10 10*, was the favorite of French, Belgian and Swiss teenagers. It aired every afternoon from five to seven.

Jacques did not contact me to offer me a job. He just wanted a guide, someone who could translate for him and who knew New York well. I picked him up at the airport and took him to his hotel. At breakfast the following morning, he explained to me, in between soft-boiled eggs and buttered toast, what *Balzac 10 10* was all about. It dawned on him that I could conduct interviews he could insert into his *Balzac 10 10*, just as I had done for the jazz program.

I made a counter offer. "What if I produced an entire show from New York that could be inserted into your own? A show within a show, if you will."

Jacques scratched his scalp. "How long a segment?"

"Oh, I don't know. An hour?"

His eyebrows rose. I corrected myself.

"A half-hour?"

"The idea's intriguing. French kids are crazy about American music and American movies. It could work. I'd say a half hour... weekly. Send me a demo and we'll take it from there."

Once Jacques left for Paris, I realized that I had no knowledge of the trends, the fads that made young people tick, the music they loved or the artists they idolized. What made me think I could pull it off? I had heard hit parade programs on the radio and had an idea of their style and content, but I had never deejayed one. I knew that Americans were masters of broadcasts that stood out for their fast transitions, their hyped and short jingles that segued into the hits of the moment, and for adrenalized deejays who wisecracked jokes before introducing their next records with the dramatics of masters of ceremonies presenting a high wire act. Such knowledge did not make me a professional radio host.

In the early sixties, two radio stations aired the best hit parades in New York, WABC and WMCA. I listened to both for hours. After a few days of total immersion, my preference went to WMCA. Its hosts were witty, on the ball and unafraid to play new records, including an unknown group from Great Britain called "The Beatles." I decided to knock on their door and ask if they could let me use a recording studio.

On a gray morning, in November 1963, I took a bus to 540 Madison Avenue, home of WMCA. I told the receptionist that I wanted to see the General Manager. Did I have an appointment, she asked? I said I didn't. When she was about to show me the door, a woman in her late-thirties happened to walk by. Could she be of assistance, she asked. I explained that I was a French journalist living in the city and that I was looking for a recording studio where I could produce a segment for a Top 40 station in Paris. The woman must have been intrigued by my story. She told the receptionist that she would take it from there and asked me to follow her. When we reached her office, I saw her name on the door. She was none other than Ruth Meyer, the Top 40 expert that WMCA's management had brought to New York from Kansas City to boost the radio station's popularity with the young.

She was smart, fast, dynamic, tough, direct and open to new ideas. Did the possibility that WMCA be mentioned in a program aired in France appeal to her? I don't think she cared. She had something else in mind. She wanted to please one of her deejays, and after all, pleasing her deejays was high on her priority list. "You should meet Joe O'Brien," she said. "Joe loves

France. He even speaks French. He'll be off the air shortly. You should meet him."

Ruth gave me a tour of the facility, then brought me to a conference room. After I had waited for almost an hour, Joe stepped in. He was a tall, skinny guy, with a typical Irish face, angular and emaciated. He was in his mid-forties, warm but shrewd, easygoing but always on his toes. I felt comfortable with him.

In 1963, he had become the number one morning man in the city. Prior to that, he had written and starred in *The Joe O'Brien Show* on the Armed Forces Network between 1945 and 1946. What surprised me, when I read his bio later on, is that he had acted and directed plays at the Great Neck Community Theater and the Hampton Playhouse in New Hampshire. In 1957, he co-founded the Cricket Theater in New York, where he directed plays including Bernard Kop's *The Hamlet of Stepney Green* and Jean Anouilh's *Ardèle*. Joe was not your regular Top 40 deejay.

When I said that the only thing I wanted was a recording studio I could rent for no more than an hour a week, Joe paused and said, "I have an idea. Come back tomorrow."

When I returned the following day, Joe greeted me with a big smile. "I have a proposal for you. Wanna hear it? Well, here it is anyway. How about the two of us anchoring that segment?"

I was stunned. "But Joe. I'm doing the program in French."

"*Je comprends,*" he answered, with a thick accent. "*En français, oui en français. Nous le ferrons en français.*"

"But..."

"I've already thought of a format. We start with a music theme, we both introduce the music numbers, we use WMCA jingles and we invite guests."

"Guests?"

"*Mais oui.* Singers, movie stars. WMCA has a lot of pull in the industry. We can get big names. *D'accord?*"

"First we have to do a demo to sell the idea to Paris," I said.

"When do we start?"

"Are you sure you can handle it? I mean... is your French good enough?"

"*Oui. Mon français, il est parfait.*"

His French was barely adequate. I often had to write his inserts phonetically. His enthusiasm mixed with an overdose of moxie more than made up for this minor handicap. He was the pro. I was an amateur.

When I showed up at the studio for our first recording, I told Joe that we would call our program *New York 10 10*. His people had scheduled Petula Clark as our first guest. In 1963, she had several hits, her biggest being "Downtown."

Joe O'Brien possessed a wide-ranging curiosity, high spirits and an unfailing humor. From the start, we decided that we would have fun doing the program and that we would never take ourselves too seriously.

Garnier loved our demo. He gave us the green light for a weekly half-hour that would air late afternoon on Mondays. *Télé Magazine*, the French equivalent of *TV Guide*, wrote a silly piece on our debut, "From now on, *Balzac 10 10* will be linked to New York thanks to a permanent correspondent. His name is Daniel Dorian. He was born on April first. It is true. He is very good looking. And that is also true." Joe also got his share of outrageous one-liners. That's the price we had to pay for fame.

From the start, we decided to introduce a bit of journalism in each program, in between our clowning, jokes, jingles and musical numbers. We brought up topics that were in the news, such as race relations, new movies, the war in Vietnam, the Indianapolis 500, the famous Cassius Clay/Sonny Liston match during which Clay KO'd Liston in one minute forty-two seconds. For greater appeal, we also offered to mail WMCA T-shirts to the first five listeners who would write to us.

Hundreds of teenagers who either wanted a T-shirt or autographed photos of Joe and me wrote us fan letters. Many asked us to find them pen pals or to communicate their admiration to Presley, Warwick or Sinatra. The kids were crazy about us.

For the 1964 Christmas show, WMCA asked twenty of the most popular performers in America to tape their wishes addressed to the young European listeners of *New York 10 10*. They recorded their *Joyeux Noël* in French.

The second show we produced featured the sweet Dionne Warwick, the third Bobby Darin who gave us great impersonations of Maurice

Chevalier and Charles Aznavour. I enjoyed Bobby Darin, his warmth, his drive and his repartees. Boy, was he quick on the draw. He helped us produce one of our most memorable *New York 10 10.*

The guest of our fourth program was Soupy Sales. While Soupy watched, Joe and I sang his banner song "Hey, Let's Do the Mouse, Yeah," making fun of his appalling lyrics and of his mannerisms. He took it like a mensch.

WMCA delivered to our doorstep the top singers and movie stars of the time, Carroll Baker, Brigitte Bardot, Kirk Douglas, Jerry Lewis, Anthony Newley, Tom Jones, and many others.

In the summer of 1965, I attended a press junket organized by Twentieth Century Fox. The Hollywood company had earned great profits that year and had to find ways to avoid sharing them with Uncle Sam. Joel Kohler, who was then in charge of publicity in New York, put together one of the most glamorous shindigs ever offered to journalists. It lasted an entire week and included breakfasts, luncheons, cocktails, dinners, movie and theater premieres with Hollywood stars in the best New York venues. It concluded with a weekend in the company of Raquel Welch at the Concord Hotel, the famous resort in the Catskills. All we guys had to do was lay our hands on a tuxedo and a bathing suit.

One of the films Joel Kohler was promoting at that time was *Morituri,* starring Marlon Brando and Yul Brenner. He had managed to persuade Brando to grant interviews to the press who attended his junket. Not a small achievement. Brando despised the media and granted interviews on one condition, at least one question had to be asked about American Indians, a cause that had always been dear to his heart.

Twentieth Century Fox had put a film crew at our disposal. David Maysles handled the sound, his brother Albert the photography. This original artist preferred handholding the camera instead of using a tripod and thus introduced a new style that would be known as *cinéma vérité.* Jean-Luc Godard once called him "the best American cameraman."

David and Albert were already famous when Twentieth Century Fox hired them. They had their own production company and had earned the respect of the industry. During their long and illustrious career, they produced many great documentaries, including *Salesman, Gimme Shelter* and *The Beatles, The First US Visit.*

Brando was staying at the Hampshire House Hotel on Central Park South. Joel accompanied the Maysles Brothers and me to his suite. We knocked. Marlon opened the door and asked us to come in. I spoke French to him from the start. He had a slight accent but his French was excellent. I was so thrilled to meet him. When he addressed me, he used *tu*, the familiar you, as opposed to the formal *vous*, putting me at ease. He suggested that I conduct the interview outside. It would be less confining and more interesting visually.

We exited the hotel, walked across Central Park South and settled on the curb, at the edge of the park. The weather that day in July could not have been better. There wasn't a cloud in the sky.

I asked Brando a few questions about his movie, about him, and then turned to the subject of race and of government responsibility in improving white and black relations in the US. Instead of answering, Brando shifted his eyes past me. Something behind my back had attracted his attention. He turned to Albert and ordered, "Point your camera over there. This woman is *ravissante*. (Ravishing)"

I did a one-eighty. A gorgeous young black woman, tall, dressed in an elegant two-piece summer outfit was ambling toward us. She was holding the hand of a five-year-old boy with curly hair and the face of an angel. What a sight! When she reached us, she looked at the movie star and said, matter-of-factly, "You're Marlon Brando."

Marlon introduced us to her as a French television crew and told her that he was answering questions on the role of government in race relations. He added that he was far less qualified than she to expand on the subject. He asked her to answer these questions instead and offered to translate her answers in French. That intervention lent uniqueness to the piece.

Twenty years later, as I was asking Albert's assistant to help me find a salesperson for my production company, I happened to mention the interview with Brando and its unusual circumstances. She informed me that the brothers had used a significant segment of it in a documentary they produced on the star in the seventies entitled *Meet Marlon Brando.*

In the middle of that glamorous week, Fox invited us to a cocktail party at Toots Shor's, the celebrity joint on West Fifty-first Street. I chose to hang out with Liz Trotta, a rookie journalist I admired. Born in 1937, like me, she carried an ambition that bordered on obsession. She had graduated from Columbia University Graduate School of Journalism, the best in the nation, and was working for WNBC.

She told me that Frank Sinatra was scheduled to show up at the party and that she'd move heaven and earth to grab an interview with the crooner, a difficult task given Sinatra's terrible reputation when it came to his handling of the media. She positioned herself at the bottom of the staircase that Sinatra had to use to access the main room, ready to wait as long as it took. The Maysles were on standby.

When Sinatra showed up at the top of the stairs and started walking down, Liz jumped up the few steps that separated her from him, extended her right arm and shoved her mic in his face. If Sinatra's eyes had been daggers, Liz's heart would have been pierced in an instant. During the entire interview that lasted three minutes tops, Sinatra's anger never let down. He would have slugged her if she had been a man. A little shaken, she turned to me and exclaimed, "Got him!" She then begged, "Daniel, I need you to come with me to the station."

Albert unloaded the camera and gave her the undeveloped footage. His brother handed her the sound reel. She grabbed both and sprinted out of the restaurant. I tagged along. By the time we arrived at WNBC's studios at Rockefeller Center, I was out of breath. She crossed the newsroom, spotted her editor and shouted, waving the reels at him, "I got Sinatra. I got Sinatra."

Liz handed him the film can and the sound reel. He took them, walked away, stopped, returned to her and asked, "Who shot that?"

"The Maysles," she answered. "You know, the Maysles Brothers."

"Are they union?"

Liz's face turned white. She looked at her editor, devastated.

"Liz, you should know better," he said.

Liz's shoulders drooped. She bent as if she had received a direct hit to the plexus. She knew that the network could not use material shot by non-union crews. I left her to her disappointment and ran back to Toots Shor's.

* * *

Back at Toots Shore's, I joined Trini Lopez and his stunning blonde girlfriend. I liked Trini. Stardom had not spoiled him. He was simple and unpretentious. He had already been signed up to Frank Sinatra's record label, Reprise Records and in 1965 made it big with "Lemon Tree." Through 1968, he would score thirteen chart singles, including "I'm Comin' Home, Cindy" and "Sally Was a Good Old Girl."

The night before, we had seen Sammy Davis Jr. perform on Broadway in *Golden Boy*, for which he had earned a Tony nomination. Joel insisted that I interview him.

He granted me one of the best interviews any star ever gave me. When I mentioned *Golden Boy*, a musical about the love between a black man and white woman, we tackled the issues of race and interracial relationships, both here and in Europe. "You have here journalists from northern and southern newspapers," he said to me. "I am sure none of you from the press has ever seen a Negro kiss a white woman on stage."

"How is it in real life?" I asked. I had my own answer to that question, having experienced a similar situation. "Well, it's according," he admitted. "There are certain places in Paris where I've never seen Negroes and whites together. If you're lucky enough to be a "celebrity," you can get away with it. When I was in Paris, I went out with white women. Nobody raised an eyebrow. But I was Sammy Davis."

The twenty-minute exchange, intercut with songs from Sammy's repertoire, filled up an entire program. At the end of the interview, Sammy took me in his arms and gave me a fat and noisy kiss that almost rivaled the one Marlon Brando would give Larry King, the avuncular CNN host, many years later, except that Sammy's was on the cheek; Brando's was on the lips.

Joel Coler called me whenever he was in a bind. Journalists were not always available to interview a star or to attend press conferences. I made a point to always be.

When Robert Taylor came to New York, five years before his death, the press had lost interest in him. Joel had to find him an escort. He asked me to spend the day with him, as a favor. I obliged.

The handsome daredevil hero of *Bataan*, *Quo Vadis*, *Ivanhoe*, *The*

Brothers Were Valiant and *The Last Hunt* turned out to be shy, taciturn and depressive. After I picked him up at his hotel on Park Avenue, we only exchanged a few words as we headed toward Fifth Avenue and Central Park. It took him a while to warm up to me. I tried to be as gentle as I could, sensing how unhappy and vulnerable he was. We had lunch, walked some more before I accompanied him back to his hotel, where I interviewed him in his room. I think he was grateful that I had spent time with him. Robert Taylor was no fool. He knew I was a fill-in. I had been a poor substitute to a press corps that had turned indifferent to him.

Joel organized intimate press conferences with movie stars once a week. I tried to attend most of them. A dozen journalists from the US and Europe and the star du jour were seated around a conference table. The questions were often flat or cliché. I always tried to set the bar a little higher with outrageous ones. For instance, I asked Jerry Lewis if he would ever consider doing Shakespeare. I confronted Burt Lancaster by telling him that there were two actors in Hollywood who had a tendency to overact. One of them was Kirk Douglas. When I asked him to name the other, Lancaster burst into laughter.

I used these sound bites and inserted them into *New York 10 10*.

Joe and I felt that our financial compensation for producing such a popular show was inadequate. Radio Luxembourg was paying each of us a mere four hundred dollars per program. We felt cheated. We could earn much more, we thought, if our half-hour could attract American sponsors. We presented the idea of going after potential sponsors to Jacques Garnier. Jacques agreed in principle. An exchange of letters between Radio Luxembourg and RKO, their sales rep in the US, followed. On March 30, 1965, the head of Eastern Radio Sales Division at RKO wrote his counterpart in Paris, "...and we agreed with Daniel Dorian and Joe O'Brien, that some American advertisers would be interested in purchasing time in their section of the *Balzac 10 10* show. American popular music seems to have a large audience in Europe, and since the program is made here in French by an American and a French disc jockey, we feel any advertisers would see an immediate advantage in sponsoring a typical American modern radio program in France."

By June, RKO had not received an answer. Radio Luxembourg was dragging its feet. In the summer of 1965, Radio Luxembourg informed RKO that the station was no longer interested. The matter was dropped, to our puzzlement. Radio Luxembourg's decision was incomprehensible. Its management had everything to gain, nothing to lose. Given the popularity of the show, the prospect of finding sponsors was better than good.

Jacques Garnier explained that his management did not feel comfortable involving talents in the business end of their operation. The people at the top were reluctant to let us cash in part of the profits derived from these revenues, no matter how small the amount would have been. They turned us down. We would have been given the green light had we faced a similar situation in the States.

A book published in France in the late seventies explains in great historical details the French's unease with money. Written by Alain Peyrefitte, a former French State Secretary and a former minister under General de Gaulle, the book entitled *Le Mal Français* (The French Disease) goes back to the sixteenth century. It blames Catholicism and the eradication of Protestantism in France, through the revocation of the Edict of Nantes by Louis XIV in 1685, for France's inability to embrace productivity, business, free enterprise and commerce. The Edict, issued eighty-seven years earlier by King Henry IV, had granted the Calvinist Protestants of France substantial rights.

"Protestant countries applied Erasmus' principles. They became tolerant and polycentric," writes Peyrefitte. "Catholic countries and their Unitarian obsession got rid of pluralism to build mono-centrism. As a result, a bumpy road for some, a faster road to democracy for others, routine here, innovation there, here the economy being scorned, there the economy being revered."

"The Prime Minister of Quebec once told me jokingly," writes Alain Peyrefitte, "Ah! If Richelieu and Louis XIV had allowed the French Protestants to settle in the New World, the first men on the moon would have spoken French, not English."

Radio Luxembourg's refusal to search for sponsors stifled our motivation. Joe had lost interest. A telephone call from Paris sealed the fate of *New York*

10 10 and opened the door to new opportunities. I cancelled the show and moved on.

In mid-September 1965, Radio Luxembourg's news editor asked me to cover the pope's visit to the United States. If I had questioned my ability to carry the assignment through, I would have walked away from it. Instead, I decided to tackle each and every task one day and one night at a time, overcoming inexperience with persistence and long hours. To secure the proper passes, line up interviews and organize live communications with Paris, turned out to be challenging. It took me twenty days and twenty nights to overcome a stifling bureaucracy, NYPD's strict rules, the discrimination most organizations displayed against foreign journalists, the fight for good locations at the UN and more importantly at Yankee Stadium.

Pope Paul VI arrived in New York on Monday, October 4, 1965. His schedule included a speech at the United Nations, a meeting at the Waldorf Astoria with the President of the United States, Lyndon B. Johnson, another with Cardinal Spellman at his residence, and in the evening a Mass at Yankee Stadium.

The Mass at Yankee Stadium was the *pièce de resistance* that I covered live from beginning to end. The news director was so pleased that he hired me as one of his freelance correspondents in the United States. I was a journalist again.

I had survived. My freelance work at USIA and Radio Luxembourg had earned me enough money to lead a decent life. On balance, the twenty-four months I had spent in New York had been more productive than my twenty-four years in France.

That achievement had come with a price. Working for myself had its rewards and its drawbacks. The days were long and, for the people who paid me, I was only as good as the last job. If I wanted to survive as a freelancer, I had to excel and be constantly on the move, like a shark. As a result, bouts of anxiety kept me pinned to my sofa, glued to the television set, watching the most stupid programs, any program, all day and often all night.

My breakup with Jo-Ann had left me bereaved. The island of Manhattan became my Màs a Tierra. One can feel isolated in a crowd.

I did something I had promised myself I would not do: I looked back and felt the irresistible need to reconnect with my past. I was twenty-seven and started to feel the weight of solitude. Wasn't it time for me to settle down?

I started fantasizing about Annick, my best friend's sister. She had left an indelible impression when I met her and her family upon my return from Algeria. Her common wisdom, her self-assurance and a sense of humor that bordered on causticity had appealed to me then. I wrote her a letter in which I expressed my desire to get to know her better. She was receptive to the idea. I decided to take a one-week trip to Paris.

When we met again, I looked at her with fresh eyes. She was sexy after all. After dinner, the two of us went out for drinks. When I took her back home, I kissed her in front of her parents' building. We promised to write to each other.

My return to New York marked the beginning of a short but intense epistolary courtship.

The frequency of our correspondence increased exponentially, fast moving from two to three letters a week to one to two a day. They dealt with a bunch of issues, including our financial situation, our respective views on religion, the way we both envisioned a life in common and last but not least, my Jewish origins.

That matter popped up two months after we decided to get married. Annick insisted on having a religious wedding and had gathered the official documents the French administration and the Catholic Church required. Lying by omission, I failed to tell her that my father was Jewish—I was not aware that my mother was Jewish then—but made a point of informing her that I had been baptized, in an attempt to reassure her and the priest.

When she examined my certificate of baptism that was required by the church, she wrote on July 7, 1964, "Why were you baptized five years after your birth? It means that it was a deliberate decision, not a natural one parents make when the baby is born. Why didn't you go through your first communion? Does your indifference toward religion stem from the fact that you have not received a religious education? Aren't you practicing, like most Catholics?"

I couldn't bring myself to reveal my Jewish origins to my future wife. A letter my mother sent me a few days before my wedding made me see things in a different light. Reacting to a derogatory remark I must have made about Jews, she wrote, "We brought you up that way (as a Catholic) because we thought it was in your best interest. I do not ask you to become Jewish. This is not my intention. But your future wife must not find out later what your true origins are. She would blame you for it."

Her advice prompted me to overcome the denial I was in. I decided to dissipate any doubts I might have cast concerning my roots. "I was shocked when I learned that my father was Jewish," I wrote to Annick. "He did everything he could to hide it from me. When I learnt that he was Jewish, I was angry with him at first. Then I tried to find 'my truth,' not socially but in my heart... I do not believe in God. I do not feel affiliated to any religion, and, as I told my mother recently, for me the Jewish religion is like a foreign country." Then I added, "Religion has always left me indifferent. What is important is to seek one's truth within."

It took a few days for Annick to answer me. When she did, she displayed a liberalism I had feared she did not possess. Many Catholics in France were staunch anti-Semites. "I have given some thoughts about your Jewish origins. I have no problem with it," she wrote back. "You shouldn't hide your origins, nor be ashamed of them. You should not act as if they were flaws. If you have a complex, a conflict in you, get rid of them. It's ridiculous because one, there is nothing you can do about it, and two, you should not consider the Jews as inferior under any circumstances."

A few days later, she added, "Your father's origins surprised me but did not bother me. Your being Jewish might have been a religious issue for me... maybe. On a human and affective level, I have no problem with it."

What became an issue was her belief that I was anti-Semitic. "Aside from the respect you have for them, why don't you like the Jews?" she wrote in the middle of August. "As far as I am concerned, the only thing that bothers me is the fact that they give such priority to social success. But their persistence in everything they undertake appeals to me." To which I replied, "I never said I hated the Jews. I hate zealous Jews as much as I hate bible-thumpers. I cannot stand sectarianism in any shape or form."

She felt that a religious marriage carried a deeper meaning than a simpler ceremony at City Hall. "These civil weddings performed one after another without any kind of reverence or meditation," she wrote, "do not convey a true and real sense of commitment."

The civil ceremony took place on Wednesday, September 2, 1964, at City Hall, in the eighteenth arrondissement, followed by a religious service at the local church. We were blessed the following year with a daughter and in 1969 with a son. Annick and I divorced in the early eighties.

Professional Fulfillment

*I provoke them [interview subjects] because I get involved,
because my interviews are never cold, because I fall in love
with the person who is in front of me, even if I hate him or her.
An interview is a love story for me. It's a fight. It's a coitus.*
—ORIANA FALLACI

The time I started my collaboration with the Canadian Broadcasting Corporation could not have been more opportune. In the sixties, French Canadians were thirsty for news coming from the US. Their love and hate for America and for all things American exacerbated their craving for stories that dealt with the best and preferably the worst of American society.

Radio Canada was still in its pioneering stage. Because it didn't have enough journalists to fill its broadcast schedule, it forgave my shortcomings and allowed me to try my hand at just about anything that had to do with reporting. Such tolerance, some would call it laxity, allowed me to venture into areas that would not have been accessible to me under normal circumstances. It is while working for CBC that I taught myself the techniques of putting together documentaries for both radio and television and, maybe equally important, the technique of interviewing people.

Asking questions of the famous and the powerful was fun. To paraphrase Forrest Gump, you never knew what you were gonna get, with a few exceptions. French politicians were predictable, pompous, stale and condescending. They barely hid their contempt for the media and displayed it overtly. When Leslie Stahl from CBS *60 Minutes*, quizzed the French

President about how Paris was buzzing with the rumors on whether his wife Cecilia had left him again, Nicolas Sarkozy tore off his lavaliere microphone and walked out.

Many French politicians turned down interviews unless they were given the questions in advance, a practice no responsible American journalist would condone. Others were wary about reporters they did not know. Giscard d'Estaing refused to grant me an interview after asking one of my colleagues, "Who is this Dorian?" This happened a few years before he was elected President of France.

To extract meaty and juicy answers from politicians, movie stars or even from the man in the street is a cat and mouse game that calls for strategy, psychology, smarts and an iota of deviousness. Some are better at it than others, but the process is more complex than one might think. Journalists have to adapt to the shy and the extrovert, the articulate and the not so articulate, the ones who are attracted to microphones and cameras and the ones who are terrified by them, the passive and the aggressive as well as the few who turn an interview to their advantage as they try to promote a product or advance their cause. A good interviewer must be uncompromising, fearless enough to ask the embarrassing questions, alert enough to foil irrelevant or self-serving answers. The aim is to cut through the bull, to get at the truth, if there is such a thing in politics, and to secure the story.

I had the advantage of being nosey, tenacious and eager to learn, but the process had not been easy. During my first interview, I kept turning the next question I was about to ask over and over in my head while my guest was still answering the preceding one. Paying attention to what he was saying would have given me the necessary clue for a meaningful follow up. It took me a couple of months to get the hang of it.

Did I wind up being a great interviewer? Depends on whom you asked. I once interviewed Ludmilla Tchérina, the ballet dancer, actress, artist and sculptor. When the camera stopped rolling, she stood up, shook my hand and said, "You are the worst interviewer I've ever had." Weeks later, Leonor Fini, the Argentine surrealist painter sat in front of me for a similar interview. When it was over, she declared, "Mr. Dorian, you are the best interviewer I ever had." Go figure! What reassured me was how my mother reacted when she replied to one of my letters in which I mentioned my interview with the ballerina. "Ludmilla Tchérina is beautiful," she wrote, "but she is stupid. I know her." Ha!

As early as 1963, I started collaborating with three news and information programs that all aired at prime time. The topics I covered for CBC were a hodgepodge of the frivolous, the serious and the fringe. They ranged from Mao's China to suicide in the US, from plastic surgery for jailers to parapsychology, from Castro's Cuba to married Catholic priests, from the Ku Klux Klan to theater in churches, from new methods of interrogating suspects to MENSA, from the merger of *The Herald Tribune*, *The Journal American* and *World-Telegram* to Ralph Nader's take on road safety. I produced a one-hour special on UFOs and also had the pleasure of doing a piece with George Balanchine's wife, Tanaquil Le Clercq, on her book, *Mourka-The Autobiography of a Cat*. In it, Martha Swope, the great theater and dance photographer, had captured the leaps, acrobatics, antics, pas de chats and entrechats of the feline ballerina.

I roamed the streets of New York and recorded its harmonious sounds as well as its cacophony, the "doo-wop" groups and the folk singers in Washington Square, the *Jazz on Wheels* in Harlem, the anti-war cries in Central Park, the voices of the underground, the hippies, the revolutionaries, the victims of society. My search for the odd, the sensational, the idiosyncratic, the extraordinary and the out-of-the-ordinary led me to every nook and cranny of a city that burst at the seams with turmoil and rebellion, a metropolis that flaunted the grandiose, the ridiculous and the shocking. New York in the sixties was home to the frustrated, the malcontent, the ambitious, the bold, the visionary as well as the genius.

My microphone was indiscriminate. I would have interviewed Al Capone or Charles Manson if I could have. I secured former General James Gavin's opposition to McNamara's theory according to which a retreat of American troops from Vietnam would lead to Communist expansion in Asia. He was the first high-ranking officer to dissent from the Johnson Administration on this issue. Herbert Aptheker, the Marxist historian and head of The American Institute for Marxist Studies, an enemy of the state by FBI standards, shared with me the observations he had gathered during his stay in Hanoi and talked about the UN Secretary's efforts to bring North Vietnam to the negotiating table in 1964.

Among the half-hour and one-hour specials I produced, one of them gave me access to the most inaccessible spot in the world, NORAD, the North American Aerospace Defense Command, a science fiction city buried under fourteen hundred feet of granite, in the heart of Cheyenne Mountain in Colorado. Few people in the world had walked through the two thirty-ton armored doors of this tightly secured military complex, with its 5,000 feet of tunnels and its six generators producing a total of 5,736 kilowatts. NORAD was a self-sufficient city equipped with reservoirs that contained 5,500,000 gallons of water and 320,000 gallons of fuel. In the mid-sixties, it employed four hundred and twenty people who were responsible for the security of the United States and Canada. The country was supposed to have been invulnerable to any nuclear attack then. NORAD still claims it is, but in spite of its state of the art technology that is updated on a regular basis, it could not detect, nor foil the attacks on New York's Twin Towers on September 11, 2001.

What turned me on the most was securing from newsmakers reactions, impressions, analysis they had never expressed publicly, not necessarily scoops, but fresh and revealing statements.

Pierre Rinfret, who had been the economic advisor to three presidents, once gave me a portrait of Richard Nixon that few would have dared express. "He is a strange man," he confided. "I can give you an example. When I started my collaboration with him in January 1966, we would address him as Mr. Nixon. For many men who worked with him, ten, eighteen, twenty years, he always was Mr. Nixon. Not Richard. Not Dick, but always Mr. Nixon. He is not a man easy to know. He is always cold. He is always precise. He is not a man, how shall I say... who is relaxed. And that for the American people is rather strange, because, as you know very well, Americans are almost always relaxed, maybe too relaxed."

Governor Nelson Rockefeller showed remarkable bipartisanship when I asked him if he agreed with the members of his party who claimed that President Johnson would not keep his promises and that he would never build his *Great Society*.

"I do not belong to the same party," he answered, "but we should give him credit for a program that is very progressive."

"Will Republicans seize the issue of racial unrest and use it against Democrats during their electoral campaign?" I asked.

"No, I don't think so. What we want is help to solve our problems, not for any political purpose, but to bring relief to the people who live in ghettos."

Not many Republicans today would give as much slack to a Democratic president and few are the politicians, on either side of the aisle, willing to choose problem solving over partisan gerrymandering.

Eugene McCarthy, the senator from Minnesota and the first candidate to challenge incumbent Lyndon Johnson for the Democratic nomination for President of the United States in 1968, was a breath of fresh air in an era plagued by war and racial unrest. No one knew him better than David Schoenbrun, a former CBS News correspondent whom I became close to.

I asked David whether McCarthy was the dreamer, the idealist, the philosopher his adversaries made him out to be.

"Yes and it is not a reproach. For once, I'd like to have a president who is a dreamer, a philosopher, a poet, or rather someone who appreciates poetry."

Few felt that McCarthy would ever make it to the presidency, except the young idealists that made up his base. This gentle mannered man who had style and, behind an apparent softness, great resolve, opposed the war in Vietnam, as they did.

McCarthy told me that he had a crisis of conscience brought about by his children. "My daughter nagged me so much," he explained, "that I finally agreed to oppose the war in Vietnam, just to have a little peace at home."

McCarthy would not stand a chance in today's environment.

Salvador Dali was fifty-nine years old when I conducted my first interview with him at Knoedler & Company, a gallery located on East Fifty-seventh Street. The occasion was the opening of an exhibit called *Dali*. I had instructed my cameraman to follow me and Dali, his Aries perched on his shoulder, as we ambled from painting to painting, pausing a minute or two to give the artist time to explain, interpret, comment on the most intriguing of the thirty pieces he had brought with him to the US. When the exhibit opened, *Time* wrote, "As usual, they were dillies. They were subtle pencil drawings of nudes, erotic washes produced by the inky wiggling of a live baby octopus, fiery battle scenes with paint laid on thick enough to thrill a pastry chef. Of course, there was also his super-surrealism, typically in GALACIDALACIDEOXYRIB ONUCLEICACID (Homage to Crick and Watson), a title so long that it resorts to a parenthetical remark. In a slick equation of Botticelli and biochemistry, Dali portrays a translucent God lifting the dead Christ into Heaven, superimposed on the molecular structure of life-bearing DNA or deoxynbonucleic acid, the discovery of which led to Nobel Prizes for Drs. Francis Crick and James D. Watson in 1962."

When I mentioned that he was one of the forefathers of the surrealist movement, Dali answered, in his cryptic Franglais "I am not the father of surrealism. To be accurate, Breton was. I came much later. Then I created havoc, because, as you know, I felt honored to be evicted from the surrealists group."

"And this piece?" I asked.

"It is the triumph of the dollar, because, even according to Marxism, the root cause of all the wars, of all human conflicts is money. Everybody wants to cling to the dollar. And when they have enough money, they will design very expensive electronic jewels. With the dollar, you can buy paintings from Vermeer, Leonardo, have mistresses, pleasures, like Napoléon, the Arabs, the Spanish Army. Everyone wages magnificent wars to catch treasures that can be enjoyed artistically, or rather ar-ti-sti-cally."

At one point, we stopped in front of two minuscule paintings that were impressionist in style. Dali blocked the camera lens with his hand. "That is serious painting. Let's move on."

To quote Forrest Gump again, Dali was the best box of chocolates ever, an inexhaustible source of unexpected treats.

"The space adventure is sublime. Finally, men, the astronauts that is, are forced to drink their own pee and probably to eat their own excrement, because, as you very well know, when in space, no one can go shopping. You can't just go and buy tomatoes up there and, you know, they're now using a process that can remove salt from seawater, rendering it potable. They are doing the same in California with urine. Therefore, an astronaut can drink his own pee and preferably his co-pilot's."

Dali cherished telling scatological anecdotes, but obsessed with the Perpignan railroad station he kept mentioning in all his interviews. Once, I asked him what his next project was going to be. "A three-dimensional painting," he said, "the most sublime idea in the history of art. It came to me like a mystically illuminated orgasm at the very center of the Perpignan railroad which is where the world spiritual activities converge, since Dali said so." Dali had a penchant for referring himself in the 'royal' third person.

At the end of one of many interviews I conducted with the eccentric genius, my assistant, Simone, ventured a question she felt was in character with the man. Pointing to his beautifully bee-waxed, long, thin mustachios, she asked sarcastically, "Maître, please tell me. Why is your left moustache higher than the right one?"

"Simple," answered Dali without losing countenance. "To establish a happy balance with my right ball that is heavier than my left one." Simone blushed. She would have disappeared in a hole if she could have.

Salvador Dali loved to startle, to galvanize, to rouse, to shock. He once imported from South America billions of flies, which he unleashed in his suite at the St. Regis Hotel, creating unbelievable pandemonium. His purpose? To create a painting with fly shit.

A rich man begged him to redecorate the interior of his four-story luxurious brownstone off Madison Avenue in the sixties. The billionaire gave him free rein. Dali could work while he and his family traveled abroad for a few months. It is said that Dali cut four round holes in the middle of each floor, starting from the top and working his way down, each larger than the previous one. The owner's bed, located on the fourth floor, wound up at the edge of a precipice. Dali, who ruined the brownstone, is quoted as saying, "This is a testimony to the originality of my design, the ever present danger. This is an apartment where your dreams must be static."

Dali approached me once with an idea for television. He would draw a portrait of Louis XIV for the camera that he would make disappear and reappear instantaneously. He suggested that I come to his St. Regis suite with a film crew.

Dali instructed the cameraman to position the camera facing a black canvas that lay on the floor, and then asked him to start filming. He grabbed a bag of Dominoes, poured white grains of sugar on the canvas tracing a thin line of white sugar as easily as he would have with a brush. The white image that appeared on the black background was unmistakable. Dali then grabbed the canvas and tilted it upwards ever so slowly. Louis XIV dissolved in front of our eyes, as the grains of sugar rolled down on the floor. Then, Dali suggested that we reverse the action in post-production in slow motion so that Louis XIV would slowly reappear. This happened long before special effects were invented.

"In France, he healed from the antagonisms and conflicts that prevailed in America in the twenties, thirties and forties. In France, they allowed him to think, to say, to write whatever he felt like thinking, saying and writing. He felt that everything in America kept him from being natural. He needed to take some distance." That is how Anaïs Nin justified Henry Miller's exile to Europe in a television interview I conducted with her in the late sixties. "Whenever he turned lyrical," she added, "Americans said that he was taking drugs or that he was out of his mind. He needed to be free. Puritanism and established conventions stifled him. When in France, he loved to live in the street. He adored cafes. He was so comfortable over there."

Miller was my hero and Nin had been his mistress. She also had had an affair with his wife June. In fact, they had a threesome. "I was twenty years old and June was already a fully matured woman," she confided in me. "Miller had forewarned me that she was capricious, that no one understood her, that she was extraordinary. The writer in me was intrigued by her complexity. And when I met her the first time, I saw her as an 'ideal' woman. She was free. She was spontaneous. She was André Breton's *Nadja*. She didn't think. She was completely irrational."

"You fell in love with her."

"Yes. I had a crush on her. I was totally seduced by her."

"It must have been a once in a lifetime experience?"

"Yes. She haunted our work. She enriched Miller's life but at the same time prevented him from working. I saw her from a woman's point of view and Miller saw her from a man's point of view. It was an exceptional threesome. We always talked about her, wrote about her. She was a *femme fatale*. She could have been the character of a novel."

Reverend Michael Allen was the Rector of St. Mark's-in-the-Bowery, New York's second oldest church. He was handsome, bright, daring, unconventional, compassionate and he loved his job. He also was a staunch militant. He was young. St. Mark's was very old.

The church sat on what had been a Dutch plantation, which Peter Stuyvesant, Governor of New Amsterdam, purchased in 1651 from the Dutch West India Company. When Stuyvesant died in 1672, his body was interred in a vault under the family chapel. In 1793, Stuyvesant's great-grandson, Petrus Stuyvesant, donated the Episcopal Church with the stipulation that a new chapel be erected and, on April 1795, the cornerstone of St. Mark's Church-in-the-Bowery was laid.

In the sixties, it shined in the thick of a battleground that pitted whites against blacks, blacks against Hispanics, rather blacks against browns as Michael often put it, Jews against Christians, the poor against the not so poor. It was the home of starving artists who begged for recognition and of drug addicts who not only wasted their lives, but their souls as well. What better environment for a man of faith.

Michael was a man of principle, a man of action who did not wait for the world to come to his church. He never hesitated to go wherever duty or need called, even if he had to travel far and at the risk of jeopardizing his physical safety.

In support of the arts, which he felt contributed to the well being of his congregation, he reached out and invited avant-garde, controversial artists, many unknown, to perform inside the church or to exhibit on its grounds, even if it meant offending the prudes.

He gave home to a very risqué and controversial musical that bore the suggestive title, *The Golden Screw*. Written and composed by Tom Sankey, it was a forerunner of *Hair*, the play that would revolutionize musicals a few years later.

When it came to the indecent and the naughty, St. Mark's competed with another church, Judson Memorial where, in 1965, a minimalist sculptor by the name of Robert Morris created a theatrical work called

Waterman Switch and starred in it along with Yvonne Rainer, the American dancer and choreographer. They both appeared nude, locked in an embrace, as they inched their way across parallel beams while Lucinda Childs, another well-known dancer and choreographer, circled the stage. Because of this performance, Judson Memorial Church was nearly ousted from the American Baptist Convention. Michael Allen luckily escaped similar punishment even though *The Golden Screw* was as controversial, if not more.

He had organized a sculpture exhibit on St. Mark's old graveyard. What an odd sight for a sculpture exhibit. Only a liberal pastor could get away with what conservative members of his own denomination might have construed as sacrilegious. I decided to cover the unusual event.

I asked my cameraman to follow the Reverend and me, as we were strolling through the yard. At one point, we stopped in front of a mobile comprised of several metallic circles mounted on top of each other, with batons swinging in and out of them. "What is this?" I asked Michael.

"I'll tell you if you turn off the camera."

I instructed the cameraman to do just that. Michael looked at me with a devilish smile and whispered in my ear, "It's a fuckin' machine."

Ha! Not only was the man daring, he also had a tremendous sense of humor. I fell in love with the guy. We became friends.

Michael witnessed first-hand the impact the war in Vietnam had on American undergrads and graduates. In 1970, he took over as Dean of Berkeley Divinity School and also as Associate Dean of Yale Divinity School, an official seminary of the Episcopal Church originally founded in 1854. It moved to New Haven in 1928 to take advantage of the resources of Yale University.

As dean, Michael had first hand knowledge of his students' discontent. The draft had impacted their morale. It had decimated their ranks.

On a Sunday in December 1972, Michael received a call from Cora Weiss. She was a peace activist since the early sixties, a co-founder of Women Strike for Peace, which played a major role in bringing about an end of nuclear testing in the atmosphere and a leader in the anti-Vietnam War movement. She organized many demonstrations, including the mammoth November 15, 1969 anti-war rally in Washington, which I covered as a correspondent. As Co-Chair and Director of the Committee of Liaison with Families of Prisoners Detained in Vietnam, she coordinated the exchange of mail between families and prisoners of war in Vietnam. The Committee also revealed the names of POWs who were still alive and accompanied some returning POW pilots back home. She would later be appointed President of the Hague Appeal for Peace.

Her call to Michael was brief. "What are you doing this coming Wednesday?" she asked.

"Nothing special."

"Great! Wednesday you're going to Hanoi."

"She tantalized me," wrote Michael, "with the possibility that if I went, I might be in Hanoi the day peace was signed, a prospect that held enormous appeal for me."

The purpose of the trip was to address human rights in the region, and to deliver Christmas mail to American prisoners of war.

Cora Weiss had already purchased Michael's plane ticket and had applied for his visa before she even called him, certain that he would not pass up this opportunity. She had made similar arrangements on behalf of the three other individuals who were going to accompany him: Joan Baez, the folk singer; Telford Taylor, an American lawyer best known for his role in the Counsel for the Prosecution at the Nuremberg Trials after World War II, for his opposition to Joseph McCarthy in the fifties and for his criticism of US actions during the Vietnam War; and Barry Romo, a former infantry lieutenant who served in Vietnam from 1966 to 1968 and who, upon his return to America, became a leading member of the Vietnam Veterans Against War Association.

Making the decision to fly to Hanoi was not easy for Michael. When he asked his fourteen-year-old daughter, she said, "Daddy, you have to go."

The Vietnam Committee of Solidarity with the American People had invited the American peace delegation to the Democratic Republic of Vietnam. It gave the four Americans a warm welcome. Others had preceded them. Herbert Aptheker and Tom Hayden had been in Hanoi seven years earlier. So had Tom Hayden's future wife, Jane Fonda, only four months before Michael's no less controversial trip.

The night they arrived in Hanoi, the US launched a bombing campaign and centered their attacks on civilian areas in an attempt to terrorize the people into submission. The four Americans were caught in the "Christmas Bombings," otherwise called "The December Raids." Michael gave a description of it in an article he wrote upon his return for *The Christian Century Magazine*. "Then all the lights in Hanoi went out. Somewhere, someone pulled the master switch and plunged the city into a darkness lightened only by the flares from the bombers and the reddening sky. Then we would make the long walk down pitch-dark corridors to the bomb shelter. The noise was unbelievable, the sharp racket of the anti-aircraft guns, the boom and swoosh of SAM missiles, the dull thud of distant bombs. It all seemed unreal until the next day when I saw the damage." His experience reminded me of the one I had gone through with my mother in 1944.

The US involvement would go on for another three months. Michael's trip contributed, as did the preceding visits of other American citizens, to the erosion of public support for the conflict.

Freelancing for the Canadian network was rewarding financially but didn't guarantee me a future. I had to find a full-time job.

Foreign Correspondent

*A reporter is always concerned with tomorrow. There's
nothing tangible of yesterday. All I can say I've done is agitate
the air ten or fifteen minutes and then boom –it's gone.*
—EDWARD R. MORROW

In May 1967, the privately owned French radio station Europe #1 asked
its US correspondent, Georges Vikar, to cover the Indianapolis 500 car
race. Jean Gorini, its news editor, expected him to go on location and
file from the side of the track. Instead, Georges stayed in his Manhattan
apartment and faked it. He asked his girlfriend to roll a vacuum cleaner in
front of the telephone receiver to simulate the roars of the Formula Ones
swooshing by the spectators as he was commenting the race he was
watching on television. Gorini wasn't duped. He fired George, leaving the
position open. I jumped at the opportunity and applied.

Gorini granted me a three-month trial period. My first assignment was
a mammoth gay parade that took place in Central Park. America had rarely
seen hordes of gays flaunting their homosexuality so overtly, young men
kissing on the lips in public, bare-breasted lesbians cavorting, transvestites
dolled up in over the top dresses and stiletto heels. Such a display of
hedonism inspired me to write a colorful piece. Gorini must have
appreciated my report. He called the following day to tell me that I had the
job. I was no longer a freelancer but a full-time foreign correspondent and
had been handed an orchestra seat to events that were going to impact the
United States politically, economically and socially for years to come. The
sixties were a pivotal decade filled with discoveries, achievements,
upheavals, threats and conflicts that shaped the future of this country.

* * *

Late afternoon, Thursday, June 23, 1967, I received a phone call from the news desk. A meeting between Lyndon Johnson and Chairman Alexei Kosygin of the USSR had just been hastily scheduled. It was going to take place the next day in Glassboro, a small town in southern New Jersey very few had heard of. I rented a car and hit the road early evening.

I did not want to be too far from where the summit meeting was going to take place. I had to find a hotel from where I could file. A road sign confirmed that I had arrived, but the absence of houses confused me. I pressed on, reached an intersection, drove past it and before I knew it, found myself beyond the town's limits. I made a U-turn, returned to the intersection and spotted a marquee that read, Hotel Franklin. It was already past eleven.

The moment I stepped inside the lobby of that small inn, I realized that I was too late. The bar area had already been taken over by Associated Press and United Press International. They had converted it into a newsroom where the continual ticking of telex machines had replaced the brouhaha of conversations usually heard over a background of elevator music. *The New York Times* had monopolized the adjacent space. The hotel's twenty-five rooms were booked. My hope of finding a telephone and a place to crash was dashed. In fact, laying my hands on a phone with which I could call long distance was more important for me than finding a bed.

Hundreds of domestic and foreign reporters had swarmed this tiny hamlet to cover the only summit meeting the US and the USSR would hold during the Johnson presidency. This get-together at the top was supposed to deal with arms limitation. It didn't. President Johnson wanted to meet his Soviet counterpart to discuss the Six-Day War. The two superpowers had recently come very close to military conflict, with the Soviet threatening to intervene if the US-supported Israeli military went too far. The stakes were high, as were the expectations. Some hoped for an improvement in the two countries' relations. The summit turned out to be disappointing. The two heads of state failed to agree on anything remotely significant.

The American and the Russian had acted like spoiled brats. Kosygin refused to go to Washington. Johnson would not travel to the Big Apple. The college town of Glassboro, which was almost exactly equidistant from

Washington and New York, met both parties' approval. The summit would be held at "Hollybush," the home of the President of Glassboro State College.

I decided to leave my rented car at the hotel parking lot and strolled along the main drag. It was past midnight, yet this village, which I understood was always dead after nine p.m., was bursting with life. Journalists were pacing Main Street and mixing with the locals who, overcome by curiosity, had forgone their bedtime to rub elbows with this sophisticated crowd. Excitement was in the air. The place felt like the Fourth of July.

At around one a.m. a woman approached me and asked me if I was French. I never knew how she found out. My looks, I guess. When I told her I was, she asked me if I needed a room. She and her husband were in the process of renovating an old house that was part of their estate. It was still in construction, but I was welcomed to stay there. "It's better than nothing," she said. The house was half a mile from The Franklin. I accepted her offer with a sigh of relief.

We walked back to the hotel parking lot, got into my rented car and drove to what was going to be my residence for the next two days. The place stood in total darkness. My generous hostess lit the way with a flashlight and took me one flight up to an empty room walled with sheetrock and still filled with the sweet and pungent odor of fresh plaster. She promised me she would run an extension cord from the main house, install a light and bring a bed and a small fridge that she would stock with soft drinks. The sodas would come in handy, but I wouldn't have much use for the bed if I were going to file stories all night. I had to have a phone of my own as soon as possible to be able to do that. Europe #1 expected pre-summit reports for the morning news.

My dear benefactor needed time to prep the place. I returned to The Franklin Hotel. To my surprise, powerful spotlights brightly lit the intersection through which I had driven twice in the dark earlier. A couple of New Jersey Bell trucks equipped with platform lifts were stationed in the middle of the road. Men were busy installing what looked like new cables. I asked one of them what was going on. Journalists were making too many phone calls, he explained. They had jammed the circuits. More lines, many more lines were needed. "Could one be installed in the house I'm staying in?" I dared asking, as I pointed out, "It's up the road, the last one on the right."

"No problem," answered the New Jersey Bell worker. "Give us an hour."

"Can you also hook a phone to it?"

"Sure thing," said the man.

I hung out at The Franklin for a while, chatting with my colleagues and gathering background information. At around two I headed back to the house. A single bed and a lamp awaited me. A small fridge had been filled with cans of Coke and Pepsi. A brand new telephone lay on the bare floor. No one had asked for my name, my address or for any type of financial reference. The line was live. I called Paris and filed my first story for the eight-thirty a.m. news, two thirty in the morning local time. In it, I mentioned the generosity of the people of Glassboro and expressed my amazement at the ease and speed with which communications had been established between nowhere in the US and the City of Light. That early morning I signed off with these simple words, "Only in America. Daniel Dorian reporting from Glassboro."

Forty-eight hours later, five hundred telephones were installed on the lawn reserved for the press, right in front of "Hollybush," for round two of the talks. I stayed online with Paris from morning to late evening and was never billed.

On August 11, 1965, Lee Minikus's attention had been drawn by some guy's erratic driving behavior. The California Highway Patrol motorcycle officer pulled over Marquette Frye and ordered him to walk a straight line. The black man failed to pass the sobriety test. A crowd of onlookers grew from dozens to hundreds as the officer radioed to have Frye's car impounded. The mob became violent. Like a spark in an oil tank, that insignificant incident exploded into what is now called the Watts Riots that would leave thirty-five people dead, over one thousand injured and more than three thousand arrested.

On July 23, 1967, Detroit police raided an unlicensed, after-hours bar known as "Blind Pig," on the corner of Twelfth and Clairmount Streets, on the city's Near West Side. Police confrontations with patrons and observers led to one of the deadliest and most destructive riots this country had ever endured. Also known as the Twelfth Street Riot, it resulted in forty-three deaths, close to twelve hundred injured and seven thousand arrests.

New Haven and Milwaukee would also succumb to unbridled violence, so would Plainfield, Tampa, Buffalo, Cincinnati, Cleveland, Durham, Memphis, Cambridge and more than one hundred other cities.

I did not cover the Twelfth Street Riot—Europe #1 had sent me to Canada to accompany General de Gaulle—but I was in the heart of it when all hell broke loose in Newark, eleven days before. Two white policemen had arrested a black driver, John W. Smith, for improperly passing them on Fifteenth Avenue. After the residents of a public housing saw Smith being dragged into the Fourth Precinct, across the street from where they stood, rumors started that the black man had been killed in police custody. The routine arrest was enough to start a racial unrest of historical proportion.

The burning desire to go where few other mortals would, to brave tornadoes or floods or to face man's own fury in order to achieve professional recognition, dulls the apprehension and fear that play havoc with most other people's nerves.

Newark during those five hot and humid days and nights in the summer of 1967 was particularly hazardous and unpredictable. Each street corner presented a potential danger. Bands of angry youths would creep behind us, throw rocks at us and disappear as fast as they had popped up. Cars were vandalized. Mobs shattered windows with bricks and set buildings on fire with Molotov cocktails. I witnessed the brutal attack on one of my white colleagues who would have been killed by the mob if another journalist, a black man, hadn't stopped the lynching party by shouting, "Don't kill him. Loot the store instead."

Guns made their first appearance during the Newark riots. Bricks, stones, baseball bats had been used as improvised weapons during preceding disturbances, but not firearms. In the Newark ghetto, insurgents armed with shotguns added an element of insecurity. Police, national guardsmen, civilians, firefighters were on edge. "If we're being attacked, we will shoot to kill," a national guardsman told me. Earlier, a policeman had pointed his shotgun at me, his finger on the trigger and lowered his weapon only when the narrow beam of his flashlight hit the press card dangling on my chest.

I had seen abject poverty in North Africa, Asia and Central America. I had witnessed it in Haiti. It was nothing compared to Newark where rats bit babies every day, where children showed physical signs of starvation with their bloated bellies, where crumbling slums, detritus in the streets, foul odors and in some instances no fresh water and no electricity made this part of America more hellish than Hell. I would never have fathomed that such poverty and despair could exist in America. The Newark ghetto was a national disgrace, a dispossessed Third World surrounded by an ocean of wealth. No wonder anger had turned unbridled. The irony though was that blacks, in their blind rage, were destroying their own properties. The few times they attempted to cross the invisible border that separated their slums from rich neighborhoods, the white establishment stopped them with everything they had.

I wandered in that ghetto for two days and two nights, filing reports every hour on the hour, day and night. I stole a few minutes of sleep here and there, mostly on the banquettes of coffee shops. To stay awake, I ate steaks whenever I could. Protein kept me awake.

On the third day, my photographer friend Jean-Pierre Laffont and I found ourselves at the corner of Broadway and Chestnut Street, outside of what was considered the dangerous zone, in a dark alley flanked by three-story slums built of black bricks. Suddenly shots were fired. Hugging the walls, sprinting crouched from tree to tree, from one front door to another, we reached a police car parked in the middle of the street, its four doors wide open. It had just been caught in an ambush. A policeman had gotten out of it in a hurry and was radioing his precinct by the passenger seat, down on his knees, "We're sitting ducks out here."

"Get the fuck out then," responded the crackling voice of a dispatcher.

"No way. We're pinned down."

"Okay. We'll send the cavalry."

Three other cops were hiding behind trees, weapons at the ready. More shots broke the silence of the night. The officer who had called his precinct retrieved a shotgun from his vehicle and returned the fire in the dark, aiming blindly at a target that might or might not have been there. I turned my tape recorder on, ran across the street and found myself behind a van, a couple of feet from where the three policemen stood. I heard an explosion.

Pieces of glass fell on my head and my back. That's when Jean-Pierre started to shoot pictures of me, using his flash, thus exposing everyone around. As I took protection against the side of the van, one of the cops shouted to my friend, "Wadda you think you're doin'? Get the fuck outta here... NOW."

The insurgents who were shooting from the roof across the street had aimed at the lamppost that was casting a weak, yellowish light on that dark corner. Reinforcements arrived. When two police cars blocked each side of Chestnut Street, the assailants had already vanished into the night. The brief clash was over. I had recorded the entire incident.

That first experience with black rage would not be my last. A few weeks later, I flew to Washington to cover a political event. I had rented a brand new Buick Skylark. I had enough time to pay a visit to a few colleagues from Agence France Presse. Their office was located at the National Press Building on Fourteenth Street. The moment I stepped in, they informed me that a flare-up had just erupted nearby. I rushed out of the building and drove to where the disturbance was supposedly taking place. At one point, I stopped at a red light, when bands of black youths carrying rocks surrounded the car. I locked the doors, managed to make a U-turn and floored it, not fast enough though. I heard the thump of rocks hitting the hood, the roof and the back of the Buick. I parked in front of the National Press Building and inspected the damage. The vehicle had been totaled, but I was untouched.

New York. I had just finished an early dinner at Carnegie Deli, on Seventh Avenue when I heard on the radio that Reverend Martin Luther King had been assassinated at the Lorraine Motel in Memphis, Tennessee. The civil rights leader had died at eight o'clock in the evening, on Thursday, April 4, 1968. I rushed to a phone and called Paris. My news editor answered. Machine guns had been sighted on the steps of the Capitol, according to an AP wire. He asked me to go see for myself ASAP. I caught the last shuttle to Washington. Forty-five minutes after takeoff, as the Eastern Airline turbojet flew over the US capital, I saw dozens of fires surrounding the Capitol. Washington looked like a city under siege.

I asked a cabbie to drive me to the Capitol. As soon as we circled it, I caught a glimpse of the machine guns. Marines had mounted them on its steps. The presence of these weapons at the foot of America's pillar of democracy was disquieting. The capital of the mightiest country on earth was on the defensive, prepared to protect itself from its own people.

It became imperative that I find a phone from which I could file my first story. I asked the driver to drop me in front of the DuPont Circle Hotel, spotted a station wagon bearing the ABC logo, crossed to it and introduced myself to the network crew. A car phone hanging on the dashboard caught my attention. I asked if I could reach Paris with it. I was told that I could. It's from the inside of that station wagon that I filed my first report, in which I confirmed the existence of machine guns on the steps of the Capitol.

The following two days were wrenching. Blacks had gone on a rampage the moment they heard the news of King's death on their transistor radios. They gathered at the intersection of Fourteenth and U Street, the heart of the black community, near the office of King's Southern Christian Leadership Conference. Angry young blacks started breaking windows. Widespread looting had begun, as it had in over thirty other cities.

By the time Washington was considered pacified on April 8, twelve people had been killed, one thousand and ninety-seven injured and over sixty-one hundred arrested. A large number of buildings had burned. Damages reached today's equivalent of over one hundred sixty million dollars.

On that Sunday morning, I decided to visit a makeshift help center where blankets, milk and sandwiches were distributed to those who had lost their homes and who had become refugees in their own backyards. Outside, an eerie calm reigned. The city was quiet, "too quiet," as they say in westerns. The sun was shining. As I observed the long line of desperate and starving people who had come to the center for help, I caught a glimpse of a band of black youths crossing the street in a hurry and walking briskly up U Street. I grabbed my Nagra recorder and ran after them.

There must have been thirty black youngsters marching in the middle of the street. None of them carried stones or clubs. They seemed to be following someone. I ran ahead of them and could not believe my eyes. Robert and Ethel Kennedy were leading the group. There wasn't a cop, a Secret Service agent or a member of the senator's staff in sight, not even a journalist. I had the luck and privilege of being the only press.

I positioned myself next to Ethel. When we reached the first scorched house, the senator shook his head in disbelief and marched on. Blacks were lining up on each side of the street. They had recognized the man who had become their "great white hope."

In some areas, nothing was left but the charred sections of walls. Stores had been wrecked; display windows had been broken open. The people who lived there had very few possessions of their own to start with. The rampage had left them with even less.

Out of nowhere, a heavy African-American woman ran toward the senator from New York and fell into his arms in tears. Robert Kennedy, tucked in between her generous bosoms, tried to console her the best he could, with immense tenderness, whispering reassuring words in her ear. The woman wouldn't let go. There wasn't one person around who didn't have wet eyes.

When the Kennedys resumed their march in the middle of the street, I asked Ethel why the senator had decided to visit this particular section of the city. They had attended the morning service at a nearby church and wanted to see for themselves the extent of the damage. I then asked her if the senator would consent to an interview. She whispered something into his ear. He whispered back. She turned to me and said he would. I positioned myself next to him and, mic in hand, asked him my first question, as we both walked up the avenue. The interview lasted for three minutes.

What I saw when I made sure that I had recorded the brief exchange left me crushed. The tape had been caught in the lid of the recorder and was a mass of tangled mess. I reloaded my machine in a hurry, took a deep breath, ran, caught up with Ethel and, huffing and puffing, explained to her what had happened as apologetically as I could. She again whispered something into her husband's ear. He whispered something back. She turned to me and gave me the thumbs up. The good senator answered my questions for the second time. "It is a great tragedy for the United States," he said, "and I would hope that, out of it all, we would take the steps that would not only maintain law and order but to insure that the injustices that still exist within our own country disappear." Not a great statement, but still a scoop given the circumstances. Robert Kennedy ended the interview with a few French words, "*C'est triste...* How do you say sad?" I heard him ask his wife. "*Triste*," she answered. "*C'est très triste,*" he repeated.

A few minutes later, we spotted a large group of people blocking the street three hundred yards ahead of us. As we approached them, I realized that these folks were none other than cameramen and photographers who had found out, much too late, about the senator's outing.

A Ford Mustang with a chauffeur was parked in the middle of the street. Robert and Ethel shook the hands of a few youngsters, waved and climbed into a chauffeured Ford Mustang, which made a sharp U-turn and disappeared. I had just shared an exclusive and moving moment with a man who could have been a great president had he not been assassinated.

Once I filed my story, I sold the interview to an NBC reporter for two hundred dollars.

I flew to Atlanta that same evening. When I arrived at the Ebenezer Baptist Church for King's funeral the following morning, sixty thousand people had gathered to pay their last respects. Family, friends and dignitaries had to jostle their way into the building. Only a press pool was allowed inside. Powerful loudspeakers had been installed outside so the crowd could hear the service. I climbed to the top of a lamppost. From there, I covered the entire ceremony and was able to spot the dignitaries and personalities entering the church: Harry Belafonte, Marlon Brando, Bill Cosby, Aretha Franklin, Stevie Wonder, Robert Kennedy, Eugene McCarthy, Jacqueline Kennedy, Nelson Rockefeller and many more. From that uncomfortable vantage point I described for my European listeners what was happening and taped parts of the service, as well as the recording of the last sermon Martin Luther King had preached at Ebenezer. In it, he described the simple funeral he wanted but didn't get. "I think about my own death," the voice of the deceased Reverend blasted through the loudspeakers, as the onlookers kept total silence, some in tears. "I think about my own funeral and I don't think about it in a morbid sense..." These words were as chilling for the thousands of people who had flocked outside the church as they were for my audience, four thousand miles away.

Fifty-eight days later, Robert Kennedy was shot in Los Angeles by a twenty-four-year-old Palestinian immigrant, Sirhan Sirhan. I did not cover the event. After two gruesome years, very little sleep and lots of running around, I had decided to take a well-deserved vacation on the French Riviera. As I lounged on the beach the morning after my arrival, I heard a bellboy yelling, "A phone call for Mr. Dorian." It was my news director who asked me to take the first flight to Los Angeles. Realizing I'd arrive too late for any meaningful coverage, he changed his mind. My vacation was saved but I never forgave myself for having missed such an important news event that, I still feel, would impact American politics for years to come.

The coverage of Charles de Gaulle's trip to Canada was exhausting. The man was indefatigable. At age seventy-seven and half blind, he had the stamina of a robust twenty-year-old.

I was familiar with the rift that existed between French-speaking and English-speaking Canadians, with the resentment and often the hate French Canadians harbored for their British fellow countrymen. Quebec's Prime Minister Daniel Johnson often spoke with me about the separatist movement, in the course of several interviews I conducted with him. Canadians on both sides of the issue were convinced that their country would cease to exist the moment Quebec gained its independence, that provinces bordering the US, such as Alberta, Saskatchewan and Manitoba, would rally the US flag and would decide to become US territory if Quebec seceded. It is in the context of that political atmosphere that General de Gaulle accepted Daniel Johnson's invitation to attend Expo 67.

The French president could have flown to Canada. Instead, he crossed the Atlantic aboard *Le Colbert*, a warship named after the minister of Louis XIV, Jean-Baptiste Colbert who had presided over the first French migration to Canada. These choices were loaded with symbolism. The approach by sea allowed de Gaulle to make an impressive, traditional landing at Quebec City without any possibility of going first to Ottawa. "Stubbornly insisting that the French-speaking Canadians were part of the French nation," wrote the Canadian author J.F. Bosher in his book entitled *The Gaullist Attack on Canada,* "De Gaulle wanted to be able to encourage and patronize them without deferring in any way to the Canadian government."

I was far too busy handling the moment to speculate on the general's political objectives. Overwhelmed by his energy and by the enthusiasm of the crowds gathered on his passage, as he traveled through twenty-two communities and delivered sixteen speeches on his ten and a half hour trip to Montreal along the so-called *Chemin du Roy*, I focused on the people's reactions to his visit.

In one much-quoted speech, de Gaulle said that the journey had reminded him of his trip to liberate Paris in 1944, a statement that said volumes about his state of mind.

On that Monday, July 24, 1967, I tried to keep up with the French president—a daunting task—and often found myself at his side. He never acknowledged my presence, maybe because he was too tall or because he had partially lost his vision. He made a stop in each community along the road that paralleled the Saint Lawrence River and shook the hands of the officials who had lined up in the hopes of being acknowledged by the tall man. He addressed mayors and other high-ranking civil servants by their full names, which was in my opinion an incredible memory stunt. His people had briefed him, of course, but the fact that he remembered the names and functions of so many amazed me. I recorded the sixteen speeches he delivered. They were, to quote J.F. Bosher once more, "full of allusions to the essential Frenchness of each occasion and of Quebec itself. All of them were tinctured with hostility to Confederation and fully in tune with a rebuff to federal government."

A luncheon had been prepared for the general and his retinue at Sainte Anne-de-Beaupré. We had installed microphones on the long banquet table and had connected them to our tape recorders in an adjacent room reserved for the press. These mics were live. They allowed us to listen to the conversations between de Gaulle and the two women who flanked him. He loved to tell women dirty jokes.

We traveled from Quebec to Sainte-Anne de Beaupré, Petit-Cap, Sainte-Anne-de-la-Pérade, Trois-Rivières, Louisville, Berthierville, Repentigny, hamlets with names that could have been those of villages in France. We reached Montréal at seven in the evening.

A half hour later, the general delivered his infamous *Vive le Quebec libre!* in front of City Hall. He had not been expected to speak that evening, but when the frenzied crowd chanted for him, he said to the Mayor of Montréal, "I have to speak to these people who are calling for me." He then stepped out onto the balcony and gave a short address that concluded with,

"Long live free Quebec! Long live French Canada! And long live France!"

The multitude of French-speaking Canadians who surrounded me could not contain their excitement and felt that the French head of state had miraculously freed them from the yoke of the British. Were these four words deliberate or were they a blunder? Few believed that the general had committed a gaffe. It would have been so out of character. De Gaulle had interfered with Canada's internal affairs and had done so on purpose. He had confided to his son-in-law, General Alain de Boissieu, "I will hit hard. Hell will happen, but it has to be done. It's the last occasion to repent for France's betrayal," a reference to what de Gaulle viewed as France's abandonment of sixty thousand French colonists to the British after France was defeated in the North American Theater of the Seven Years War in 1763.

Pierre Trudeau, who had just been appointed Minister of Justice, wondered what the French reaction would have been if a Canadian Prime Minister had said "Brittany to the Bretons." De Gaulle's bombshell produced serious tensions between Canada and France. Most Canadian and some French newspapers condemned it. Given the cool reactions from the federal government, everyone wondered whether the general would be welcome in Ottawa or if he would dare show up in the Canadian capital, as was originally planned.

The following day, the French president visited Expo 67, which had been the pretext for his Canadian tour in the first place. He hopped from pavilion to pavilion, leaving us journalists in the dust. Incapable of keeping pace, I chose to lag behind in the company of the elegant Couve de Murville, de Gaulle's Foreign Minister and Roger Vaurs, a high-ranking official. The two men had decided to take their time and let their president outdistance them.

De Gaulle was already inside the US pavilion when we reached its entrance. A security guard stopped us and asked Couve de Murville for his ID. The foreign minister explained that he was part of the French delegation and that he did not have papers on him. The guard refused to let him in, unaware that he could have triggered an international incident. Lucky for him, Couve, as he was familiarly called, had a great sense of humor. He shrugged his shoulders, turned to us and said with a disarming smile, "Okay, then. We'll walk around the building. Their loss."

Europe #1 asked me to go to Ottawa ahead of de Gaulle to get reactions to his *"Vive le Quebec libre!"* I arrived in the Canadian capital. When I learned that the general had cut his visit short, I decided to take a nap. I woke up forty-eight hours later.

De Gaulle had failed to acknowledge that these people he had come to liberate were not French citizens, even though they used a French dialect sprinkled with gallicized English words and expressions, spoken with such a funny accent that we, the French, could not understand. No, they were not French. They were North Americans. De Gaulle had never forgiven Roosevelt and Churchill for having mistrusted him during World War II. He had let his resentment for Anglo-Saxons blind him to reality.

As I cringed at the Frenchman's arrogance, I realized that maybe I had become a turncoat. Was I no longer French? Had I stopped thinking, reasoning, rationalizing like a Frenchman? Possibly.

Europe #1 asked me to organize the coverage of the 1968 Summer Olympics in Mexico City. I had already made two trips to work out the details of our setup for a live coverage. In April, I returned to the Mexican capital to finalize all arrangements. Maurice Siegel, the head of news, decided to accompany me. It's not that he didn't trust me. He came along to impress upon high-ranking Mexican officials to give us what we needed. He had clout. I didn't.

The forty-nine-year-old journalist had a clear conception of how news should be handled. It had to be dramatic and "personalized." Maurice expected his journalists to be aggressive, competitive, even theatrical. He wanted them to breathe life into their reporting, to provoke strong emotions, even to shock when they covered historical moments, whether they were coups, wars, revolutions, assassinations, or natural disasters. News had to be entertaining.

Sylvain Floirat, a powerful French businessman, had taken over the ownership of Europe #1 at the request of the French government. He exerted considerable influence on Maurice Siegel, and by extension, on the news operation of the station. News aired by Europe #1 had to meet the owner's approval. If it didn't, as was the case now and then, Siegel would receive a phone call.

It didn't take great insight for me to realize that Maurice was as much a political animal as he was a journalist, juggling between his duties as head of the news department and the pressures exerted by the men in power. This did not mean he acted as a doormat. He knew which battles to wage and when to wage them and never shied away from a confrontation, even with Floirat. His bottom line was to insure that Europe #1 remained number one.

I was never pressured into giving my reports an orientation that suited the political correctness of the moment. But my editor's repeated demands for stories on riots, protest movements, opposition to the war in Vietnam, poverty or racism could have been construed as a form of partiality. The French media was fond of news that demeaned America.

Europe #1's main competitors were Radio Luxembourg, another private station, and various state-owned outfits that weren't as free, precisely because the government owned them. Whichever party was in power scrutinized their news broadcasts like watchdogs. In fact, the CEOs of these outfits were often replaced, their more visible journalists demoted or taken off the air after the opposition had won an election. They'd make a comeback once their party regained power. That's the way things worked in France.

Europe #1 and Radio Luxembourg enjoyed a little bit more leeway but did not escape the scrutiny of politicians, owners or sponsors. A hard look at history seems to confirm that the so-called freedom of the press was a myth in the land of Zola and Voltaire.

State control in France peaked between 1944 and 1954. On August 26, 1945, Charles de Gaulle, head of the provisional government, nationalized the written and audio-visual press. The Gaullists felt that in order for it to be objective, it had to be made into a public service operation. All newspapers, radio stations and publishing companies were collectivized and sequestered. They were then given to journalists or publishers who were believed to have joined the resistance or were entrusted to corporations that would manage them without owning them. Ten years later, Prime Minister Pierre Mendès-France privatized the written press, but the government retained indirect control over circulation. A cooperative headed by the representatives of the Ministry of Information retained the monopoly of the paper used by all publications and determined the "fair" allotments of its stocks until 1986. The partial privatization of radio only happened in 1982 under François Mitterrand's presidency. Jacques Chirac privatized television four years later, but allowed state-owned television stations to operate. They still do.

The press in France gives the appearance of being free but faces government control at all levels. Agence France Presse, the largest French news agency, gets half of its revenues from the government. To exert additional control, the state determines which commercial sector can advertise in newspapers, radio and television stations, thus creating an artificial balance.

In 2010, the daily paper *Le Monde* claimed that national intelligence services had spied on it to discover its sources in the Woerth-Bettencourt case named after Liliane Bettencourt, the L'Oreal heiress. The scandal that involved alleged tax evasion and money laundering had embarrassed President Sarkozy's government because of allegations by Liliane Bettancourt's former bookkeeper that the billionairess and her late husband had made numerous illegal cash donations to conservative politicians. Sound familiar?

French journalists can protect their sources in theory, but the law does not protect the public servant who releases documents that should not have been classified but still were, which clearly indicated an abuse of power. Protection of sources has been under siege in France. That is not to say that America has been immune to these assaults. But the American press benefits from laws that protect its sources. The "reporter's privilege" in the US has been recognized in the Inter-American Declaration of Principles of Freedom of Expression, which states in Principle Eight that, "every social communicator has the right to keep his/her source of information, notes, and personal archives confidential." The most famous illustration of such principle is the series of articles by Washington Post reporters Bob Woodward and Carl Bernstein, which uncovered the Watergate scandal, ultimately leading to the resignation of President Richard Nixon. In France, such scandal would have never made it to the front page of the major dailies.

In 2010, an organization called *Reporters Without Borders*, ranked France forty-fourth in the world for its freedom of the press status behind Tanzania, Uruguay, Ghana and Jamaica. In this Press Freedom Index, the

US ranked twentieth, Finland first.

The coverage of Apollo 4 on November 9, 1967, took me to Launch Complex 39, from where I had anchored USIA's *Report from America*, three years back. The aim of the mission known as Apollo-Saturn 501 was to launch a Saturn V rocket without a crew on board. It was a dress rehearsal that would determine the future of the Apollo Program. If successful, and it was, it would allow NASA to pursue President Kennedy's goal to put a man on the moon by 1970.

The event gave me the opportunity to familiarize myself with Cape Canaveral, its launching pads, its huge Vertical Assembly Building, the fourth largest building in the world by volume, and with the crawlers-transporters, a pair of fourteen million dollar mammoth tracked vehicles used to transport the tall Saturn V rockets along the Crawlerway from the VAB to the Launch Complex. Cape Canaveral, later named Cape Kennedy, was impressive.

I had spent the past two to three years covering assassinations, mayhem and destruction. My colleagues were as worn out as I was by the string of depressing events that had plagued the United States in recent months. With maybe the exception of the first heart transplants, the space program was the only positive story I was asked to report on.

Apollo 7 aroused far more interest than Apollo 4 because it was to be the first manned US space mission. It was scheduled to take off on October 11, 1968, from Launch Complex 34 at 11:02:45 EST.

I flew from New York to Orlando the preceding day and drove in a rented car to Cocoa Beach in less than an hour. Accompanied by a few colleagues, we tried the first restaurant we could find and were in for a surprise. The menu, as thick as the Bible, offered such exotic fares as fried locusts, fried ants, turtle soup, hippopotamus stew, gazelle, crocodile and snake. While Walter Schirra, Donn Eisele and Walter Cunningham were about to explore space, we were venturing into unknown gastronomic territory. To this day, I don't know which of the two took more courage. Surprisingly though, we found the food quite good. I'd make a point to dine there every time I covered a space flight. The ASPCA would probably close such a place down nowadays.

Once back in my motel room, I studied NASA's flight plan, a book as fat as New York's telephone directory. Frustrated by the space lingo—try to understand "Passive Thermal Control" or "TLI burn"—I turned in.

I arrived at the entrance gate of Cape Canaveral at eight sharp the following morning, retrieved my pass at the press building and was escorted to the open press stand, the vantage point from which the media would witness the launch, almost four miles away from where the rocket stood, so far yet so close.

Droves of still and movie cameras were on standby. The press stand was packed with journalists from all over the world. These seasoned reporters who had witnessed all kinds of upheavals in their lives had left their jaded outlook of the world at the entrance gate. We all felt like kids waiting to be dazzled by some magic. "T-minus twenty-one seconds and counting. We have completed our power transfer. The Saturn V 1B vehicle, which now weighs one point three million pounds, is ready to go." If you are convinced like I am, that you witness nothing less than a miracle every time a 747 takes off and flies, then you'll understand how I felt when I laid my eyes on this massive phallus erected against the deep blue of the Florida sky. "This thing will never fly," I thought to myself.

The voice of Jack King, Chief of Public Information and Public Affairs Officer for NASA, broke out through the loudspeakers. Its unemotional and neutral undertone contrasted with the excitement and anticipation that filled the hearts and minds of everyone in attendance.

"Ten, nine, eight, seven, six, five, four, three, two, we have ignition. Commit lift off. We have lift off." The dragon spat a huge bowl of fire. The Saturn V rocket hesitated in an apparent standstill that only lasted a couple of seconds but felt like an eternity. Was it going to fall back in its flames? The ground trembled, as if a seven-magnitude earthquake had rocked it. The strong vibrations filled me with a mix of apprehension and euphoria. The thunderous, deafening roar intensified in a crescendo. The press stand would have been pulverized if it had been installed any closer to the launch pad. It seemed that Saturn V took forever to clear the tower as it rose in the air slowly and majestically. It picked up speed, leaving a long trail of fire and white condensation behind it. At two minutes and twenty-eight seconds into the flight, we witnessed the separation of the first stage. "We've got ignition and we're up to thrust on the second stage," announced mission control. Three minutes later, Saturn V became a speck in the sky. It then disappeared from view, leaving us in total awe.

As Saturn V lifted off, Walter Cronkite, who stood a few feet from me, lost his cool. "It's terrific. Look at it going!" he exclaimed, as excited as a ten-year-old. "This big glass window is shaking and we're holding it with our hands. Look at the rocket go..."

Apollo 7 lift off wasn't any less spectacular, but Cronkite had toned down his delivery while describing its launch. I hadn't. There is no way that the people who listened to my live reports in France and elsewhere could have missed my exhilaration.

The Manned Spacecraft Center, located southeast of Houston, took over the monitoring of the flight and all communications with the astronauts before Apollo 7 started its first orbit. Consequently, the entire press corps had to rush to Orlando Airport to catch a flight to Texas. We would follow the same routine for the subsequent Apollo missions, spending one day in Cocoa Beach and nine to ten days in Houston.

Apollo 8 was, in a way, every bit as spectacular as the landing on the moon because it accomplished so many firsts. Its astronauts were the first humans to pass through the Van Allen radiation belts, which extend up to fifteen thousand miles from Earth. At fifty-five hours and forty minutes into the flight, they became the first humans to enter the gravitational sphere of influence of another celestial body. When the spacecraft came out from behind the moon for its fourth pass across the front, the crew witnessed Earthrise for the first time in human history.

Contrary to other launches that took place late morning, Apollo 8 lift-off happened at seven fifty-one a.m., on December 21, 1968, three days before Christmas Eve. When we took our position in the press stand at six a.m., total darkness enveloped the launch pad, as powerful beams lit the tall rocket, adding drama to the sight. It felt like watching a science fiction movie. At the time of lift-off, the day had barely broken.

In Houston, I always stayed in a motel across from the Space Center. Its location was so ideal that journalists had to book their rooms weeks in advance. The balmy weather of southern Texas made most of us who came from the cold behave as if we had been vacationing at Club Med. The media took the motel swimming pool by storm and competed in crazy water polo games, *The New York Times* vs. *The Daily Telegraph*, CBS vs. *The Diario of Mexico*, *The Miami Herald* vs. *The Vancouver Metro*. News editors were mostly interested in takeoffs and landings. They wanted few status reports in between these events. Apollo 9 spent ten days in low orbit, between March 3 and March 13, 1969. Apollo 10, the dry run before the moon landing, lasted nine days from May 18 to May 26. We had ample time to frolic.

During the coverage of the two flights that preceded Apollo 11, I hung out with Jean-Claude Héberlé, my rival and nonetheless friend. He was at the time the correspondent of a French government-owned radio station.

Forty years later, my children asked my close friends to write a few words under the theme "I remember" for my seventieth birthday. This is what Jean-Claude wrote:

> The story takes place in 1969, in Houston, Texas. In a few days, in a few hours, the Apollo 10 astronauts will circle the moon. The entire planet is on pins and needles. Hundreds of journalists who flocked to the Space Center from the four corners of the world and who communicate in at least thirty foreign languages, have already spent hours, days, weeks boning up on the fat document given to them by NASA. It describes the mission in all its technical details, with hundreds of pages of copy, drawings, graphs, photographs and schedules. Aware that they will have to report live, these journalists better know this document almost by heart, because, at the other end, in Paris or anywhere else, their colleagues, who are comfortably cooped up in their little studios and who know diddly-squat about space flights or the English language, will delight in asking them questions about everything, including the sex of angels and how old their doormen are.
>
> We're staying in a small motel managed by a nice Canadian couple. We occasionally take a break at poolside

and fast realize that we're haunted, obsessed. We can't help but talk about space.

Daniel and I have devised a system that will pay off. We will play a game and cram at the same time. One of us stands at the edge of the pool, the other on the diving board. The one at poolside throws a question on a particular flight event to the other who counts to three, then jumps. He must come up with the right answer before hitting the water. For example, "How many seconds between the end of such and such maneuver and the opening of the airlock?"

" One, two, three." He jumps.

"Thirty-seven seconds."

Splash, he's in. The answer was correct. He gave it in time. We switch positions for the next question and repeat the motion ad nauseum.

Our coverage will be flawless. We will leave the competition in the dust.

Once the Apollo 10 mission is over, we will go for a last swim and will refrain from asking questions to each other. Relieved, we will fall into a deep sleep on our lounge chairs. We won't dream. We will just bask in the Texas sun."

It is astounding to see how fast humanity has taken space exploration for granted. After Apollo 11, the public at large lost interest. Today, shuttle flights to the space station barely make the first page of our dailies and are the object of brief mentions in television newscasts. We have all become as indifferent as Pablo Picasso who, following the first moon landing, declared, "It means nothing to me. I have no opinion about it, and I don't care." It can be argued, in his defense, that *Les Demoiselles d'Avignon* is a far more intriguing endeavor than any space launch. Propulsion holds no ambiguity, no paradox, no mysticism, no emotion. Conversely, art confounds, baffles, touches our inner selves. It bypasses our brain to target our soul directly. This is why we can forget or take for granted a space venture but are haunted by Van Gogh's *Starry Night*.

I would never deny the glory of the Apollo flights achievements.

Having had the privilege to witness them from so close might not have rattled my soul, but it revived the amazement, the wonder that used to strike me after I had read Jules Verne and Antoine de Saint-Exupéry.

Europe #1 wasn't my only source of revenue. I was still freelancing for CBC and for CKAC, a private radio station in Montreal, and was also writing articles for *L'Express*, the French equivalent of *Newsweek* or *Time*. I had plenty to report. Nineteen sixty-seven and nineteen sixty-eight were the most turbulent years of the decade. The war in Vietnam had divided the country. The Democrats were in shambles and the Republicans were bent on recapturing the White House. That suited me fine. There's nothing as lethal for a journalist as peacefulness and harmony. We need bad news to thrive. We feed on conflicts.

Europe #1 expected thorough pre-presidential election coverage, preferably sprinkled with sound bites from political personalities. Finding French-speaking people to interview was challenging. I had set my sights on Governor Nelson Rockefeller, who was fluent in French and was running for the presidency against Richard Nixon. He had been governor of the state of New York since 1959 and had tremendous influence within the Republican Party. I was ready to move heaven and earth for an interview with him.

I first called his press secretary and hit a wall. I couldn't get past his assistant who would end every telephone conversation with, "I'll give him the message, sir." The lady had no idea who she was up against. I called two to three times a day, until she gave up and decided to pass me on to her boss.

Rockefeller's press secretary was all business and no charm. My first conversation with him was brief. It concluded with a vague promise. "Call me back in a few days and I'll see what I can do." I called back and this time the assistant suggested that I put my request in writing. So I did, to no avail. I waited a week and called again. The press secretary picked up the phone. Had my luck turned? He remembered me. How could he not have? I begged. My insistence either annoyed him, wore him down or both. He threw me a bone to get rid of me. There was a governors' conference at the Hilton Hotel, he explained, that would be followed by a press conference. After that, the governor would speak to a few journalists, top reporters from *The New York Times*, *The Journal* and the three networks. It was then, the man assured me, that he would arrange for me to ask the governor a few questions.

The room at the Hilton was packed with the usual suspects, their writing pads in hand, cameras and tape recorders at the ready. The second the governor stepped in, the din stopped. The clickety-clack of shutters and the pops from flashes filled the silence for a brief moment. Once the press conference ended and most of its participants left, the governor stepped away from the podium and was surrounded by the handful of journalists he had handpicked for an intimate "give and take." I recognized Walter Cronkite, Peter Jennings and my friend Lou Cioffi from ABC.

I remained in the back, a few feet away from the group, patiently waiting for the press secretary to come and get me. The mini press conference was about to end and nothing was happening. The man was avoiding looking at me, a body language that clearly indicated that he had once again given me the runaround. I took a deep breath, grabbed my tape recorder and crossed the auditorium. The press secretary rushed toward me and laid his hand on my chest, in an effort to stop me from reaching his boss. I pushed him hard and sent him tumbling into the empty chairs. Startled by the noise, everyone turned to me. I seized this short distraction, held my mic at arm's length like a lance, and attacked Rockefeller head on. "Governor, do you think that the recent riots in Newark and Detroit have impacted national unity?" I asked in French. The interview lasted a few minutes. After giving me his last answer, Rockefeller exclaimed in English, "You're very patient, you know. You have a lot of patience." My American colleagues applauded. One of them said, "way to go!" My persistence had paid off, but I doubt my editor would ever be aware of the hurdles I had to surmount to secure this material.

From then on, the governor called me 'Frenchy', not offensively but in an affectionate way, and never turned me down for interviews. The last one he granted me was at the occasion of the opening of the Michael C. Rockefeller exhibit at the New York Metropolitan Museum. He had given the museum the collection of Asmat art his youngest son, Michael, had assembled before his disappearance in New Guinea, late 1961. During that interview, he had been quite emotional. The death of his son had affected him. As was often the case, Jean-Pierre Laffont took photos of the event.

One of them reveals the governor's fondness for me, as he answers one of my questions, his hand covering mine in a caring gesture. I liked him too. He had a heart.

Any European attending a National Convention for the first time is bound to question the soundness, rationality and seriousness of the American political system, given the chaos, the brouhaha and the puerility of these proceedings. When Republicans and Democrats gather every four years to choose their candidate for the presidency, they throw a party that makes the carnival in Rio look tame and organized. But the hoopla, the funny hats, the trepidations, the chanting, the hysteria as well as other exuberant and often comical manifestations are smokescreens for serious business. Not only will each party elect its candidate for the highest office of the land, it will also come up with a platform that will define its mission and provide a list of its political objectives for the next four years.

When I landed in Miami in the late afternoon of August 4, 1968, the searing and muggy air knocked me down, mellowing me out as effectively as a couple of valiums. It sapped my energy. The following day I recovered the moment I entered the excessively air conditioned Miami Beach Convention Center. The Republicans were fired up, poised to reclaim the White House. The Democrats had been weakened by an unpopular war and racial violence. They were on the defensive. The future looked good for the Grand Old Party.

The outcome of this nomination process was predictable. Richard Nixon, Eisenhower's former VP, emerged as the frontrunner from the start. His two opponents, the liberal Nelson Rockefeller and California Governor Ronald Reagan lagged far behind. Nixon's significant lead killed the suspense and somewhat lessened the interest my radio station had in the proceedings. Still, the Democrats had been at the helm for eight years. The end of their reign would also mark the end of a tumultuous era in American history. That alone was a matter of great import.

Jacques Sallebert, the head of the French Broadcasting System, had secured a cubicle in a corner of the convention floor, next to Agence France Presse. It was my base to which I'd always return after having roamed the place, spoken to delegates, conducted interviews, chased after caucuses and snooped around for juicy stories.

On the evening of Wednesday, August 7, 1968, an AP wire alerted me that riots had erupted in a section of Miami known as Liberty City. The disturbances were contained in a small area. They would have remained unnoticed had they erupted elsewhere. But blacks had rebelled in the city Republicans had chosen for their convention and, what is more, the night before the nomination. The incident was newsworthy, so I decided to check it out. Jacques Sallebert dispatched one of his cameramen to accompany me. He was a tall and muscular fellow named Jean-Claude Luyat. A photographer from AP joined us.

The three of us exited the convention center at around eight-thirty and took a taxi. The cabbie refused to take us to our final destination, dumping us in the middle of nowhere. "That's as far as I'll go," he told us categorically. Liberty City, he said, was straight ahead. Luyat grabbed his Aries. I took hold of my heavy and cumbersome Nagra and we started to walk in the direction of trouble.

Liberty City, also listed as "Model City"—what an oxymoron—was home to a large and poor African-American population in North West Miami. We knew we had reached it when we found ourselves surrounded by blacks, in an area blanketed by four-story housing projects, all identical, all built in cement.

Each floor featured long and narrow open galleries that extended the length of entire blocks and linked these low-income buildings to one another. They were mobbed by a restless crowd on edge, ready to burst. The oppressive humidity made matters worse.

We ventured deeper into the ghetto, unnoticed for a while, but it didn't take long before a bunch of black men and women, who were assembled on the second floor gallery of one of these buildings, spotted us. They followed us from above, some of them raising their fists and heaping profanities on us. An empty bottle crashed on the pavement a few feet from where I stood, then another one. A heavy black woman ran frantically along the gallery, pushing and shoving her way through the crowd, holding a chair at arm's length. She flew down the first staircase she could find, hit the street and sprinted after me. I tried to get away, but she was surprisingly faster than I thought she would be. She crashed the chair on my back with unexpected strength. It must have been a cheap piece of furniture. It exploded in hundreds of pieces. No one had ever attacked me with such hostility. I was unharmed but shaken.

Jean-Claude Luyat and the journalist from AP picked up speed. I tried to keep up with them, but the weight of my Nagra slowed me down. Suddenly, a dozen young blacks emerged from nowhere and chased us. One of them grabbed the strap of my tape recorder from behind me and pulled it hard, making me fall on my ass. He snatched the expensive machine and disappeared with it. I picked myself up and ran. His cohorts, energized by what they saw, redoubled their efforts to catch me. One of them got hold of my jacket and tore it off. Another ripped my watch off my wrist. It was a solid gold Movado my father's best friend had given to me before he passed away. A third tripped me up and punched me in the face before I hit the pavement. The rest of the pack swooped down on me like bees on the warpath and kicked me in the stomach and in the face with a vengeance. I felt like a pig about to be slaughtered. I shouted hysterically, "I am French. Please, I am French." A young man smashed a baseball bat on my skull. I staggered under the blow but remained conscious. A thought came to me in a flash; these were my last moments on earth. Another youth hit me again with his baseball bat. All lights faded.

When I came to, I found myself lying in the back of a police car, weak and numb. As I tried to raise myself in the sitting position, I heard someone say, "Take it easy, boy. Stay down." I managed to look at myself in the rear view mirror. What I saw scared the hell out of me. That face, torn, cut, bloody and swollen couldn't possibly be mine. A blinding lamp dazzled me. Jean-Claude Luyat, his camera mounted with a flood lamp, was filming me. The newsman that I was had turned newsmaker.

I would have been dead if that police car hadn't showed up. An ambulance pulled in next to it. I was taken to the nearest hospital where I had to go through a battery of tests. Miraculously, I suffered no fracture, though I still can feel an indentation on the top of my skull. A young intern sewed more than twenty stitches inside my mouth.

As soon as I woke up at five the following morning, I picked up the telephone in my hospital room, called Europe #1 and informed Bruno Dahl, the man in charge of correspondents, of my whereabouts. He already knew. My story had made the first page of the leading French newspapers. Bruno asked me if I was up to participating in a live Q&A for *Europe Midi*, the newscast that included public participation. I said I'd try. He called me back an hour later and connected me to the studio. Journalists and listeners asked me detailed questions about my ordeal. I answered the best I could, my speech hampered by the stitches inside my mouth. One of them wanted to know if I felt any resentment. I answered that I could not blame all blacks for the actions of a few.

I was released from the hospital the day Richard Nixon was officially nominated by his party. I flew back home and took a cab to Westchester, a suburb of New York, where my wife and my three-year-old daughter had spent the week at a friend's house. I knew my physical appearance would justify the apprehensions my wife felt whenever I had to cover race riots. I got out of the cab and rang the bell of her friend's brownstone. The hostess opened and took me to the living room where my three-year-old daughter was playing. When she saw me, she burst into tears and ran into her mother's arms. I tried to pick her up, but she became hysterical. My face was still swollen and scarred, my lips had stitches and my black eyes made me look like Frankenstein's monster. I had spooked my daughter out of her wits. The scene reminded me of *Somebody Up There Likes Me*, a movie in which the boxer Rocky Graziano, played by Paul Newman, returns home disfigured by a succession of bouts and triggers identical reactions from his kid.

My youth, the passion I felt for my work, my eagerness helped me fast forget the incident. It did not traumatize me. I proudly perceived it as a sort of baptism of fire and I looked forward to covering the next event.

The mere mention of the 1968 Democratic Convention brings back the vivid memory of the foul smell of stink bombs and of the stinging and blinding of tear gas that turned the lobby of the Chicago Hilton where I stayed into hell. Mid-afternoon, on Wednesday, August 28, 1968, two days after the start of the Democratic Convention, ten thousand protesters had rallied legally at Grant Park. When a young boy disrespectfully lowered the American flag, police broke through the crowd and began beating him. Protesters threw food, rocks, bags of urine and chunks of concrete at them, first chanting "Hell no, we won't go," referring to Vietnam, then switching to "Pigs are whores." Police responded by spraying mace at demonstrators and innocent bystanders indiscriminately. Protesters upped the ante with chants of "kill, kill, kill." An empty coke bottle hit my head. Tom Hayden, one of the leaders of Students for a Democratic Society, an organization opposed to the war, encouraged the protesters to move out of the park. If they were going to be tear-gassed, he felt, then the whole city would have to be tear-gassed as well. If blood were spilled in Chicago, it would be spilled throughout the city. That's what incited the crowd to storm the Hilton Hotel. I was told later that the commotion had disturbed the Democratic candidate Hubert Humphrey, as he was taking a shower. This day would be known as "Police Riot Day."

The preceding Sunday, anti-war leaders had been denied city permits that would have allowed them to sleep in Lincoln Park and to demonstrate outside the convention site. That night, William Burroughs took to the stage and addressed the crowd. Jean Genet, who came to Chicago as a reporter to cover the convention for a French magazine, spoke next. The French novelist, playwright and poet had been prohibited from entering the US and had traveled from Canada illegally with his Black Panthers friends. "I am pleased that white America is threatened by these dogs," he said, alluding to the German Shepherds the Chicago police were using to intimidate and attack the protesters, "these dogs who dispensed the same brutality against blacks in Alabama. It's therefore good that American dogs devour American whites." I didn't need a Ph.D. in psychology to guess how the Chicago police felt after hearing these provocative words. The coldness in their eyes expressed their profound contempt for the foreigner who had come to their town to insult the white race and who, by the same token, had humiliated them. For their part, the multitude of hippies loved these inflammatory remarks. They craved words that would feed their anger and incite them to action. These amateur anarchists were bent on creating havoc. They were determined to do battle with one of the most repressive and cruel police forces this country had ever assembled, knowing full well that they didn't stand a chance. Yet, they seemed eager to be immolated in the name of their convictions.

Law enforcement had received strict orders from the top to crush the rebellion at all costs. Mayor Richard Daley had raised an army of forty thousand cops and National Guardsmen.

The following day, I recorded the black comedian and social critic

Dick Gregory when he addressed the same crowd that was now surrounded by hundreds of police and National Guard on the ready. "You can look around and you can see from the amount of police and the amount of federal soldiers, you must be doing something right," he said. Rows and rows of policemen armed with billy clubs shoved the demonstrators, leaving behind hordes of youngsters lying on the pavement and bleeding from blows in the head. Tear gas grenades exploded everywhere. Chaos reached an intensity I had rarely seen.

"I was chanting Om... Om, a holy prayer with a hundred kids joining me under a fucking tree," said Allen Ginsberg, "when the tear gas came from all these cops advancing on us behind a fucking National Guard tank. There was no reason to it."

"They were like vicious dogs, yapping, snapping, every bit as hysterical as their fucking handlers," Burroughs added. "Me, I wallowed in this violent maelstrom, like a dog rolling with relish all over the putrefied corpse of a dead skunk."

Photojournalist Art Shay wrote:

> By the happy circumstance of being a lucky photojournalist (I was shooting for *Time*), I was in a gaggle of journalists blinded by tear gas who stumbled out of Lincoln Park, across City Street, and into the minuscule lobby of the Lincoln Hotel.
>
> Ten feet into the door, coughing and wiping tears with me were small, sturdy, egg-bald Jean Genet, the Gallic Sartrian bête noire, his momentary girlfriend of the week, poet Allen Ginsberg, and adding machine company heir and heavy user William S. Burroughs. For lagniappe, there was William Styron leaning on a plastic-marble wall.
>
> My first picture was of Genet tissuing a slight wound on his left forehead and muttering imprecations against the police in French, as Allen Ginsberg comforts him. Fortuitously I included the small wooden sawhorse in the lobby displaying a long green and yellow sign dispensed by the city, "Welcome to Chicagoland."

It wasn't Ginsberg's first confrontation with law enforcement. In the several interviews I had conducted with him while covering anti-war protests and in particular the march against the Pentagon in March 1967 during which I, incidentally, was locked up and forced to spend the night inside the US Department of Defense headquarters, the bard consistently expressed his staunch opposition to the war and condemned any form of repression unconditionally. He once told me "cops had a 'provincial' hatred for culture, freedom and for conscience."

I felt as unsafe in the streets of Chicago as I had in the streets of any American ghetto, as I stood with my friend Paul Slade, from the French magazine *Paris-Match*, sandwiched between protesters and the National Guard, their rifles at ready, bayonets fixed. I was also roughed up on the convention floor, but wasn't punched by ground security, as was Dan Rather, the future CBS anchorman. Inside, the convention had turned as tumultuous as outside.

Given these circumstances, you'd think that the place was secure. In fact, the people in charge of security had outdone themselves. They had issued the press four passes we had to swipe to release a narrow and claustrophobic turnstile located at the entrance of the Chicago International Amphitheater, a large structure adjacent to the Union Stock Yards. These passes made of lead were electronically encoded and bore a different color, one for each day. The technology was way ahead of its time.

On Thursday, August 29, 1968, I arrived early at that entrance and reached for my right pocket where I kept my valuable papers. The pass wasn't there. I feverishly checked all my pockets over and over again. It was lost. I was crestfallen. I turned to a French colleague and said jokingly, "You know what, let me try my Amex card." I slid it in the slot and the turnstile opened, as if by magic. So much for security.

Most of that day, I hung out with two delegates, Theodore Bikel, the folk singer, and Robert Ryan, the actor. Both men were opposed to the war in Vietnam. Bikel, who spoke French fluently, had granted me many interviews in the past. I liked him. He was easygoing and warm. Ryan, who always played bad guys in movies, was concerned about the state of things in America and bent on trying to make a difference. In fact, his presence as a delegate surprised me. I would never have imagined then that a Hollywood actor would get involved in politics, let alone accept being a delegate for his party. This was way before Ronald Reagan's presidency.

Acknowledging that there was "division in the American House" five months earlier on March 31, 1968, Lyndon B. Johnson had declared in the name of unity, "I shall not seek and I will not accept the nomination of my party for another term as your President." His successor and Vice-President had won the nomination of his party on that fourth day of the convention, but the prospects for the Democrats of carrying the day against a Republican Party that had coalesced behind Richard Nixon were low. President Johnson's decision not to run did not produce an ounce of unity. In fact, the Democratic Convention had shown to the world how divided America was. The violence and chaos displayed during these four days of August 1968 had put on view a party in disarray. The Democrats had committed suicide. They would have to wait almost a decade before regaining power for a brief period, to lose it again for another twelve years.

That convention had given us the kind of stuff reporters dream of: action, violence, suspense and controversy. But it also left a bad taste in the mouths of those who loved their country. In its immediate aftermath, many of us were left with sadness and anger. The main issue for which the young demonstrators had fought remained unsettled. They would have to wait another five years before the signing of the Paris Peace Accords with Hanoi, on January 27, 1973.

I remained with Europe #1 another year. Eisenhower's funeral in Washington on March 30, 1969, was the last significant event I covered for the French radio station. It gave me one more occasion to stand next to General de Gaulle in the Capitol Rotunda where Eisenhower's body lay in state. The Frenchman had come to pay his respects to his companion-in-arms for whom he nourished great affection.

I'd have to move back to France if I was going to pursue a career in journalism. It was out of the question. America had become my home.

On this side of the Atlantic, the political scene had gotten boring under the Nixon Administration. The country had quieted down. The blacks didn't burn their houses anymore, the opponents to the war had lost their oomph, and the hippies had turned bourgeois. This new order had taken the fun out of reporting. Nixon's tenure would be marked by only two surprises, the first when he and Henry Kissinger opened relations between the US and China, the second when Nixon's staff was caught orchestrating the breaking and entering into the Democratic National Committee headquarters, triggering a scandal that would lead to his resignation.

I had mouths to feed. My wife was expecting another child. I was thirty-two. It was time for me to settle down. I spread the word that I was looking for a steady job.

In July 1969, I received a phone call from the Director of Air France's operations in the US. He needed an assistant director for his public relations department. Would I be interested? I'd be given a nice office, a secretary, free air travel and I'd work regular hours. I resigned from Europe #1 and took the job.

29

The Final Stretch

Life is the sum of all your choices.
—ALBERT CAMUS

Until now, the White House had been my office, the Capitol and the United Nations my hangouts. I had been reporting the facts. I now had to embellish them.

My stay at Air France, though not always inspiring, might have contributed to making me a little more American than I already felt. My travels as a foreign correspondent had given me the opportunity to familiarize myself with America and the American way of life. But my involvement with the battle to secure landing rights in New York for Concorde—the first commercial supersonic aircraft—helped me grasp in a palpable way the power of grassroots, a civil right ingrained in the American DNA, an entitlement endemic to the American persona, the ultimate expression of freedom. Something most foreigners have trouble understanding fully.

The introduction to the US of this amazing aircraft spoke volumes about the French and British resentment to what they felt was American protectionism, and, in contrast, revealed the average citizen's determination to fight tooth and nail to preserve his quiet environment. The outcome this confrontation between the people of Queens and two of the most powerful European powers had turned out to be irrelevant to me. What was not irrelevant was that average people had formed a coalition powerful enough to threaten the future of the Concorde. This is something I learned to respect.

The turf war between France and the UK, as they introduced their awesome flying machine to the world, also disclosed appalling pettiness.

The French and the British had been working on the design of a supersonic aircraft since the late fifties. Construction of two prototypes began in 1965: 001 built by Aerospatiale in Toulouse and 002 by BAC at Filton, Bristol. In an effort to honor the treaty between France and the UK that led to its creation, they called the airplane Concorde, a word that the French dictionary defines as harmony of feelings or of wills. The English cognate for it is concord, without an e. So, in this battle of egos between two old foes, that little vowel at the end of the name spelled victory for the French.

In the UK, the aircraft was initially referred to as Concorde until it was officially changed to Concord by Harold MacMillan, England's PM, in response to a statement by Charles de Gaulle in which the general dashed Britain's hopes of joining the Common Market.

At the rollout, which took place several months later at Aerospatiale in Toulouse, the British Minister for Technology, Tony Benn, announced that he would change the spelling back to Concorde, thus creating a nationalist uproar. Benn appeased his fellow countrymen by stating that the suffix 'e' represented "Excellence, England, Europe and *Entente Cordiale.*" Yeah, right! In fact, the former Minister received a letter from an irate Scotsman claiming, "You talk about 'e' for England, but part of it is made in Scotland." The nose cone of the aircraft had indeed been built in Scotland. Benn replied, "It was also 'e' for *Ecosse,*" the French name for Scotland, "and I might have added 'e' for extravagance and 'e' for escalation as well." What mattered the most to the French was that the e had been reinstated. The country's honor had been saved.

Concorde flew at 1,350 miles per hour, (Mach 2.04), almost twice the speed of sound. A record. It consumed a ton of fuel per passenger on the Paris-New York run, also a record. What a sleek aircraft it was with its double-delta shaped wings and its needle-like droop nose. A French daily compared it proudly to a beautiful white bird.

The plane was new, sexy, way ahead of its time. I proposed we make a promotional movie that would highlight the technical prowess of this new aircraft and flaunt the advantages of supersonic travel.

My director of photography took a few standard shots of takeoffs and landings, but he and I wanted something more dramatic, a sequence that would illustrate the grace and power of this incredible machine. We positioned ourselves at the end of the runway.

After a half hour wait, the Concorde made its grand appearance, slowly turned at the far end of the runway and positioned itself for takeoff, pointing its nose at us like a prehistoric bird stalking its prey. Then the thunderous noise of its Rolls-Royce/Snecma Olympus 593 engines being revved up pierced the silence of this pristine morning. Concorde, enveloped by the distorting heat waves its powerful jet engines had generated, hesitated before rolling toward us majestically. Its roar amplified as it built up speed. Its needle nose dashed straight at us, like an arrow. The moment the aircraft lifted off, almost grazing us, my camera man's body made a fast hundred-eighty-degree turn to film its belly and to follow it up as it climbed. The powerful thrust of the engines had flattened us down to the ground. My exhilaration almost matched the one I felt when witnessing an Apollo lift off.

Most opponents of the Concorde claimed it was deafening at takeoff. It was counter-argued that the decibel level produced by a New York subway entering a station was higher than that produced by Concorde. These observations didn't silence the people adverse to the SST. The most vocal among them was Carol Berman, a New York Democrat who had been part of the leadership of *The Emergency Coalition to Stop the SST*. Concorde was flying over her Lawrence home on approach. Starting in May 1977, she fomented a series of protests at Kennedy Airport during which as many as a thousand cars drove along the main airport roadway at peak time, driving at five to ten miles per hour.

As soon as the US government lifted the ban on Concorde in February 1977, the Port Authority of New York opposed the federal decision to grant it landing rights and barred it from operating to and from JFK.

The development costs of the supersonic had neared two billion dollars. British Airways and Air France had bought each aircraft for forty-six million dollars a piece. A lot was at stake. The French and British governments and their two flagship airlines pooled their resources. British, French, American lawyers, government officials, executives, public relation and advertising specialists were called upon to fight the interdiction in every conceivable way. They called themselves the Concorde Group. As member of that group, I battled the opponents of progress, even appeared in several TV news shows as well as entertainment programs such as "What's My Line," unabashedly promoting the supersonic.

The French felt that the US government had conspired against the Concorde to protect the interests of American airlines and by extension the US economy. They refused to admit that the opposition to the SST was a grass-root reaction, born out of the discontent of the people from Queens and Brooklyn who didn't want the noise to impact their quality of life. They blamed the federal government and dismissed localism as the source of the problem. They could not fathom that average Joes, who lived in communities as small as Rockaway, Ozone Park, Lawrence, Inwood, Canarsie or Long Beach, could unite and create a political body powerful enough to exert pressure on local institutions, such as the Port Authority. If a similar situation had arisen in France, the government would not have let the people living near and around Charles De Gaulle Airport interfere. It would have made a unilateral decision in favor of the aircraft, regardless of the opposition. I don't think that executives from Air France or French government officials ever believed in the grass-root theory. It was beyond their comprehension and maybe beyond their culture.

Air France who had been my employer for close to nine years, did not pay well, was too sedentary for my taste and had become routine. It was time for me to reinvent myself once more. In 1979, my friend Eliane informed me that Sygma-USA, the photo news agency she had created with her husband Jean-Pierre, was looking for a director. She knew I had been the correspondent of Europe #1 and therefore felt that I possessed the journalistic competence to assume this responsibility. She recommended me to Hubert Henrotte, the head and creator of Sygma-Paris, the man who invented modern photojournalism.

He was relieved to have found in me a candidate who might put his New York subsidiary back on its feet—and I did. He allowed me to head this dynamic company for almost a year.

Whatever happened in the four corners of the planet impacted my life and that alone was rewarding. One day it was the Soviet invasion of Afghanistan, another El Salvador, the next Somalia or Ethiopia. If my undivided attention wasn't given to the Shah of Iran's flight into Egypt or to Cuban refugees, it was given to the Pope in Africa or to Mount St. Helens' eruption. While I lived some fascinating but also difficult moments—it is not easy to manage news photographers—I was way too busy to think about anything other than world news.

Circumstances outside my control precipitated my departure from Sygma. I had earned enough money and some wiggle room to start anew at age forty-two. I was still young, yet not that young to start all over again. The odds were not in my favor. I had no other choice but to move on.

I decided to start my own film production company. A real challenge. Eight years from then, I'd turn fifty. Most producers who were starting in the profession were in their early thirties, and those who were my age and had survived were well established. Besides, the city was overpopulated with moviemakers. The number of film production companies in New York neared a thousand. The competition was brutal.

Lacking the know-how to produce feature films, I was ready to try my hands at just about everything else, travel films, public service announcements, corporate presentations, documentaries, anything that required a camera. Such was the dream. I just had to find a way to realize it quickly. My savings were not going to last forever.

Like a restaurant owner in search of a chef, I had to find a talented cameraman. Without one, I had nothing to sell. Laying my hands on a reliable director of photography proved to be challenging. Where could I turn?

By mid-afternoon on that first day, I made two executive moves: I named my company DDC Productions, DDC standing for Daniel Dorian Communications, and I called my editor friend Bob Duffus to ask him to get me the names of cameramen who were freelancing for the production companies that were his clients, most of them specialized in TV commercials.

A few hours after having made these decisions as President, General Manager and sole employee of a production company that had so far produced diddly-squat, I was emotionally spent, anxious and filled with self-doubt. I didn't sleep much that night.

The next morning, Bob gave me the names and phone numbers of a few cameramen with excellent credentials. These guys were making tons of money shooting TV ads, I thought. They didn't need the work, but what the hell... I had nothing to lose. I called the first name on the list. "Jim?"

"Yeah?"

I cleared my throat. "My name is Daniel Dorian and I'm starting a film production company." I can imagine what went through the guy's mind when he heard this world-changing piece of news. "Are you still with me?"

"Yep."

"Um... I'm... I'm looking for a cameraman."

"For a specific job?"

"No... not exactly. At least not for the moment, but..."

"Listen, Dude, why don't you call me back when you have something concrete to offer."

I called a few other names from Bob's list and faced similar rejection. What was going on? I was begging them to allow me to work on their behalf; I was ready to slave sixteen hours a day to find jobs for them and they were not interested? Of course they weren't. Why would they be? I had produced and directed a few travel films. So what? They knew my chances of finding work for them were close to nil.

At the end of that second day, my enthusiasm had shrunk considerably but I never asked myself what I'd do if I didn't make it. I was down but didn't think for an instant that I would fail. I had chosen a difficult path and was convinced that something would eventually break. I just had to give it some time. I would never have taken such a risk had I not been as insanely confident as I was.

Obstinacy and patience paid off. It took me less than a year to build a sustainable business and a list of prestigious clients, among them three major European governments and a few leading US corporations. DDC thrived for close to thirty years.

30

I Am an American!

The making of an American begins at the point where he himself rejects all other ties, any other history, and himself adopts the vesture of his adopted land.

—JAMES BALDWIN

The Immigration and Naturalization Service of the US Department of Justice granted me a green card on May 14, 1964, allowing me to reside in the US as a permanent resident. On September 1, 1982, eighteen years later, I received citizenship at the United States District Court for the Southern District of New York.

It took me eighteen years to acquire the US nationality. Maybe I felt that I didn't have to become an American to prove my love for America. Maybe I had been too lazy or too busy to make it happen earlier. I had procrastinated.

My friend Ralph Friedman told me as early as 1980 that I'd lived in the country long enough, and if I loved America as much as I claimed I did, I should become an American citizen. In other words he urged me to put my money where my mouth was. When he realized that his admonishments, sarcasm and persistence had no effect on me, he took it upon himself to order the application forms from the Department of Justice and handed them to me. I filled them out and shortly thereafter was sworn in, along with a few hundred other immigrants, all folks from Africa, India, Pakistan, China and South America. I was the only Caucasian in that big room downtown where we all pledged allegiance to the flag. It made me feel like a minority.

Being accepted as an American turned obsessive. Owning the certificate that attested I was American was one thing, but being integrated as one was another. I wanted to blend in as opposed to so many French people I knew who had also immigrated and who insisted on keeping their French identity, going as far as to accentuate their French accent, hoping that it would give them an edge in society or in business.

Americans thought the French were oh-so-charming. "Let me introduce you to my French friend," they would say with the pride of a collector who's just come across a rare item while displaying a genuine sign of affection for its place of origin.

"We have a true Frenchman in our midst," others would brag. Really? Are there any fake ones? I guess there are. People often mistake French Canadians or Belgians for French. How sophisticated, even exotic to have a French friend and what is more, a French friend from "gay Paree."

I had not been ostracized the way blacks or Puerto Ricans were, but I felt that being treated as a foreigner was a form of discrimination, even if whoever did it had a great opinion of me. I had been cast as a minority and that is what I intended to fight against. "In the first place," wrote Theodore Roosevelt, "we should insist that if the immigrant who comes here does in good faith become an American and assimilates himself to us, he shall be treated on an exact equality with everyone else, for it is an outrage to discriminate against any such man because of creed or birthplace or origin. But this is predicated upon the man's becoming in very fact an American and nothing but an American." That was my case.

I would have spoken with a southern accent if I could have. I didn't sound as French as Maurice Chevalier, but couldn't be mistaken for a Yank either. There were still traces of Paree in my speech, hard as I tried to erase them. Some would say, "I detect an accent," then would pause a second or two and, in a eureka moment, would ask in a sort of affirmative way, "French?" impressed with themselves for having guessed right. Most people would say, "I detect an accent, but I can't really..." Darn it! I might as well have pasted a sticker on my forehead that read, "Don't try to guess. I AM FRENCH." Had all these people dug deeper, they would have realized that I appreciated the things many of them appreciated, shared the same values, cherished and abided by the same Constitution. Those who knew all that still couldn't overlook my accent and insisted on sticking the French label on me.

Me? I saw myself as ninety-five percent American and five percent French, only because of my love of good food. Actually, I felt more American in some respects than most Americans who had inherited their nationality willy-nilly and had never been asked to choose. I, on the other hand, had given up my French citizenship and had elected to be an American. It had been a decision of the heart and of the mind.

If I wasn't perceived as an American in the States, my French friends thought I was too American. I had conditioned them to think that way. When conversations with them turned to politics, and they always did, I always took the defense of America and American positions, particularly when they dwelled on freedom and the American way of life. Any criticism of the United States made my blood boil, so much so that many of my close French friends refrained from expressing their animosity toward America in my presence.

When in France, and whenever a stranger would ask why a Frenchman like me would be so passionate about America, I'd say with pride, "Because I *am* an American." In certain circumstances, I even spoke French with an American accent, which I now admit was silly.

Unlike most immigrants, I refused to seek comfort in a French ghetto, surrounded by folks speaking my mother tongue. I avoided the New York French community but worked almost exclusively with the French since my arrival in the United States, making it easier for me to survive and to escape poverty as fast as I did. I attended the Actors Studio but gave a French poetry recital. I produced a hit parade show for a French network. I was the correspondent of various French outfits. I worked for Air France and was the director of a French news agency. The first client of my production company was French. I hadn't severed my ties with the old continent.

My life might have turned out differently if I had chosen to start at the bottom. Instead of capitalizing on my Frenchness, I could have taken a menial job at an American company and climbed the ladder the American way. I could have been a mail boy at NBC or CBS and might have grown into a national correspondent. That would have been an achievement, but it wasn't the correct approach for me.

After all, I was a 'zero generation' citizen. My true purpose was to be integrated instead of being perceived as that carefree, happy-go-lucky guy who carried a baguette under his arm, smoked Gauloises, ate stinking cheese, drank Bordeaux wines for breakfast and stole the hearts of all the women he encountered. DDC's acquisition of American clients such as the Home Insurance Company and Citicorp, might have validated my assimilation into American society, but it was my first cross-country trip that created a bond between me and America.

Nineteen eighty-three was a terrible year for DDC. The phone hadn't rung for weeks. No work in sight. I had never been in such a pickle. I had nothing but time on my hands, so, why not do something that would pull me out of my rut while giving me the opportunity to spend time with my boy. I decided to drive to the West Coast and back with him and his cousin. They were in their mid-teens.

The three of us took to the road at five a.m. on a warm day in July. My anxieties faded the moment I crossed the George Washington Bridge and drove through the first toll. Unknown territories lay ahead. Bad luck wouldn't last forever. I had still to live the best years of my life. Route 80 would never end. It was going to take us to lands of mind-boggling beauty, strewn with expansive lakes as big as oceans, with cornfields and wheat fields as far as the eye could see, to roaring waterfalls. It was going to lead us to snow-covered mountains that we would climb, to whitewater torrents on which we would raft, to white-sand deserts we would cross, to thick forests we would explore, to vast prairies we would roam and where we would come face to face with hundreds upon hundreds of bison, to streams where we would watch bears fishing salmon, to steep canyons we would descend, to ranches where we would ride wild horses, to Tombstone where we would relive the gunfight at OK Corral. The land was going to fill me with the enchantment and magic of my neighbor's garden in Paris when I was a little boy.

Index

CPSIA information can be obtained at www.ICGtesting.com
Printed in the USA
BVOW02s0330031115

425354BV00002B/2/P